Selected Letters of Alessandra Strozzi

Selected Letters
of Alessandra Strozzi

Bilingual Edition

TRANSLATED WITH AN INTRODUCTION AND NOTES BY

HEATHER GREGORY

UNIVERSITY
OF CALIFORNIA
PRESS

BERKELEY
LOS ANGELES
LONDON

University of California Press
Berkeley and Los Angeles, California

University of California Press, Ltd.
London, England

© 1997 by the Regents of the University of California

The Italian text of the letters is reprinted from Alessandra Macinghi
negli Strozzi, *Lettere di una gentildonna fiorentina del secolo XV ai figliuoli
esuli,* edited by Cesare Guasti (Florence: G. C. Sansoni, 1877), and
*Una lettera della Alessandra Macinghi negli Strozzi in aggiunta alle LXXII
pubblicate da Cesare Guasti nel 1877* (Florence: G. Carnesecchi e Figli,
1890).

Library of Congress Cataloging-in-Publication Data

Macinghi Strozzi, Alessandra, 1407 – 1471.
    [Lettere di una gentildonna fiorentina del secolo XV ai
figliuoli esuli. English. Selections.]
    Selected letters of Alessandra Strozzi / translated with an
introduction and notes by Heather Gregory.
        p.   cm. — (Biblioteca italiana; 9)
    Includes one additional letter from Una lettera della
Alessandra Macinghi negli Strozzi in aggiunta alle LXII
pubblicate da Cesare Guasti nel 1877 (Florence: G. Carnesecchi
e figli, 1890).
    Includes bibliographical references and index.
    ISBN 0-520-20389-5 (alk. paper). — ISBN
0-520-20390-9 (pbk.: alk. paper).
    1. Macinghi Strozzi, Alessandra, 1407 – 1471 —
Correspondence.   2. Nobility — Italy — Florence —
Correspondence.   3. Women — Italy — Florence —
Correspondence.   4. Florence (Italy) — History — 1421 –
1737 — Sources.   I. Gregory, Heather.   II. Title.   III. Series.
    DG737.58.S7A5   1997
    945'.5105'092 — dc20
    [B]   95-51561
                                                       CIP

Printed in the United States of America

08   07   06   05   04   03   02   01   00
9   8   7   6   5   4   3

The paper used in this publication meets the minimum requirements
of ANSI/NISO Z39.48-1992 (R 1997) (*Permanence of Paper*). ∞

FOR KATE AND JAMES

Contents

Acknowledgments

ALESSANDRA STROZZI'S LETTERS, despite their great interest, hold pitfalls for the would-be translator, and I have undertaken this task with considerable trepidation. I would like to thank Gene Brucker, who first suggested it to me and who was unfailingly helpful and encouraging during the protracted period over which the translation was prepared.

Dale Kent was kind enough to read draft translations of several of the letters when I had just begun the project, and her detailed comments and general observations were very helpful. I would also like to thank Louise George Clubb for specific comments, for her editorial advice, and for her encouragement. F. W. Kent introduced to me the letters of Alessandra Strozzi more than twenty years ago as a likely subject for my Honors dissertation at Monash University, and has given me much help in the research and writing I have undertaken on fifteenth-century Florence in the years since then. I am very grateful for his comments on this translation. The mistakes which remain are of course my own.

My husband, John Knott, has assisted me at every stage of this undertaking, and I would like to take this opportunity to express my gratitude. I could not have begun it without his support, and it would have been a much more arduous task without his help.

Introduction

THE LETTERS OF Alessandra Macinghi Strozzi are among the richest and most revealing autobiographical materials to survive from fifteenth-century Florence. They reveal a woman who fought stubbornly to preserve her family's property and position in adverse circumstances, and who was an acute observer of the political and social life of Medicean Florence. They tell the modern reader much about social and political status in this society, and about the concept of honor (*onore*), which could link the destinies of members of the same extended family or lineage.[1] But perhaps their greatest importance lies in the fact that Alessandra Strozzi's letters enable us to trace her inner life over a period of almost twenty-three years, revealing with great immediacy the anxiety and resignation, pain and sorrow, and (more rarely) joy and triumph with which she responded to the events through which she lived.

The lives of most men and women who lived in Renaissance Florence are obscure by modern standards, and the details of women's lives in particular are often lacking. For this reason—and despite the fact that seventy-three of her letters to her sons are extant—there are many gaps in our knowledge of Alessandra Macinghi Strozzi's life. Nevertheless, a fairly full picture of her life can be assembled, at least for the period after her marriage to Matteo Strozzi.

Alessandra Macinghi was born into the merchant patriciate, the elite class of Florentine society, probably in

1. The term lineage is used here to mean the largest kinship group, consisting of a number of households (between thirty and thirty-five in the case of the Strozzi, which was a large lineage) sharing a common family name and whose members were aware of their common ancestry. This is the body to which Alessandra Strozzi sometimes refers in her letters as the *casa,* or house.

1408.[2] The Macinghi were a small lineage whose members seem to have lived mainly in the *gonfalone*[3] of Lion Bianco, in the quarter of Santa Maria Novella. The first member of the Macinghi family to hold the office of prior[4] did so in the last quarter of the fourteenth century, and so the Macinghi were still "new men" within the Florentine elite at the time of Alessandra's birth. But unlike the Strozzi, the family into which she was to marry, the Macinghi steadily improved their political standing during the sixty years of Medicean dominance, from 1434 to 1494.[5]

2. Filippo Strozzi stated, in a final entry in his mother's book of accounts, that she was sixty-three when she died in 1471, giving 1408 as her date of birth. This is likely to be correct, as both Filippo and Alessandra seem to have been careful in recording such information. Cesare Guasti, the nineteenth-century editor of Alessandra's letters, stated that her age was given as twenty-one years and two months in a *catasto portata,* or tax document of 1427: *Lettere di una gentildonna fiorentina del secolo XV ai figliuoli esuli* (Florence: Sansoni, 1877), XL. If correct, this would make her year of birth 1406. The only *portata* which I have seen for Matteo Strozzi's household for 1427 does not give Alessandra's age.

3. Each of the four quarters of the city was in turn subdivided into four *gonfaloni* or neighborhood districts. It was in these districts that the most basic processes of political eligibility for the high offices of the Florentine state were carried out.

4. The highest executive office in the Florentine state. The priors were "elected" (their names drawn from a bag containing name-tickets of citizens eligible for the highest political office) for a two-month period of office, this short period being designed to ensure that they could not entrench themselves in power.

5. See Dale V. Kent, "The Florentine *Reggimento* in the Fifteenth Century," *Renaissance Quarterly* 28 (1975): 626, 636, 637; and Ann Morton Crabb, "A Patrician Family in Renaissance Florence: The Family Relations of Alessandra Macinghi Strozzi and her Sons" (Washington University, St. Louis: University Microfilms International, 1980), 17, for differing views of the Macinghi family and their political antiquity.

Alessandra's father was Filippo di Niccolò Macinghi and her mother was Caterina di Bernardo Alberti. Caterina died when Alessandra and her brother Zanobi were young children, and her father married again and had three more children (Antonio, Caterina, and Ginevra) with his second wife, Ginevra di Albertuccio Ricasoli. As an adult Alessandra had a close and affectionate relationship only with her full brother, Zanobi. Filippo Macinghi must have been wealthy, because even with five children to provide for, he managed to set aside a dowry of 1600 florins for his eldest daughter, a large sum by the standards of the early fifteenth century. He died in 1420, two years before Alessandra's marriage.

Alessandra married Matteo Strozzi on 10 June 1422. She was probably only fourteen at this time, the earliest age considered marriageable for girls of her class. Matteo was twenty-five and was of very good birth but only modest wealth. The Strozzi were one of the largest and most prestigious lineages in Florence, and they had enjoyed a leading position in politics and business since the end of the thirteenth century. Matteo was a member of one of the two wool merchants' guilds, but appears to have devoted most of his time to politics and fashionable humanistic studies,[6] and was a friend of some of the leading figures of Florentine politics and society at this time. This match would have been considered a very good one for a girl from the Macinghi family, whose members, while respectable and wealthy, were not particularly distinguished. The Macinghi and Strozzi were residents of adjoining *gonfaloni;* marriage alliances were common between such neighbors, and were considered politically useful.

6. See Richard A. Goldthwaite, *Private Wealth in Renaissance Florence: A Study of Four Families* (Princeton: Princeton University Press, 1968), 38−52.

No portrait of Alessandra survives and it is unlikely that one ever existed, so her appearance is unknown. It seems probable that she was attractive in her youth, as physical beauty was considered important in a prospective wife, even one with a substantial dowry, particularly as she came from a family of lesser social prestige than that into which she married. The first four years of Alessandra and Matteo's marriage did not produce any children, but she then gave birth to three daughters and five sons in fairly rapid succession: Andreuola (1426), Simone (1427), Filippo (1428), Piero (1429), Caterina (1431), Lorenzo (1432), Lessandra (1434), and Matteo (1436). Five of these children survived to adulthood.

Alessandra and Matteo were separated by his extended absences from Florence on diplomatic missions during the early 1430s. Then, during 1433 and 1434, a bitter struggle for power took place in Florence. The city was officially governed by a guild regime, with most political offices reserved for members of the seven merchant or professional guilds. Although the constitution made political parties illegal, many citizens within the political class were in fact divided into two opposing factions. Most members of the Strozzi lineage belonged to the so-called Oligarchical faction, a loose alliance of various powerful patrician families, while the Medici faction was supported by the wealth of the Medici bank, the greatest in Europe at this time. In September 1433, the leader of the Medici faction (Cosimo de' Medici) and a group of his kinsmen and close associates were exiled from the city to prevent their anticipated assumption of power. A year later the Medici faction staged a far more successful coup d'etat, and in turn exiled many of their opponents. In November 1434 Matteo Strozzi was exiled to Pesaro, where he was treated as an honored guest by the ruling Malatesta family; three other Strozzi were exiled at this time, and the great majority of the lineage's adult male members had

their names removed from the lists of politically eligible citizens.

Alessandra joined Matteo in his exile, although she was not legally compelled to do so. Her husband died in Pesaro a little over a year later, in 1435 or early 1436, probably of the plague. Three of their children—Andreuola, Piero, and Simone—also died of the plague at this time. Alessandra then returned to Florence with her surviving children and remained there, except for occasional journeys, until her death on 2 March 1471. She did not remarry. Women who made a second marriage were usually very young when widowed, and often had no children, or at least no sons; it was considered to be against a boy's best interests to be raised in a stepfather's household. Also, both Christian doctrine and popular sentiment encouraged widows to remain chaste and devote themselves to their children and the management of their husband's estate. By remarrying, Alessandra would also have deprived her sons of the use of some of their inheritance, because the lands which (under Florentine law) represented her dowry, restituted to her after Matteo's death, would have passed to her new husband during his lifetime. She may also have followed her own inclination in not remarrying: a widow was much more her own mistress than a wife could ever be.

It would have been usual for a young widow in such circumstances to turn for help to her father-in-law or a brother-in-law, but Matteo had no brothers and Simone Strozzi had died before his son. Matteo's closest male kinsmen, his first cousins Jacopo, Filippo, and Niccolò di Lionardo Strozzi, had left Florence voluntarily in the years after 1434 and had established a very successful bank with offices in Bruges, Barcelona, and Naples. This branch of the Strozzi lineage was very cohesive, and Jacopo, Filippo, and Niccolò were willing to help their cousin's sons, mainly by taking them into their bank to

give them the training in business which Florentine boys of the merchant class usually received during their teenage years. There was an additional reason for Alessandra's sons to leave Florence: because their father had been a legal exile, their future prospects were considered poor if they remained in the city. Filippo and Lorenzo appear to have learned their business lessons well, and with the patronage of King Ferrante of Naples they went on to make an even greater fortune than their cousins', through their own bank and cloth warehouse in Naples. They were not legally exiled from Florence until 1458, when one of the periodic threats to Medicean dominance led to a range of restrictive measures against their opponents, actual or prospective.

Although Alessandra maintained some contacts with her own family, at least until the death of her brother Zanobi in 1452, she identified herself strongly with the Strozzi lineage, and after her return to Florence she had extensive dealings with her Strozzi kinsmen-by-marriage. She devoted herself wholeheartedly to the interests of her children, while much of her time was spent in the routine business of the Florentine property owner: managing tenants, collecting rents, and paying taxes. She was both literate and numerate, writing fluently in Tuscan and keeping household accounts. She had almost certainly been taught to read and write by her mother or another female relative, as girls were not usually taught by tutors. She wrote a "merchant" hand which was without any of the graceful and deliberate form of the humanist script which some Florentine boys of her class were learning at this time, but which is nevertheless as clear and legible as the handwriting of most of her contemporaries, male or female. While she had obviously received a basic education, Alessandra was not "lettered" in the contemporary sense of the word, being unable to read Latin, and her letters appear to be without literary allusions. She makes no ref-

erences to books, and if she possessed any they would probably have been devotional in nature.

Alessandra stated on various occasions that she did not enjoy using a pen and complained about how much she disliked writing letters, giving the strong impression that she wrote only out of necessity. But when she did write it was usually at far greater length and with far more detail than was needed. In fact there was little real need for her to write to her sons at all, as their brothers-in-law, Marco Parenti and Giovanni Bonsi, kept them faithfully informed about family business and Florentine politics. Alessandra wrote long letters because she wanted to, even though (so far as we can tell) this seems to have been rather unusual for a woman. She would also, no doubt, have preferred to dictate her letters to a secretary, professional or amateur.

The present translation of Alessandra Macinghi Strozzi's letters is based on the edition published by Cesare Guasti in 1877, entitled *Lettere di una gentildonna fiorentina del secolo XV ai figliuoli esuli*, with the addition of another letter published by Isidoro del Lungo thirteen years later.[7] From the seventy-three extant letters, thirty-five have been translated here, either in full or in part. The selection has been based on two main criteria. First, it was important that the letters included were those which carried forward the story of Alessandra's life, both because of its intrinsic interest and for the sake of comprehensibility. For this reason, none of the letters omitted is chronologically isolated, and most date from the periods from which (relatively speaking) a large number of letters survive. (For example, of the thirty-seven letters which are not included, twenty-five were written between April 1464 and

7. Guasti, *Lettere di una gentildonna* (cited above); *Una lettera della Alessandra Macinghi negli Strozzi in aggiunta alle LXXII pubblicate da Cesare Guasti nel 1877* (Florence: Carnesecchi, 1890).

February 1466.) Second, letters were chosen for inclusion because of the extent to which they illustrate the range of attitudes, concerns, and activities which were characteristic of their author. In this process I have tried to balance as well as possible the desire to show the full range of her activities with the need to make the selection representative, and to make it clear that some topics were of particular importance to her and that she returned to them frequently.

Some passages have been omitted from most (but not all) of the letters translated here. This has been done so as to enable as many letters as possible to be included. The sections omitted are discrete paragraphs and often consist of discussions of matters which arose frequently, such as the sending of flax from Naples to Florence, or minor financial transactions. Where passages have been omitted in this fashion, a brief summary of the material concerned has been provided.

Due possibly to both her comparative lack of formal education and her impatience with the physical chore of putting pen to paper, Alessandra's prose is often lacking in clear grammatical structure. Punctuation in the modern sense was not used in Renaissance Italy, and her letters are generally made up of very long sentences and infrequent stops, which often give a breathless and headlong air to her narratives. Perhaps more troublesome for the modern reader is the fact that her use of personal and relative pronouns is often ambiguous, and it can be difficult to determine precisely to whom or what she is referring. In this translation, punctuation has been kept to a minimum to preserve some of the flavor of the original. So far as the ambiguities are concerned, it will be seen that some remain even after translation.

One aspect of Alessandra's style which may be disconcerting for the reader is her abrupt shift between the second person singular and the second person plural. Al-

though most of her letters were addressed to only one of her sons, during the period when Filippo and Lorenzo both lived in Naples she would sometimes switch to addressing them both, using the *voi* form to indicate this, as distinct from the *tu* form of the singular. Both these forms have been rendered simply as "you"; where there is any danger of a plural subject being mistaken for a singular one, I have added a qualification in parenthesis, for example, "[both of] you."

Alessandra Macinghi Strozzi's letters form a mirror in which much of the patrician society of fifteenth-century Florence is reflected. She wrote frequently about her feelings for her children and her concern for their welfare; she also wrote a great deal about money and whether they had enough of it for their needs. Mundane considerations such as the price of grain and wine also figure prominently. She was interested in births and deaths among her circle of relatives and friends, and wrote frequently about the plague and efforts to avoid it. The political arena also engaged her attention, peopled as it was by friends and enemies, particularly after the legal exile of Filippo and Lorenzo in 1458. She also wrote a good deal about marriage. In the early letters she described fairly briefly the marriages arranged for her two daughters, and in the later letters she wrote at length about the need for her sons to marry and produce children, and discussed possible wives for them.

The letters reflect family relationships in an unusually forthright way. Because they were written unselfconsciously, intended to be read only by the recipient and possibly by other family members, they express a range of emotions which often elude the student of past family life: love, tenderness, maternal pride and disappointment, anger, sorrow, and resignation. The softer side of Alessandra's personality is shown in her attitude toward her youngest child, Matteo, and other boys in whom she took

an interest. Her tenderness for Matteo seems to have been compounded of two main elements, his own attractive personality and the fact that he was her youngest child, born after his father's death and named after him, so that for her he was in some sense his father "remade." [8] In an early sequence of letters to Filippo (written in 1448 and 1449) she expressed her reluctance to part with Matteo so that he could join his brother in the Strozzi business in Naples, using any available argument to delay his departure. After keeping Matteo in Florence in July 1449, contrary to Filippo's wishes, she wrote: "You should be patient for the sake of his health for a month and a half or two at the most, because once he is dead neither of us will have him" [Letter 3]. Perhaps the best known of her letters is the one she wrote to Filippo in September 1459, on learning of Matteo's death in Naples at the age of twenty-three. "I've heard how on the 23rd [of August] it pleased Him who gave him to me to take him back. . . . Being deprived of my son has given me the greatest grief, and while I've lost a son's love it seems as if I've suffered an even greater loss through his death" [Letter 11]. Her last letters reveal the love which illuminated the last years of her life, for her grandson Alfonso. He was born in December 1467, and in March 1469 she wrote to Filippo (absent on business in Naples) about his son's infant cleverness. She reported his sayings and first steps and claimed that she was teaching him to read; "I know you will laugh at what I've written and say I'm a fool, but I know it gives me pleasure and comfort and will make you want to see him even more" [Letter 33]. In the last of her letters to be

8. On the tradition of naming children after deceased family members and its significance, see Christiane Klapisch-Zuber, "The Name 'Remade': The Transmission of Given Names in Florence in the Fourteenth and Fifteenth Centuries," in *Women, Family and Ritual in Renaissance Italy,* trans. Lydia Cochrane (Chicago: University of Chicago Press, 1985), 283 – 309.

preserved, of April 1470, Alessandra wrote eloquently that "Alfonso is well, and so are the rest of us" [Letter 35].

During the 1440s, when Filippo and Lorenzo were in their teens and early twenties, Alessandra wrote them letters full of advice and admonition. Lorenzo (who was four years younger than his elder brother) was rather wild and extravagant in his late teens, and on more than one occasion she reproached him for his apparent thoughtlessness. The adult Lorenzo appears to have been a loyal and generous person, and he had an affectionate relationship with his mother. In February 1465 she told Filippo that "you make me angry by saying he's the one I love most" [Letter 21], but it seems this was true, at least after the death of Matteo. Alessandra feared that Lorenzo's good nature would lead him into difficulties. After the death of Jacopo Strozzi (his employer in Bruges) she advised him to avoid becoming entangled in the affairs of Jacopo's widow and heirs: "Things to do with inheritance are very risky and can lead to a lot of trouble and aggravation, and you don't want to get involved in that" [Letter 15].

Filippo, the eldest son, emerges from his mother's letters as difficult and not particularly lovable. When he was in his early twenties Alessandra gave him predictable advice about working hard and treating Niccolò Strozzi, the cousin who had taken him into his business, with appropriate reverence. She urged Filippo to do his utmost to succeed in business, so as to "rebuild your house," by which she seems to have meant the Strozzi lineage as a whole [Letter 5]. Filippo was to succeed in this endeavor, both literally and metaphorically. The sentence of exile was eventually lifted from him (and from Lorenzo) in September 1466, and he returned to Florence two months later, already a very wealthy man. (He began to acquire the many properties needed to assemble the site for his greatest undertaking, the Strozzi palace, from late 1474 onward. The foundation stone of the palace was laid in

1489.) While devoted to her eldest son, Alessandra was by no means in awe of him or uncritical of his behavior; for her, wealth was never an end in itself. Alessandra seems to have believed that Filippo lacked both Christian and family piety and generosity, and was too fond of cash in hand. In March 1464 she told him, in answer to a request that she spend money "more usefully," that when she died "I won't have any cash in my coffers, because I will have spent it on my soul instead, which is the most useful thing I have" [Letter 16].

Filippo named his first child, a boy, after his godfather, Alfonso Duke of Calabria. This saddened Alessandra because it flouted the Florentine convention that a man name his first son after his father, if dead. But Filippo was clearly devoted to his mother, and shortly before his second child was born—a girl, as it turned out—he told her of his intention to name his next son Alessandro after her. This was an extremely unusual step, and one of which she profoundly disapproved, despite the implied compliment to herself; "I've had many other griefs, and I've endured them, and so I endure this one. I would have put up with having him called Alessandro, just as I put up with Alfonso . . . but I realized then that you didn't like your father's name" [Letter 34]. Such disagreements encapsulate the tragicomedy of family life with astonishing immediacy. During her sons' exile Alessandra stated many times that she wished to leave Florence and live with one or both of her sons, but this never happened. It is not clear whether her sons simply preferred to live at a distance from their mother, or whether the reason given by Filippo, that he needed her to look after his interests in Florence, was the true one. She commented in April 1465 that "I love you and feel much more tenderness for you than you do for me. And the reason is because I can only do badly without you, but you can do everything without me" [Letter 23].

Alessandra loved her daughters and remained involved with both of them all her life. She did the best she could for them in arranging their marriages, in what were difficult circumstances: when Caterina was married it was only eleven years since her father had been exiled, and they had not yet experienced that spectacular improvement in their fortunes which Filippo brought about from the 1460s onward. As it turned out, Caterina's marriage appears to have been a great success, while her sister Lessandra's was something of a disaster, at least in material terms. But Alessandra's daughters did not occupy the central place in her life that her sons did; although she noted the birth of Caterina's first child, Piero Parenti, she said little thereafter about him or any of Caterina's other children, or about Lessandra's. This difference may be accounted for partly by the fact that in this society a mother's intimate relationship with her daughters was generally confined to the period of their childhood. After they had married, daughters became members of another family and lineage for all practical purposes, whereas a mother and her son (or sons) could, and often did, spend a large part of their adult lives together. Sons' sons continued the family unit and the family name (that is, the name of the family their mother had joined on her own marriage), but daughters' sons continued someone else's family. For this reason women were culturally predisposed to invest their emotional capital in their relationship with their sons, if they had any. This is certainly true of Alessandra, even though she was physically separated from her sons for more than twenty years, and was in frequent personal contact with both her daughters, at one time even sharing her house with her daughter Lessandra, son-in-law Giovanni Bonsi, and their children.

Filippo and Lorenzo were in their mid or late thirties before they married. Both had informal liaisons before they married, Filippo with a domestic slave, Marina, and

Lorenzo with a lower-class Florentine woman, Caterina di Chimenti da Sommaia, who lived in Naples. Alessandra wrote to Filippo that she had heard about Marina and understood "why you want to put off getting married for a year and why they're so slow in finding you a wife" [Letter 17]. Caterina da Sommaia bore Lorenzo two children, Violante and Giovanluigi. Before the birth of the first, Alessandra asked Filippo to tell her how Lorenzo was, "and if he has had an heir, because Tommaso [Ginori] told me he was expecting one. You'll both be unmarried for so long that you'll have a dozen of them" [Letter 24]. Her attitude of tolerant amusement toward these informal liaisons owed nothing to Christian doctrine and everything to Florentine social custom. Such relationships were certainly accepted, particularly for unmarried men; the strictest standards of sexual morality and propriety were, by contrast, expected of both unmarried and married women of the patrician class. Illegitimate children were acknowledged and often seem to have been treated kindly, although they did not have the status of legitimate children; Alessandra's description of the marriage she helped to arrange for the illegitimate daughter of Jacopo Strozzi in 1459 provides a good example [Letter 10].

Her sons' status as exiles made it hard to find them appropriate wives, as most families of high status were reluctant to send their daughters away from Florence. All negotiations had to be relayed to Filippo and Lorenzo by letter, and their views ascertained by the same means, a wearisome business. The actual negotiations were carried out by their long-suffering brother-in-law, Marco Parenti;[9] Alessandra's role was limited to that of reporter, persuader, and adviser, at which she had only a very lim-

9. On Marco's relationship with his brothers-in-law, see Mark Phillips, *The Memoir of Marco Parenti: A Life in Medici Florence* (Princeton: Princeton University Press, 1987), particularly 150–65.

ited degree of success. Both Filippo and Lorenzo were reluctant to marry, despite their mother's urging, Lorenzo's unwillingness in particular leading his mother to remark in exasperation that "if all men were so afraid of getting married the world would be empty by now" [Letter 29]. On another occasion she was moved to tell the cautionary tale of their cousin Filippo di Lionardo Strozzi, which pointed a different moral. He had married unwisely and became infatuated with his foolish wife; "there was no need to wonder at her, the wonder was at him, the silly old fool" [Letter 26].

Money was of great practical importance, and it occupied a major place in Alessandra's letters. During the 1440s and early 1450s she suffered real financial hardship, before Filippo and Lorenzo started to make substantial amounts of money in independent business ventures. During this period she had difficulty paying her taxes, and on one occasion arranged to consolidate her debts to the government and repay a monthly sum until they were discharged. Even after this period Alessandra continued to use her letters to record her disbursement of sums of money on her sons' behalf, because it was good merchant practice to record such transactions, and this may have been one reason why some of her letters survive. While both Filippo and Lorenzo became rich men, and Caterina's husband Marco Parenti was in very comfortable circumstances, Lessandra's husband, Giovanni Bonsi, was frequently in debt and had eight mouths to feed. In January 1466, at a time when Filippo and Lorenzo were considering both employing him and lending him 200 florins for a year, Alessandra told them how he had suffered due to poor harvests and losing money in various schemes. She described how Giovanni had pawned his clothes, and how Lessandra tried to hide the fact that her underskirt was worn out. She advised her sons against the loan, nevertheless, on the grounds that Giovanni would

probably not be able to repay it in the time proposed. She also warned them that his great need of money for himself might expose him to temptation if they employed him in a position where he had to handle large sums [Letter 32]. Alessandra gave such advice in spite of the fact that her sons were rich men and her daughter and son-in-law were reduced to borrowing 80 florins (from their brother-in-law Marco Parenti) for a dowry investment for one of their daughters. (Her sons in fact lent Giovanni a substantial amount of money, although whether they did so on this particular occasion is not clear.)

Death tended to overshadow life during the fifteenth century. The Black Death had swept through Italy more than one hundred years earlier, and the plague was still a common and unwelcome visitor in the later fifteenth century. Alessandra frequently discussed both the severity of a current epidemic in Florence and her decision either to stay and endure the greater risk there or take refuge in the house of a relative in the countryside. She also frequently urged Filippo to neglect his business rather than his health and to leave Naples when necessary to escape the plague. But this was only one of many serious threats to life, such as childbirth, death by misadventure of one kind or another, various imperfectly understood illnesses and diseases, and of course old age. When Caterina was expecting her first child, Alessandra expressed her fear that she would die in childbirth, an anxiety exacerbated by the possibility that the final installment of her dowry, which was about to mature in the State Dowry Fund, would thus be lost; "we could lose her and the money at the same time" [Letter 4]. Death retained much of its grim mystery, as in many cases its cause was highly conjectural. Her description of Benedetto Strozzi's death is a good example: "he wasn't in a bad way, and he was always going out and didn't seem really sick. They say he had a tumor on his body, but from the symptoms they think he died of the

plague" [Letter 9]. Many died prematurely, leaving behind widowed husbands or wives and young children: "he
had three daughters and two sons and his wife is seven
months pregnant" [Letter 9], Alessandra wrote in Benedetto's case. The theme of the brevity of earthly life and
its many disappointments echoes through her letters. "She
was so happy when she gave birth to a boy, but it has so
soon turned to bitterness," she wrote about one friend,
Gostanza Pandolfini, when the death of her husband,
Pandolfo, left her alone with eleven children; "all our
hopes in this world come to little, and we can only hope
in God" [Letter 28]. Alessandra herself had no need for
the memento mori. She thought frequently about her
own death, and seems to have considered it imminent
from the age of about forty-five. In December 1449, more
than twenty years before her death, she wrote of her desire
to see Filippo again if God let her live long enough [Letter
4], and this became a frequent refrain. In the last of her
letters she described an earthquake, and various revolts
which had just occurred in Prato, one of Florence's subject cities. "I thought we were close to the end of the
world. So it's good to put your soul in order and be ready"
[Letter 35].

Most of what Alessandra has to say on the subject of
religion is related to the conduct of everyday life rather
than to formal religious observance. She believed that
good works helped secure the soul's salvation and that
God rewarded good Christians in this life. For example,
in January 1466 she commended Filippo for having helped
the son of an enemy who was in dire straits in Naples.
"You gave Brunetto's son food to eat and clothes to wear,
and you gave him shelter and money and sent him back
here; out of the seven acts of mercy you have performed
three. You have done very well and you didn't hold what
his father had done to you against him. God will help you
prosper even more, because he who is charitable can only

meet with good in return" [Letter 30]. Her faith was strong and did not waver even in the face of personal calamity; she believed that God always took people at the best time for their souls' sake, no matter how inexplicable this might seem to those who loved them.

References to practices such as pilgrimage and the veneration of saints' relics are relatively infrequent. Alessandra considered undertaking a pilgrimage to Rome during the Jubilee year of 1450 to earn the offered plenary indulgence, but did not in fact go [Letter 4]. She invoked the protection of St. Sebastian for Filippo during an outbreak of the plague [Letter 18], and during a difficult period in 1465 she suggested that her sons might "arrange to do some good works to honor him [Christ] and His Blessed Mother the Virgin Mary, and the Angel Raphael, so that just as he looked after Tobias and . . . brought him back to his father and mother, so he may return you both to your mother" [Letter 29]. She also mentioned making offerings for the souls of the dead members of the family on All Souls' Day, a very common Italian custom. Considered in context, however, and in proportion to the space given to other topics, these matters do not seem to have occupied her thoughts a great deal.

It is difficult to summarize the content of Alessandra's letters relating to Florentine politics. It must be kept in mind that she and her sons followed the deliberate policy of not committing to paper anything of importance about political matters, because their letters were often opened and read while in transit; it is not clear how this was done or by whom, but the motive is clear enough. The Medici regime saw the exiles of 1434, and later their sons, as potential plotters against their regime, and kept a close watch on their correspondence for evidence of such intentions. From the end of 1458, after Filippo and Lorenzo had been legally exiled, they were also specifically forbidden to write about politics. If Alessandra ever wrote about

secret political matters—and it is by no means clear that she did—such letters would have been sent by a trusted carrier and would not have been preserved. Sensitive information was usually conveyed by word of mouth, and for this reason the political references in her letters were generally limited to facts in the public domain (such as the names of those elected to political offices or comments about current political developments) and references to her sons' own political position, which were deliberately cryptic. Number codes were sometimes substituted for names, to make such passages difficult for an unauthorized reader to decipher [Letter 28].

It is clear, nevertheless, that Alessandra took a keen interest in politics. She knew many of the players on the Florentine political stage personally, whether as friends or enemies, as the political class was quite small. For example, her brother-in-law Niccolò Soderini (with whom she was not on friendly terms) was Gonfalonier of Justice [10] for two months in 1465–66. He had been expected to introduce some important reforms during what was a period of unrest and discontent among the political class, but achieved little. She reported with a certain relish the verdict of his brother Tommaso that "he went in like a lion and will leave like a lamb" [Letter 31]. Alessandra was extremely well informed about the latest political developments, despite the fact that (by her own account) she went out relatively little except to attend Mass. Her son-in-law Marco Parenti was a keen student of Florentine politics and was probably her most important informant about day-to-day developments, but she had a wide range of other contacts who clearly told her a great deal about

10. The Gonfalonier, or Standard-Bearer, of Justice was the ninth member of the Priorate, or Signoria (together with the eight priors), and was the head of the Florentine state. He could exert great influence on political events, particularly in times of crisis.

the discussions which took place in the formal and informal forums of the city. When she wrote, during a crisis in
January 1466, about the deliberations of a consultative
group of leading citizens, that "no one has heard anything, because anyone who reveals anything will be declared a rebel and so everything has been kept very secret"
[Letter 31], she was describing a very unusual state of
affairs.

From the few comments she made about Florence's
leading family, we can deduce that Alessandra had considerable reservations about the Medici. It seems she accepted the need for Filippo's assiduous cultivation of their
favor, but she showed absolutely no enthusiasm for them
on a personal level. She noted on one occasion that Lucrezia Tornabuoni, wife of Piero de' Medici, had sent
Filippo "a fine letter for love of the flax you sent her," and
commented that Lucrezia "would do well to reward you
with something she doesn't have to spend any money
on . . . by saying a good word on your behalf to Piero"
[Letter 23]. On another occasion she told Filippo that a
family connection who was also an exile, Niccolò Ardinghelli, had been given permission to visit the city because his wife was the mistress of the seventeen-year-old
Lorenzo de' Medici [Letter 22]. In one of her last letters,
in 1469, she told Filippo how his young wife, Fiammetta,
had been invited to the wedding of Lorenzo de' Medici
and Clarice Orsini. Fiammetta had used the impending
birth of her second child as an excuse not to go, but since
the baby's birth, Lucrezia Tornabuoni (the mother of the
bridegroom) had sent a further message "to say she really
wanted her to come, and we shouldn't say no" [Letter 34].
It is with this type of detail that the letters illuminate the
fine background textures of Medicean politics.

The letters of Alessandra Macinghi Strozzi can be used
to illuminate a number of matters of current and con-

tinuing interest to historians. First among these is the question of the nature of the Florentine family and the role of women within it. During the 1950s and 1960s it was generally assumed by historians of Renaissance Florence that the lineage (or family in the broadest sense) was basic to patrician Florentine society, and that men who shared a common surname would generally (but not invariably) act together in political, social, and business life, motivated by a perception of common interest.[11] Such common interest might concern tangible things such as business profit or political success, or intangibles such as honor and reputation. Due to the prevailing historiographical concerns and style, the basis of such assumptions remained unexplored in detail, and the notion that the significant ties in question were those between men was not seriously questioned.

This state of affairs began to change after the publication in 1968 of Richard Goldthwaite's *Private Wealth in Renaissance Florence: A Study of Four Families*. This work challenged prevailing assumptions by considering the economic framework of the lives of selected members of four Florentine lineages.[12] What was ultimately most significant about Goldthwaite's work was not perhaps his controversial conclusion, that there were few remaining significant family ties for Renaissance Florentines outside their households. Still more important was the way in which his work, and the controversy it aroused, ensured

11. An example of an important work in which this assumption is made, at least in regard to political life, is Nicolai Rubinstein's *The Government of Florence under the Medici, 1434–1494* (Oxford: Oxford University Press, 1966), although many other examples could be given.

12. *Private Wealth in Renaissance Florence* (cited above). This work is based largely on a study of account books and other financial records.

that further research and writing in this area were directed toward a detailed examination of the types of historical evidence which could elucidate domestic and kinship relations, most importantly diaries and account books, domestic chronicles (*ricordanze*), and private letters. Goldthwaite's work was followed in 1977 by that of F. W. Kent, *Household and Lineage in Renaissance Florence: The Family Life of the Capponi, Ginori and Rucellai*, which presented a very different argument but was in some respects complementary.[13] This study used a wider range of evidence and considered other areas of life (in addition to business and property) to argue that broader kinship ties were still of great importance to patrician Florentines. In common with that of Goldthwaite, however, Kent's work emphasized the presence of close and loving ties within the household. The nature of domestic relationships was one in which there had previously been limited interest, despite the earlier appearance of Iris Origo's brilliant study of the lives of Francesco Datini and his wife, Margherita, *The Merchant of Prato: Francesco di Marco Datini;*[14] nor had any great interest previously been shown in the role of women in Renaissance Italian life. But the winds of change were blowing in many areas of history writing, and the attention of many historians was turning to the neglected denizens of the past, including women and children. From the 1970s onward, historians began to look to cognate disciplines (such as anthropology, ethnography, and sociology) for inspiration when writing about kinship relations. Contemporaneously, the new possibilities provided by information technology led social historians to attempt more ambitious and inclusive

13. Francis William Kent, *Household and Lineage in Renaissance Florence: The Family Life of the Capponi, Ginori and Rucellai* (Princeton: Princeton University Press, 1977).

14. Iris Origo, *The Merchant of Prato: Francesco di Marco Datini* (Harmondsworth: Penguin, 1963).

studies than had previously been possible.[15] Over the last twenty years, a large body of detailed and groundbreaking research has been published which relates to the lives of women in Renaissance Florence and how they fitted into what had previously been assumed to be a predominantly male system of lineages and alliances.[16]

The letters of Alessandra Macinghi Strozzi have much to contribute to our understanding of these matters. They reveal the ties which bound the members of the Strozzi lineage together, ties which were created and kept strong by a sense of mutual obligation: to employ one another,

15. The most notable example is David Herlihy and Christiane Klapisch-Zuber, *Les Toscans et leurs familles: une étude du catasto Florentin de 1427* (Paris: Presses de la Fondation Nationale des Sciences Politiques, 1978), translated into English as *Tuscans and their Families: A Study of the Florentine Catasto of 1427* (New Haven, Conn.: Yale University Press, 1985).

16. See in particular Christiane Klapisch-Zuber, *Women, Family and Ritual in Renaissance Italy* (cited above); David Herlihy, *Medieval Households* (Cambridge, Mass.: Harvard University Press, 1985); Gene Brucker, *Giovanni and Lusanna: Love and Marriage in Renaissance Florence* (Berkeley: University of California Press, 1986); Julius Kirshner, "Pursuing Honor While Avoiding Sin: The *Monte delle Doti* of Florence," *Studi Senesi* 41 (1978); and Anthony Molho, *Marriage Alliance in Late Medieval Florence* (Cambridge, Mass.: Harvard University Press, 1994). Among more recent short studies see Sharon Strocchia, "Remembering the Family: Women, Kin and Commemorative Masses in Renaissance Florence," *Renaissance Quarterly* 42 (1989): 635–54, and "La famiglia patrizia fiorentina nel secolo XV: la problematica della donna," in *Palazzo Strozzi Meta Millenio 1489–1989, Atti di Convegno di Studi,* ed. Daniela Lamberini (Rome: Istituto della Enciclopedia Italiana, 1991), 126–37; Elaine G. Rosenthal, "The Position of Women in Renaissance Florence: Neither Autonomy nor Subjection," in *Florence and Italy: Renaissance Studies in Honour of Nicolai Rubinstein,* ed. Peter Denley and Caroline Elam (London: Westfield College, University of London Committee for Medieval Studies, 1988), 369–81; and Heather Gregory, "Daughters, Dowries and the Family in Fifteenth Century Florence," *Rinascimento,* 2d ser., 27 (1987), 215–37.

to help find a husband for a kinsman's daughter, to rejoice in each others' political success, and to give advice in financial matters. Alessandra was not of course a member of the Strozzi lineage by birth, and her letters show the extent to which it was possible for a woman to assume the interests and loyalties of the lineage into which she married. (It may be significant in this regard that after the death in 1452 of her only full sibling, her brother Zanobi, Alessandra appears to have been unusually detached from what remained of her own family, partly as the result of a long inheritance dispute.) To her, the interests of her sons and the interests of the Strozzi lineage were virtually inseparable: as Filippo and Lorenzo made their own fortunes, Alessandra saw their efforts as able to mend the fortunes of the whole lineage,[17] and when the honor of the lineage was damaged (for example, by the failure of Giovanfrancesco Strozzi's company in late 1464, and his subsequent poor behavior) she saw this, by extension, as reflecting poorly on her sons.

This collection of letters almost inevitably raises the question of whether daughters suffered unfair treatment and emotional neglect at the hands of their parents in patrician Florentine society. While this obviously cannot be answered satisfactorily on the basis of a single source, certain relevant observations can be made. Alessandra's first priority was certainly the welfare of her sons and (Strozzi) grandson and the preservation and increase of their patrimony. She showed a continuing interest in her daughters' happiness and welfare, however, and certainly did not adopt the more ruthless option to which some Florentine fathers resorted, of placing their daughters in a convent

17. Others saw their success in the same way. See Francis William Kent, "'Più Superba de quella de Lorenzo': Courtly and Family Interest in the Building of Filippo Strozzi's Palace," *Renaissance Quarterly* 30 (1977): 311–23.

rather than dowering and arranging marriages for them.[18] When comparing her attitude toward her sons with that toward her daughters, it must also be remembered that our judgment is based on letters written to the former, which inevitably reflect their concerns more than their sisters'. It seems overwhelmingly likely that she also wrote some letters to her daughters, and these would have been written from a rather different perspective. It is clear from the references to Caterina and Lessandra in their mother's correspondence that she saw them frequently and that they were in no way cut off from their own family; unlike in her own case, these women continued to play a part in the life of their natal lineage.

Alessandra Macinghi Strozzi's letters have been much quoted by historians and are among the most famous written by any woman of the Italian Renaissance, although their full scope has been relatively little known. While it is impossible for the letters of any single person to convey the full flavor of life in a past period, her letters virtually achieve this for fifteenth-century Florence, so rich is their emotional range and so diverse their subject matter. They convey to us with great clarity the fact that five centuries ago, life was different in many respects, but was also, curiously, very much the same. The details of her life, and the lives of her family and friends, are preserved in her letters for us to inspect at our leisure, when most of the world in which they were written has long since disappeared.

18. On this particular strategy for providing respectably but cheaply for daughters, see Molho, *Marriage Alliance in Late Medieval Florence* (cited above), 173–77.

TEXT AND TRANSLATION

Lettere

I

Al nome di Dio. A dì 24 d'agosto 1447.

Carissimo figliuolo. A'dì passati ebbi una tua de 16 di luglio, alla quale farò per questa risposta.

E'n prima t'avviso come, per grazia di Dio, abbiàno allogata la nostra Caterina al figliuolo di Parente di Pier Parenti, ch'è giovane da bene e vertudioso, ed è solo, e ricco, e d'età d'anni venticinque, e fa bottega d'arte di seta; e hanno un poco di stato, ch'è poco tempo che 'l padre fu di Collegio. E sì gli do di dota fiorini mille; cioè, fiorini cinquecento ch' ell' ha avere di maggio nel 1448 dal Monte; e gli altri cinquecento gli ho a dare, tra danari e donora, quando ne va a marito; che credo sarà di novembre, se a Dio piacerà. E questi danari sono parte de'

Letters

This is the earliest surviving letter of Alessandra Strozzi. It was written to her eldest son, Filippo, to tell him about the marriage she had arranged for his sister Caterina, who was to be married to a young man called Marco Parenti, a silk merchant. The letter also deals with taxes, the education of Alessandra's youngest son, Matteo, and the need for Filippo to be suitably grateful to Niccolò Strozzi, his father's cousin, who had taken him into his business in Naples.

In the name of God. 24 August 1447.

Dearest son, in the last few days I have received your letter of the 16th of July, which I will answer in this one.

And first I must tell you how by the grace of God we have arranged a marriage for our Caterina to the son of Parente di Piero Parenti. He is a young man of good birth and abilities and an only son, rich and twenty-five years of age, and he has a silk manufacturing business. And they take a small part in the government, as a little while ago his father was [an officeholder] in the College.[1] And so I am giving him one thousand florins of dowry, that is, five hundred florins that she is due in May 1448 from the Fund,[2] and the other five hundred I have to give him, made up of cash and trousseau, when she goes to her husband's house, which I believe will be in November, God

vostri e parte de'mia. Che s'io non avessi preso questo partito, non si maritava quest'anno; però che, chi to' donna vuol danari; e non trovavo chi volesse aspettare d'avere la dota nel 1448, e parte nel 1450: sicchè, dandogl'io questi cinquecento tra danari e donora, toccheranno a me, s'ella viverà, quegli del 1450. E questo partito abbiàn preso pello meglio; che era d'età d'anni sedici, e non era da 'ndugiar più a maritarla. Èssi trovato da metterla in maggiore istato e più gentilezza, ma con mille quattrocento o cinquecento fiorini; ch'era il disfacimento mio e vostro: e non so come la fanciulla si fussi contentata; che, dallo stato in fuori, non v'è grascia, che ci è de' soprossi assai. Ed io, considerato tutto, diliberai acconciar bene la fanciulla, e non guardare a tante cose: e parmi esser certa la starà bene come fanciulla di Firenze; che ha la suocera e 'l suocero che ne sono sì contenti, che non pensan se non di contentalla. O! non ti dico di Marco, cioè il marito, che sempre gli dice: Chiedi ciò che tu vuogli. E come si maritò, gli tagliò una cotta di zetani vellutato chermisi; e così la roba di quello medesimo: ed è 'l più bel drappo che sia in Firenze; che se lo fece 'n bottega. E fassi una grillanda di penne con perle, che viene fiorini ottanta; e l'acconciatura di sotto, e' sono duo trecce di perle, che viene fiorini sessanta o più: che quandro andrà fuori, arà in dosso più che fiorini quattrocento. E ordina di fare un velluto chermisi, per farlo colle maniche grandi, foderato di martore, quando n'andrà a marito: e fa una cioppa rosata, ricamata di perle. E non può saziarsi di fare delle cose; che è bella, e vorrebbe paressi vie più: che in verità non ce n'è un'altra a Firenze fatta come lei, ed ha tutte le

willing. And this money will be partly yours and partly mine. If I hadn't taken this decision she wouldn't have been married this year, because he who marries is looking for cash and I couldn't find anyone who was willing to wait for the dowry until 1448, and part in 1450. So as I'm giving him this five hundred made up of cash and trousseau, the 1450 [money] will be mine if she lives until then.[3] We've taken this decision for the best because she was sixteen and we didn't want to wait any longer to arrange a marriage. And we found that to place her in a nobler family with greater political status would have needed fourteen hundred or fifteen hundred florins, which would have ruined both of us. And I'm not sure it would have made the girl any happier, because outside the regime[4] there's not a great choice, and this is a big problem for us. Everything considered, I decided to settle the girl well and not to take such things into account. I'm sure she'll be as well placed as any girl in Florence, because she'll have a mother- and father-in-law who are only happy making her happy. Oh and I haven't told you about Marco yet, [Caterina's] husband, he's always saying to her "If you want anything ask me for it." When she was betrothed he ordered a gown of crimson velvet for her made of silk and a surcoat of the same fabric, which is the most beautiful cloth in Florence. He had it made in his workshop. And he had a garland of feathers and pearls made [for her] which cost eighty florins, the headdress underneath has two strings of pearls costing sixty florins or more. When she goes out she'll have more than four hundred florins on her back. And he ordered some crimson velvet to be made up into long sleeves lined with marten, for [her to wear] when she goes to her husband's house. And he's having a rose-colored gown made, embroidered with pearls. He feels he can't do enough having things made, because she's beautiful and he wants her to look even more so. There isn't a girl in Florence to compare

parti, al parere di molti: che Iddio gli presti santà e grazia lungo tempo, com'io disidero.

Del mandare Matteo di fuori, non vorrei per ora; però che, perchè sie piccolo, pure ne sono più accompagnata, e posso mal fare sanz' esso; almanco tanto la Caterina ne vadia a marito: poi mi parrebbe rimanere troppo sola. Per ora non ho il capo a mandarlo: che se vorrà esser buono, lo terrò qua; che non può esser preso per le gravezze insino a sedici anni, ed egli ebbe undici di marzo. Hollo levato dall'abbaco, e appara a scrivere; e porrollo al banco, che vi starà questo verno: dipoi vedrèno quello vorrà fare; che Iddio gli dia quella virtù che gli fa bisogno.

De' fatti del Comune, t'avviso che ho debito fiorini dugento quaranta, e sono istata molestata da no' meno di quattro Ufici, che hanno a riscuotere pel Comune: da se' mesi in qua non ho mai avuto a fare altro, che andare ora a questo Uficio e ora a quest'altro. Ora, per grazia di Dio, mi sono accordata co' loro per ensino a febbraio; che pago, tra tutti, il mese fiorini nove o circa. Aspettasi che la gravezza nuova esca fuori per tutto ottobre; che se mi fanno il dovere, come dicono, di non porre albìtro a vedove e pupilli, non arò duo fiorini; che forse non farò tanto debito. E poi che 'l Duca è morto, istimasi non se ne pagherà tanti, se già il Re di Ragona non ci dessi noia; che già ha cominciato presso a Monte Varchi, a un castello che si chiama Cennina. Dicevasi, quando l'ebbono, che si riarebbe l'altro dì, chè non vi potevano istare. Sonvi già stati tre settimane, e ancora sono atti a starvi; che v'era drento tal contadino, che solo del grano e della roba vi

with her and she's beautiful in every way, or so many people think. May God give them his grace and good health for a long time, as I wish.

About sending Matteo away,[5] I wouldn't want to do so for the present because although he's so little he keeps me company and I'd be in a bad way without him, at least at the present time while Caterina's getting ready to go and live with her husband. After that it seems to me I'll be on my own too much. For the present I'm not inclined to send him away. If he wants to be good I'll keep him here. He can't be taxed[6] until he's sixteen and he was only eleven in March. I've taken him away from learning arithmetic and he's learning to write.[7] I'll put him at the writing desk and he can stay there this winter. After that we'll see what he wants to do. May God give him those abilities which he's going to need.

So far as the Commune[8] is concerned, I must tell you that I owe them two hundred and forty florins and that I've been persecuted by no less than four Offices[9] trying to recover [money] for the Commune. For the last six months I've done nothing but go to one Office after another. Now by the grace of God I've reached an agreement to pay them all, up until February, nine florins à month or thereabouts. They say the new tax may be imposed for all of October. If they do the right thing by me as they say they will, not imposing the assessment on widows and orphans, I won't have two florins [to pay], so perhaps I won't have so many debts. And since the Duke of Milan is dead[10] they think we won't have to pay so much [tax], if the King of Aragon[11] doesn't give us trouble, which he's already begun [to do] close to Montevarchi[12] at a castle called Cennina. It was said when they took it that it could be retaken in a day because they wouldn't be able to stay there. They've already been there for three weeks and look like [they're] staying because it's in such [good] countryside. It's said there was so much grain and

lasciò si dice ne vi verebbono un anno. Dicesi che innanzi si riabbia, si spendrà più che quaranta migliaia fiorini. Iddio provvegga a' nostri bisogni.

Dice la Caterina, che tu faccia ch'ell' abbia un poco di quel sapone; e se v'è niuna buon' acqua o altra cosa da far bella, che ti prega gliele mandi presto; e per persona fidata, chè se ne fa cattività.

Non ti maravigliare s'io non ti scrivo ispesso, che sono infaccendata ne' fatti della Caterina. Ristorerotti quando Matteo arà apparato a scrivere: ma non guardare a me. Fa' che per ogni fante mi scriva, se no' dovessi dir altro che tu sta' bene, e Niccolò. Non so come tu ti porti nelle faccende che tu hai a fare, come se' sollecito: che Iddio il sa, il dispiacere ebbi quando intesi non potevi venire quando fusti a Livorno; perchè tal cosa si dice a bocca, che non si dice per lettera. Che a Dio piaccia vi rivegga sani enanzi ch'io muoia. Fa' sopra tutto, figliuol mio, che tu ti porti bene en modo, che dove l'anno passato mi desti tanto dolore de' tua tristi modi, tu mi dia consolazione: e considera allo stato tuo, e quello che Niccolò ha fatto inverso di te, che se' degno di baciare la terra dove e' pone e piedi. E dico quello medesimo per tuo amore, chè se' più obrigato a lui che a tuo padre o tuo' madre, quando penso quello ha fatto di te, che niun altro l'arebbe fatto; sicchè fa' ne sia conoscente, e non essere ingrato del benificio hai ricevuto tu e' tua, e ricevi tu continovamente. Non mi voglio distendere in più dire; che mi debbi oggimai intendere, chè non se' un fanciullo; che di luglio n'avesti diciannove, e bastiti. Fa' sopra tutto masserizia; che ti bisogna, chè sta' peggio non ti credi. Nè altro per questa m'accade dirti. E Dio di male ti guardi. None scrivo a

goods they could live off it for a year. It's said that before they [the Florentines] retake it they will have spent more than forty thousand florins. May God provide for our needs.

Caterina says you should arrange it so she can get some of that soap and if there's any good water or anything else [in Naples] to make [her] beautiful she begs you to send it quickly and by a trustworthy person, because otherwise he [the carrier] might do something mischievous with it.

Don't be surprised if I don't write often, because I'm very busy arranging everything for Caterina. You'll be paid back when Matteo has learned to write, but don't expect letters from me. Do write by every messenger though, if only to say that you're well and that Niccolò is.[13] I don't know how you're going with your tasks or whether you're keen to do them. God knows the disappointment I suffered when you couldn't come to Florence while you were at Livorno, because you can say things in person which you can't put in a letter. May it please God to let me see you again safe and well before I die. In the past year you've made me very unhappy with your bad behavior.[14] Above all my son, you must behave better and give me comfort instead. You should consider your position and think what Niccolò has done for you and be worthy to kiss the ground he walks on. And I say this out of love for you, because you have a greater obligation to him than to your father or mother, when I think of all he's done for you, which no one else would have done. So do be aware of this and don't be ungrateful for the kindness he has shown to you and yours, and that you constantly receive from him. I don't want to say any more. You should understand because you're no longer a boy: you were nineteen in July, which is [old] enough. Above all, do be careful with money; you must, because you're in a worse position than you realize. Nothing more for now. May God keep you from harm. I haven't written to Nic-

Niccolò della Caterina, che n'è stato avvisato da Giovanni e Antonio. Raccomandaci a lui. E se se' cassiere, portati en modo abbia onore; e tieni le mani strette, ch'io n'abbia avere più dolore ch'io abbia avuto.

2

Al nome di Dio. A dì 8 di novembre 1448.

A dì 6 di questo ebi una tua de' dì 16 del passato, alla quale farò per questa risposta.

Tu mi di' de' fatti di Matteo, come t'ha scritto una lettera di nostro istato: ed è vero; e stiàno ancora peggio che non dicie. Iddio lodato di tutto. E dell'aver mostro la lettera a Niccolò, ha' fatto bene: però che lo stato nostro è noto agli strani, ben debb'esser noto a quegli che ci sono parenti e continovamente ci aiutano: chè Niccolò non ha ora a dimostrare la buona volontà inverso di voi, chè sempre è stato di buon animo a farvi del bene; ed èciene di te tale isperienza, che ne so' chiara; e tu più di me ne debb'essere chiaro. Tu di' che, veduto che qua Matteo, sì per amore della morìa, che porta pericolo a starci, e sì perchè e' perde tempo e non fa nulla, Niccolò è contento lo mandi costà, e ch'io lo metta in punto. Egli è vero che qua è cominciato la morìa, e chi ha 'vuto

colò about Caterina because I know he's heard all about it from Giovanni and Antonio.[15] Remember us to him, and if you're the cashier, act in a way that does you credit and keep a strict tally so I don't have any more grief than I've had already.[16]

2

Alessandra continues her discussion with Filippo about whether Matteo, now twelve, was old enough to join him in Naples. She refers to her lack of ready money and her desire to conserve what she had in order to provide her sons with some capital to develop an independent business eventually.

In the name of God. 8 November 1448.

On the 6th of this month one of your letters arrived, of the 16th of last month. I will answer it here.

You mention the business about Matteo, and how he has written you a letter about the position we're in. [What he says] is true, and in fact things are even worse than he said. May God be praised for everything. And about having shown the letter to Niccolò, you've done the right thing. When strangers know our business, it's only right that our relations, who are always helping us, should know about it too. Niccolò doesn't have to show you how well disposed he is toward you because he's always been prepared to do the right thing by you and we've had so much experience of this that I'm sure of it and you should be even more so. You say that as Matteo's here it's dangerous to stay here because of the plague,[1] and that because it's wasting time and achieving nothing, Niccolò is happy for me to send him there and that I should arrange it. It's true the plague has started here, and those

d'andare in villa, se n' è ito; e ancora per le ville n' è morti, e quasi per tutto il contado ne muore quand' uno e quand' un altro; e la brigata si sta per ancora in villa; e credo, non faciendoci altrimenti danno, che torneranno ora a Firenze. Istimasi che questo verno non farà troppo danno, ma che a primavera comincierà a fare il fracasso: che Iddio ci aiuti! e Matteo m' ha sentito dire che, sendoci morìa, non ho danari da partirmi: ed è vero. Io non so come io me lo mandassi, che è piccolo, ancora ha bisogno del mio governo, ed io non so come mi vivessi; che di cinque figliuoli, rimanessi con una, cioè l'Alesandra, che ogni ora aspetto maritalla; che il più possa istar meco non sono du' anni. Che quando vi penso, n' ho un gran dolore, di rimanere così sola. E dicoti che a questi dì andò Matteo in villa di Marco, e stettevi se' dì; ch' io non credetti tanto vivere ch' e' tornassi; e non avevo chi mi faciessi un servigio; che mi pareva essere impacciata sanza lui, poi mi scrive tutte le lettere. Da altra parte, ebbe in questa state un gran male, e credetti che morissi: ma il buon governo lo scampò. E ragionando col maestro dell'andar di fuori, mi disse: Voi l'avete poco caro, se lo mandate; però ch' egli è di gientile compressione; e se avessi un male fuor del vostro governo, sì mancherebbe: sicchè, se l'avete caro, no lo partite sì tosto da voi. E per questo, e perch' io me ne veggo bisogno, me n' uscì il pensiero. È vero che, or fa un anno, n' avevo voglia: ma avevo ancora la Caterina in casa; che non mi pareva esser sì sola. Ma poi senti' come Lorenzo si portava tristamente, e che d' amendue avevo avuto tanto dolore, che sendo morti no n' arei avuto maggiore, ch' io, tra una cosa e l' altra, diliberai non ne mandar più fuori, se grande bisogno non m' era: e l' ho detto co Marco e con Antonio degli

who can go to their country houses have gone, but people are also dying from the plague in the country and nearly everywhere in the country [2] someone dies of it now and then. For the present the household [3] is in the country but I think they'll come back now, so long as there are no more deaths. They say there won't be too many deaths this winter but a lot of people will die in the spring. May God help us. Matteo has heard me say that even if we had the plague here I wouldn't have the money to leave, and it's true. But I don't know how I could send him away because he's little and still needs me to look after him. And I don't know how I could go on living if out of five children I was left with only one, Lessandra, as I'm expecting to arrange a marriage for her any time now. She won't stay with me more than two years longer. I feel very sad when I think about being left so alone. I must tell you how in the last few days Matteo has gone to stay in the country with Marco and he's been there for six days. I didn't think I could live until he came back and I've had no one to run errands for me. It's been inconvenient without him here because he writes all my letters for me. We should also keep in mind the fact that he was very sick this summer and I thought he would die, but he was saved by being well looked after. I was talking to the doctor about him going away, and he said "You have little love for him if you send him away, because he has a delicate constitution and if he were sick and didn't have you to look after him he would die. So if you love him you won't part with him so soon." And because of this and because he needs to stay, I've given up the idea. It's true I did consider it a year ago but I still had Caterina at home then, so it didn't occur to me that I'd be so alone. But then I heard how Lorenzo was behaving so badly [4] and I've been so unhappy over you both, it couldn't have been worse if you were dead. So what with one thing and another I decided not to send any more sons away if there was no great need. I've dis-

Strozzi. Amendue mi dicono per ora nollo mandi: ma se pure a primavera ci sarà la morìa grande, come si stima; essendo migliorata a Siena e per tutto il camino per ensino a Roma, lo potre' mandare: chè sarebbe pazzia la mia a mandallo ora, chè ora siàno nel verno; chè diliberando mandarlo, nollo metterei per via: sicchè per ora non vi porre pensiero. So i' meglio di niuno il bisogno vostro; e che se voi non ve ne guadagniate, non bisogna istare a fidanza d'altro. Io per me m' ingegnerò, per ogni modo e masserizia, di mantenervi questo poco ch' i' ho, se 'l Comune non me lo toglie; chè non posso più difendermi. Iddio sia quello che m' aiuti; e a voi dia virtù e santà, come disidero.

Del lino, istarò a tua fidanza; e se me lo mandi, mandami drentovi libbre 10 di mandorle per la quaresima; che verranno bene nella balla del lino. Chieggotele perchè sento costà n' è buono mercato, e qua son care. Fa' di mandarmele, chè so è poca ispesa.

Di Marco, t' aviso ch' è buon giovane, e molto bene tiene la Caterina, e tutti se ne porta bene, e molto me ne contento; che è di buona virtù; ma ha troppa gravezza, chè ha da undici fiorini. Tutto ha pagato per ensino a qui; e se non peggiora, ne sono molto contenta di lui: che Iddio gli dia della suo' grazia. La Caterina non è per ancora grossa; che al temporale che è, l' ho molto caro: ma istà magra della persona, che somiglia suo padre. Iddio la faccia pur sana.

A dì 4 di questo ti scrissi: manda' la sotto lettere di Marco; e perchè il fante si partì prima ch' io non credetti, credo l'arai a un' otta con questa. E per quella ti scrissi della casetta di Niccolò Popoleschi, che s' è venduta a Donato Ruciellai, che ci è a confini, cioè in sulla corte,

cussed it with Marco and with Antonio degli Strozzi. They both tell me not to send him away at the moment or even in the spring if there's a serious outbreak of the plague as they expect. [But if] it's better at Siena and all the way to Rome, I could send him then. [They say] I would be mad to send him now because it's winter and I wouldn't want to lose him by deciding to send him away. So for the moment I'm not considering it. I know better than anyone what you need and that you wouldn't stay reliant on someone else [5] if you didn't have to and weren't profiting by it. So far as I'm concerned I will try in every way I can to save for you what little I have, if the Commune doesn't take it from me, because I can't protect myself any longer. [6] God knows what will help me. May He give you abilities and good health, as I wish.

About the flax, [7] I'll leave that up to you and if you do send it, send me 10 pounds of almonds for Lent in with it because they'll fit well into the bale of flax. I'm asking you for them because I've heard they're cheap there, and they're dear here. Do send them because I know it won't cost much.

I must tell you about Marco. He's a good young man and treats Caterina very well and behaves well to everyone and I'm very happy about it. He has great abilities but too much tax, eleven florins. [8] He is up to date with his payments and if it doesn't get any worse I'll be very happy about him. May God give him grace. Caterina isn't pregnant so far, which at present I'm glad about, but she stays thin [9] because she takes after her father. May God keep her well.

I wrote to you on the 4th of this month; it was enclosed in a letter from Marco. Because the servant left earlier than I thought, you should get it at the same time as this one. In that letter I told you about Niccolò Popoleschi's little house, that it's been sold to Donato Rucellai and that it borders on this one, that is on the courtyard side, and

che per verun modo non si vole lasciare uscire di mano. Filippo, rispondi presto, chè lo voglio iscrivere a Iacopo a Bruggia.

Nè altro per questa. Iddio di male ti guardi. Per la tua Allesandra fu di Matteo degli Strozi in Firenze.

3

Al nome di Dio. A dì 13 di luglio 1449.

Per Soldo ebbi l'utima tua, che fu de' dì 3 del passato; e non ho fatto prima risposta, aspettando farla per Matteo: farolla per questa.

Avvisoti come Soldo giunse qui a' dì 15 del passato, ed era di malavoglia. Anda'lo a vicitare più volte, e ragionammo insieme del mandare Matteo, come ero contenta di farne la volontà di Niccolò e tua, veduto il gran disidèro avete di tirarlo innanzi e farlo da qualche cosa; non guardando a la consolazione mia, ma all'utile vostro, come sempre ho fatto, e così farò insino al fine. E pensa se m'è dura cosa, quando penso come io rimasi giovane allevare cinque figliuoli, e di poca età come savate. E questo Matteo mi rimase in corpo, ed òmello allevato credendo che altro che la morte no 'l partissi da me; e massimamente, di

that we wouldn't want by any means to lose our chance of [buying] it.[10] Answer quickly Filippo, because I want to write to Jacopo [11] in Bruges about it.

Nothing more for now. May God keep you from harm. From your Allesandra, widow of Matteo degli Strozzi, in Florence.

3

Matteo was now thirteen and it was normal for Florentine boys of the merchant class to start learning their trade at this age. But in his case this meant leaving his mother and home for a distant city, even though he would be working for a kinsman and with his elder brother, Filippo. Here Alessandra explains to Filippo why she had delayed his departure for another few months.

In the name of God. 13 July 1449.

I received your last letter, written on the 3rd of last month, from Soldo.[1] I haven't answered earlier because I was waiting to send it with Matteo. I will now answer in this letter.

I must tell you how Soldo arrived here on the 15th of last month and [how] he was sick. I went to see him many times and we talked about sending Matteo [to Naples], how I was happy to do what you and Niccolò wanted about it, seeing how much you want to take him away and make something of him, not thinking of my own comfort but of what will be useful to you, as I have always done and as I will do to the end. You should consider how hard it is for me, when I think how I was left while I was still young to bring up five children as young as you all were. I was still pregnant with Matteo and I've brought him up thinking that nothing but death could part him from me,

tre, avendone due di fuori, mi pareva fussi a bastanza. Ora veggo quanto me n'avete iscritto, e mostromi le ragioni che questo è l'utile e l'onore vostro; e simile me n' ha detto Soldo: ho diliberato non guardare che di tre figliuoli niuno n'abbia a' mie' bisogni, ma fare il ben vostro. E sì t'avisso come l'ho messo in punto d'ogni cosa; cioè, un mantello nuovo in quella forma mi disse Soldo, e un gonnellino pagonazzo, e un farsetto di quello medesimo, e camice, e altre cose che mi pare sia di bisogno; e simile e coltellini, e pianelle fratesche, e palle, e tutto quello ha' chiesto a Matteo, è comperato. Ebbi da' Capponi, con parola di Soldo, per comperare quello e' fa di bisogno, fiorini otto.

Ora, dovendo partire a questi dì, il fanciullo è ito a vedere e a far motto a questi mia e vostri parenti. Infine, tutti m' hanno gridato ch'i' ho poco caro questo fanciullo, e ch' i' sono una pazza a mandallo per questo tempo; sì per la morìa ch'è per tutto, e sì pel gran caldo ch'è, che le persone grandi e che son usi a cavalcare, è loro ispiacevole il camminare, non che al fanciullo, ch'è di gentile compressione: che se pella via non ammalassi di morbo (che non sare' gran fatto), per gli alberghi che hanno a fare, son certa nol condurrebbe sanza una febbre; chè conosco la natura sua: e seguendone men che bene pella via, non riuscirebbe il pensier tuo, ed io non sare' mai più contenta, e detto mi sarebbe Ben ti sta. Che insino a Neri di Gin Capponi mi mandò a dire ch'i' ero una sciocca a mandallo. E più iermattina ci vennono dua Frati dell' Osservanza di san Francesco, ch'erano molto amici di vostro padre, e sì mi sconfortorono del mandarlo ora; ch'è troppo gran pericolo. E tanto m' hanno detto loro, e gli altri che ci voglion bene, ch'io iscrissi duo versi a Soldo, che per verun modo non volevo mandallo ora; ma più qua a settembre, che sarà migliorato la cosa, e passato il caldo,

and more than anything else having two out of three away seemed more than enough. But now I've seen your letter, explaining to me how this will bring you both honor and profit, and Soldo has said something similar to me. So I decided not to consider the fact that out of three sons, I'll have none to look after me, but to do what's best for you instead. So I must tell you that I organized everything, a new cloak in the style Soldo told me about and a short gown and a doublet of the same material, and also some little knives [2] and monk's sandals and some balls and everything you wanted for Matteo, has been bought. I drew out eight florins from the Capponi [bank] with Soldo's surety to buy what he needed.

As he had to leave in a few days the boy went to see my relatives and yours and have a word with them. As it happens they've all made a great fuss about it, [saying] I can't have much love for this boy and that I'm a madwoman to send him at this time because of the plague being everywhere and the great heat and that [even] for adults and those who are used to riding it is unpleasant to travel, let alone for the boy, who has a delicate constitution. If he doesn't get sick with the plague on the way, which would be surprising, I'm sure he wouldn't complete the journey without catching a fever in the inns they have to use, because I know what he's like. And if things went badly your plan wouldn't succeed and I would never be happy again, and they would have told me it served me right. Even Neri di Gino Capponi [3] sent [a message] saying I was a fool to send him. And then yesterday two Brothers of the Observant Franciscans, who were great friends of your father, came here and discouraged me from sending him now, because the risk is too great. They said so much to me and [so have] all the others who wish us well, that I wrote a couple of lines to Soldo [saying] that I didn't want to send him at present, by any means. But later on in September it will be better and the heat will be over. I will send him

lo manderò. E non avendo altra compagnia, manderò Agnolo da Quaracchi, o Pagolo che stette con Niccolò quando era qua. E pertanto abbiate pazienza, pella salute sua, un mese e mezzo o due, il più; chè quando fussi morto, noll'aresti nè tu ned io. A fine di bene fo tutto; sicchè dillo con Niccolò, che gli è 'n punto, e non ha se non a salire a cavallo: e altra ispesa non bisognerà fare, dal cavallo in fuori: che abbia pazienza do' mesi, che certo lo manderò. Che Iddio gli dia della suo' grazia, com' io disidero.

Raccomandaci a Niccolò. Non gli ho fatto risposta, che ho 'vuto tanta faccenda tra ordinare Matteo e accordarmi con que' delle Vendite e ordinare d'andare in villa, che ma' più non v'andai, ch' io non n' ho 'vuto agio. Poi Matteo è stato in villa, e sono stata sola. Abbiatemi per escusata. Per la tua Allesandra, in Firenze.

Domattina, se a Dio piacerà, n'andrò in villa. Iscrivimi ispesso, e dove sete.

[then]. And as I won't have any other company I'll send for Agnolo from Quaracchi[4] or that Pagolo who stayed with Niccolò when he was here. And so you should be patient for the sake of his health for a month and a half or two at the most, because once he is dead neither of us will have him. I'm doing everything for the best so discuss it with Niccolò, [tell him] it's all arranged and that he [Matteo] will have nothing to do but jump on a horse and there'll be no more expense apart from the horse. He should be patient for two months and then I'll send him. May God give him grace as I wish.

Five short paragraphs: she was sending Filippo a power of attorney; more about the adjoining house owned by Donato Rucellai; the death of a member of the Macinghi family from the plague; Ginevra di Niccolò Soderini[5] was going to write to him about flax; Soldo would tell him about a financial matter.

Remember us to Niccolò. I haven't answered his letter because I've had too much to do, what with getting Matteo's things ready and reaching an agreement with the Officials for Sales[6] and getting ready to go to this house in the country (not having been there before), so I haven't had the time. Then Matteo went to the country and I've been alone. You'll have to make my excuses. From your Allesandra, in Florence.

Tomorrow morning, God willing, I'll be going to the country. Write to me often and [let me know] where you are.[7]

4

The plague was still raging in Florence and the subject of death clearly occupied Alessandra's mind as she wrote to Filippo. Niccolò's brother, Filippo di Lionardo Strozzi, had died in Barcelona some months earlier, and several other relations had

4

Al nome di Dio. A dì 26 dicembre 1449.

Fu' avvisata da te, e prima da Soldo degli Strozzi e da Matteo di Giorgio, della morte del nostro Filippo; che n'ebbi un gran dispiacere, ed ho, considerando il danno che getta a noi prima, e poi a tutta la casa; che la virtù sua era tanta, che a tutti dava riputazione. Non si può riparare a questa morte: convienci avere pazienza a quello vuole Iddio. Ancora morì F. della Luna; che n'è stato un gran danno. E qua morì Antonangiolo Macigni, e molti altri nostri parenti degli Strozzi. E a questi dì è morto la Margherita di Pippo Manetti con dua figliuoli: sicchè questa volta ci è tocca la nostra parte. A Dio piaccia per suo' misericordia far fine. E pe' rispetto della morte di Filippo, ho tue lettere e da Iacopo, come Niccolò e lui s'hanno accozzare a Barzalona: che Iddio die loro buon viaggio. Avvisimi ch'io faccia onore a Niccolò, che iscavalcherà in casa nostra; e come ne menerà Matteo seco a Barzalona, e ch'io lo metta in punto. Così ho fatto, e aspettolo co' letizia; chè ho gran voglia di vederlo. Io m'ingegnerò di fargli quello onore che a me fia possibile. So non potrei nè saprei fare quello onore che merita; ma arammi per escusata quando farò quello ch'io potrò, e fia volentieri: che Iddio lo conduca a salvamento. Ieri senti'

recently died of the plague in Florence. Alessandra was also concerned that Caterina (who was expecting her first child the following February) might die in childbirth, and the final installment of her dowry might thus be lost. She discusses whether they should insure against this possibility.

In the name of God. 26 December 1449.

Two paragraphs: she had had many letters from Filippo which she had not answered; she had been ill, and had gone to stay with Marco and Caterina and then with her brother, Zanobi Macinghi, at Antella.[1]

I heard from you and first from Soldo degli Strozzi and Matteo di Giorgio Brandolini[2] of the death of our Filippo, which has made me very sad and still does, considering the harm it will do to us first and then to the whole family.[3] He was such a good man, he gave a good reputation to [us] all. There's nothing we can do about his death; we must endure whatever God wills. F[rancesco] della Luna[4] has also died, which has been a great loss. And Antonangiolo Macinghi has died and [so have] many other Strozzi relations. Margherita di Pippo Manetti died today[5] and two of her children, so this time our immediate family has been hit. May God in his mercy bring it to an end. About the death of Filippo, I've [heard from] your letters and from Jacopo's how he [Jacopo] and Niccolò met in Barcelona.[6] May God give them a good journey. You tell me I should honor Niccolò, who will be staying with us, and how he will be taking Matteo with him to Barcelona and that I should get everything organized. I've done so and I'm looking forward to his arrival because I'm eager to see him. I'll try to do him as much honor as I can. I know I can't do him all the honor he deserves because I don't know how to. He'll have to excuse me when I do whatever I can and do it willingly. May God bring him

49

ch'era a Roma: istimo si partirà di là fatto le feste, e qui l'aspettiàno a dì 4 o 5 di gennaio.

Credo che da Marco se' avvisato come la Caterina è grossa; ed ha a fare il fanciullo a mezzo febbraio. A me parrebbe, essendo in quello stato, pigliarne sicurtà che no si perdessi que' cinquecento fiorini s'hanno avere dal Monte; che si perderebbe l'avere e la persona a un'otta: che se Iddio facessi altro di lei innanzi aprile, ce gli perderemmo. I' l'ho detto con Antonio degli Strozzi: in ogni modo gli pare si spenda fiorini 12; che così costerà di sicurtà per questi tre mesi, cioè gennaio e febbraio e marzo. Aspetterò Niccolò, poi ci ha essere tosto, e farò quanto me ne dirà. Marco no gli pare si faccia; che dice ch'ella istà sì bene della persona, che no gitterebbe via questi parecchi fiorini: e a me pare di volègli gittare, e stare nel sicuro. No gliene iscrivere però nulla, a ciò no l'abbia per male; ch'è faccenda tocca a noi. Priego Iddio ne la tragga al tempo debito con salute dell'anima e santà del corpo, come disidero.

Ho pensiero, piacendo a Dio, qua d'aprile venire per quel santo Perdono a Roma: e se per niuno modo tu potessi fare di venirvi, a ciò ch'io ti vedessi innanzi ch'io morissi, mi sarebbe una gran consolazione; che vedi ch'io non ho altro bene in questo mondo che voi tre mia figliuoli; e per la salute vostra mi v'ho levati a uno a uno dinanzi, non guardando a la mia consolazione: e ora ho tanto dolore di levarmi dinanzi questo utimo, ch'io non so come mi viverò sanza lui; chè troppo gran duolo sento, e troppo amore gli porto; chè somiglia tutto il padre, ed è fatto un bello garzoncello in questo tempo è stato in villa;

here safely. Yesterday I heard he was in Rome; I imagine he'll leave there after the [Christmas] festival and we'll expect him here on the 4th or 5th of January.

Three paragraphs: cloth for shirts and flax; a list of their debtors in Pesaro; another discussion about the neighboring house belonging to Donato Rucellai.

I gather you've heard from Marco that Caterina is pregnant and expecting the child in the middle of February. As that's the case I think we should take out some insurance so we won't lose the five hundred florins they're owed from the [Dowry] Fund,[7] as we could lose her and the money at the same time. We could lose it if God has other plans for her. I've discussed it with Antonio degli Strozzi and he thinks we should spend the 12 florins, which is what it would cost for insurance for these three months, that is for January, February and March. I'll wait for Niccolò, who'll be here soon, and do as he advises me. Marco thinks we shouldn't do it; he says that as she's keeping so well in herself we shouldn't throw away these few florins. It seems to me better to throw them away and be sure. For that reason [I won't] write to him about it, so he won't take it badly, because it's our business. I pray God will bring her through it at the proper time and healthy in body and soul, as I wish.

I'm thinking of going to Rome, God willing, later on in April for the Holy Indulgence.[8] If by any chance you could come too, so that I could see you again before I die, it would be a great comfort to me. You see there's nothing else I care about in this world except you, my three sons, and I've sent you away one after the other for your own good and not considering my own happiness. Now I am so sad at sending away this last one. I don't know how I can live without him, because I feel so unhappy and love him too much because he is just like his father. And he's become such a beautiful boy while he's been in the

che avendol veduto prima, e vedendo ora, è rimutato. Piaccia a Dio n'abbia consolazione. E per tanto ti priego, poi ch' i' rimango così isconsolata, darmi un poco di rifrigiero in questa mia venuta costà a Roma: che Iddio mi presti tanta vita ch'io vi rivegga tutti, come disidero.

Da Lorenzo ho lettere d'ottobre, che sta bene: iscrivigli spesso, che faccia bene. I' ebbi la procura mi mandasti: quando bisognerà altro, te n'avviserò. Nè altro per questa. Iddio di male ti guardi. Per la tua Allesandra, in Firenze.

5

Al nome di Dio. A dì 8 di febbraio 1449.

A' dì 30 del passato per Niccolò ebbi una tua de' dì 4 di dicembre, e dipoi a' dì 7 di questo ebbi un'altra tua de' dì 24 passato. Farò per questa appresso risposta.

Veggo Niccolò alla partita sua t'ha lasciato il carico del governo di costì, e tutto ha rimesso in te: che mi pare abbi usato inverso di te una gran liberalità, e grande onore t'ha fatto, e grande amore veggo ti porta; e hanne fatto ora tale isperienza ch'è noto a ciascuno: e, secondo le parole tue, mi pare tu lo conosca. E pertanto i' ti ricordo che tu faccia onore a chi n' ha fatto a te: che, secondo m' ha detto Niccolò, che portandoti bene a questo punto, e faccendo il

country; if you'd seen him before and saw him now you wouldn't know he was the same boy. May God let him be a comfort to me. And because I'm so sad I beg you to give me a little comfort from this trip to Rome. May God let me live long enough to see you all again, as I wish.

I've had a letter from Lorenzo which he wrote in October. He says he's well. Do write to him often because it will be good for him. I received the power of attorney you sent me and I'll let you know if I need anything else. Nothing more for now; may God keep you from harm. From your Allesandra in Florence.

5

Niccolò Strozzi had just visited Florence, leaving Filippo in charge of the business in Naples during his absence. Alessandra lectures Filippo on the importance of making the most of this opportunity. She also refers to Matteo's departure and to the birth of her first grandchild, Piero Parenti.

In the name of God. 8 February 1450.[1]

On the 30th of last month Niccolò brought me a letter from you, written on the 4th of December, and since then, on the 7th, I've received another from you of the 24th of last month. I will answer [both letters] in this one.

I see Niccolò left the running of the place to you when he left Naples, and has trusted you with everything. He's been very generous to you, it seems to me, and has done you a great honor and loves you very much. He is now testing you in a way which is clear to everyone, and judging by what you say I think you know it. And so I must remind you to honor the person who has honored you. From what Niccolò has told me, if you do well at this

debito tuo come t' ha ordinato, ti darà ta' luogo e aiuto, che tu rileverai la Casa tua, e me fara' contenta. E m' ha detto molti pensieri ha fatto sopra a' fatti tua; che n'ho preso assa' conforto. Ed è cosa ragionevole, che faccendo 'l debito tuo, adoperando la virtù, che faccia quello che dice: sì che tutto sta in te, l'utile e l'onore tuo, e la consolazione mia. E pertanto ti priego, consideri i' luogo dove se' rimaso, e lo 'ncarico t' ha lasciato Niccolò, che tu governi en modo abbia onore; chè ora si coglie il fatto tuo, e ha' fare pruova di te in questo tempo Niccolò non v'è. Che se farai il contradio, mi dice se' spacciato, e che ma' più gliene dica nulla, ch'i' perdere' tempo. So che conosci il bisogno tuo: e sopra ciò non dirò altro, se no che l'opera loda il maestro. Priego Iddio che ti dia quella grazia e virtù che ha' di bisogno.

Niccolò per grazia di Dio si condusse, come ho detto di sopra, qua a' dì 30 passato, e qui en casa iscavalcò. Non ci è stato continovamente a mangiare, ch'è ito duo dì a casa Antonio degli Strozzi, e una mattina a casa Francesco della Luna, e una sera a cena co' Lionardo Mannelli: tutto i' resto del tempo è stato qui a mangiare e abergo continovamente. E così ci è stato la Lena sua sirocchia, e la moglie di Bernardo Tanagli, e la Ginevra d'Antonio da Ricasoli, e la Checca; e tutto il parentado ci è venuto a vedello: e Marco ancora ci venne di Mugello; che v'è la Caterina in parto, che ha fatto il fanciullo, e sta bene. Sì che gli è stato fatto grande onore da tutto il parentado: ed ècci venuto a vicitallo de' maggiori cittadini di Firenze. Io gli ho fatto in tutte le cose quello onore che m'è stato possibile, e volentieri: e quello non s'è fatto, è suto per non potere nè sapere più. Aràmi auto per escusata. Èmi stato la venuta sua di consolazione: e dispiacere m'è suto la partita del mio Matteo; che ancora non sono in me.

stage and do your duty as he's taught you, he will give you such a position and such help that you will rebuild your family[2] and make me happy. He's told me what he thinks about your concerns and I've taken great comfort from that. It makes sense that if you do the right thing and use your abilities, you can do what he says [you can]. So it's all up to you, whether you advance yourself in the business and give yourself a good reputation and give me some consolation. For that reason I beg you, considering your position and the responsibility Niccolò has left you with, to manage everything in a way which does you credit. What you do will be noticed and you have to prove yourself while Niccolò's away. If you do the opposite he says it will be the end and I should never mention it again, because I'd be wasting my time. I realize you know what you need to do and I won't say anything else, except that the work praises its craftsman. May God give you grace and the abilities you need.

As I said, Niccolò arrived here by the grace of God on the 30th of last month and he stayed here with us. He didn't always eat here because on two days he went to Antonio Strozzi's house and one morning to Francesco della Luna's,[3] and one evening he went to supper with Lionardo Mannelli.[4] The rest of the time he was here both to eat and sleep. And so his sister Lena was here, and Bernardo Tanagli's wife and Ginevra d'Antonio da Ricasoli[5] and Checca[6] and all the [other] relations came here to see him. Marco even came all the way from the Mugello because Caterina gave birth there; she had a boy and is well. So he [Niccolò] was greatly honored by all our relations and the most important citizens of Florence came here to visit him. I showed him as much honor as I possibly could and did it willingly and anything I didn't do was because I didn't know how to do it or couldn't do it. He'll have to excuse me. His visit was a comfort but my Matteo leaving has made me so unhappy I'm still beside myself with grief.

Non mi distendo sopra il fatto suo per ora, che nulla ne potre' dire; ma per altra te n'avviserò. Partironsi di qua a' dì 6: che Iddio die loro buon viaggio e conducagli a salvamento.

Matteo andò con Niccolò, e andò volentieri, e bene a punto. Grande amore gli dimostrò, in questi parecchi dì che ci è stato, el fanciullo: molto gli piace l'aspetto suo, e credo gli piacerà più l'un dì che l'altro. Prego Iddio che gli dia tal virtù e grazia, ch'io ne sia consolata. Fa' di scrivere ispesso a Lorenzo. Nè altro per questa. Iddio vi conservi nella grazia sua, come disidero. Per la tua Allesandra, in Firenze.

6

Al nome di Dio. A dì 22 d'ottobre 1450.

L'utima ti scrissi fu a dì 5 di giugno, e per allora t'avvisai quanto era di bisogno. Dipoi ho 'vuto più tue, e a niuna ho fatto risposta, perchè tu vegga che Matteo non ci è, e che oramai è di bisogno uno di voi torni qua; che

I won't go on about it any more for the moment as I can't really say anything, but I'll give you some advice in another letter. They left here on the 6th; may God give them a good journey and keep them safe.

Four paragraphs: about the insurance bond they had taken out on Caterina's dowry and that it was nearly time to arrange a marriage for Lessandra; Niccolò's advice to Alessandra was not to make the trip she had been planning to Rome; more about the neighboring house belonging to Donato Rucellai; about Filippo sending her some flax from Naples.

Matteo went with Niccolò and went willingly and in good order. He [Niccolò] showed the boy great affection in the few days he was here. He liked the look of him very much and I think he'll like him more with every day that passes. May God give him such virtue and grace as will give me comfort. Do write to Lorenzo often. Nothing more for now; may God keep you in his grace, as I wish. From your Allesandra in Florence.

6

Alessandra begins by complaining to Filippo about the chore of writing frequent letters, now that Matteo was no longer at home to act as her scribe. She advises him not to beat Matteo, but to correct him gently if he makes a mistake. She then describes Caterina's position in her husband's family, the status of the Parenti and their likely usefulness to the Strozzi.

In the name of God. 22 October 1450.

I wrote to you on the 5th of June and told you everything you needed to know about. Since then I've had a lot of letters from you and I haven't answered any of them. Now that Matteo isn't here I need one of you to come

i' sono oggima' d'età da volere essere governata, e son poco sana, e fatica mi pare lo scrivere. E poi questo andare pelle ville fuggendo la morìa, m'ha ancora isviata dallo scrivere. Ma ho detto alle volte a Marco e 'Antonio Strozzi ti scrivino due versi per mie' parte. Ora di nuovo ho due tue, l'una de' dì 23 di settembre, l'altra de' dì 4 d'ottobre. Farò risposta.

Veggo che 'l pensiero di Niccolò è di menarne seco di costà Matteo; che l'ho caro, chè di meglio ne sarà assai a essere presso a te. Ma fa' che tu no gli dia busse: fa' che abbia discrezione di lui; che, a mie' parere, ha buono sentimento: e quando errassi, riprendilo dolcemente; e farai più frutto per questa via, che colle busse. E questo tieni a mente. E' m'ha iscritto molte lettere, e così 'Antonio e a Marco, che sono sì bene iscritte e dettate, che basterebbe a un uomo: che me ne conforto assai di lui, e vorre'lo presso a me. E se Niccolò facessi la via di qua alla tornata sua a Napoli, non so s'io mel lasciassi uscire tralle mani. Che Iddio dia lor grazia, che piglino buon viaggio.

La Caterina istà bene, e 'l suo fanciullo; e Marco e Parente si portano benissimo di lei, e pella suo' persona non gli manca, se non ch' ha mala suocera. Ma ben ti dico non sono parenti da farne conto di servigio niuno; ma a noi basta che lei istie bene. Priego Iddio a tutti dia di suo' grazia. Istannosi in villa presso a Giovanni Portinari; ed io mi sto all'Antella con Zanobi, chè v'è sano. Alle volte vengo a Firenze, quando ho faccenda, per due dì. Ora ci sono istata tre dì, aspettando il lino desti a Giovanni Lo-

back, because I'm at an age where I need to be looked after and I'm not well and writing seems like hard work. And then this going to the country to escape the plague has also stopped me writing. But now and then I've asked Marco, and Antonio Strozzi, to write you a couple of lines on my behalf. Now I've had two [letters] from you again, one of the 23rd of September and the other of the 4th of October. I'll answer them here.

I see Niccolò's thinking of keeping Matteo with him there.[1] I'm glad because it's much better for him to be close to you. But do be sure not to beat him and do be understanding with him. He seems to me to have the right ideas, and when he makes a mistake you should correct him kindly because you'll get better results that way than by blows. Do keep this in mind. He's written a lot of letters to me and to Antonio and Marco; they're so well written and phrased they'd do credit to a grown man. He's a great comfort to me and I'd like to have him close to me; if Niccolò comes here on his way back to Naples, I don't know if I can let him [Matteo] slip through my fingers. May God give them grace to have a good journey.

Three paragraphs: about flax, fennel, sheep's milk cheese, and other matters; she will do as Filippo wishes when Francesco returns; it was pointless trying to arrange a marriage for Lessandra while the plague was raging.

Caterina's well and so is her boy, and Marco and Parente are very good to her. Her situation couldn't be better except for the fact that she has a bad mother-in-law. But I must say they're not relations to put themselves out for you, although it's enough for us that she's well placed. May God give his grace to them all. They're staying in the country close to Giovanni Portinari and I'm staying at Antella with Zanobi because it's healthy there. Sometimes I come to Florence for a couple of days when I have business to do. At the moment I've been here for three days waiting for the flax you gave Giovanni Lorini, which

rini. Non è giunto per ancora. Nè altro per questa. Iddio di male ti guardi. Per la tua Allesandra, in Firenze.

La morte di Francesco sanza dubbio è danno a tutta la Casa. Iddio gli perdoni. E la tratta d'Anton de' Signori è stata molto utile. Iddio lodato di tutto.

7

Al nome di Dio. A dì 10 d'aprile 1451.

L'utima ti scrissi fu a dì 11 di dicembre, e non t' ho iscritto poi, che ho 'vuto male di stomaco, e non ho potuto istar chinata a scrivere. Sommi medicata un mese, e assa' bene sono migliorata; e se non fussi la quaresima, credo sarei guarita. Verranne la pasqua, se a Dio piacerà: penso guarire.

Del mese passato, d'Antonio Strozzi fusti avvisato come abbiàno maritata la Lesandra a Giovanni di Donato Bonsi, ch'è giovane dabbene e virtuoso e dassai, ed ha tante buone parti in sè, che i' tengo certo ch'ella istarà bene quanto io. Per quello sento di lui, e quanto n'ho veduto in questa state passata in villa di Riccardo Macigni, molto ne sono contenta; e benchè sieno sette frategli, lui sta di per sè dagli altri. Truovasi ora a Roma per certe faccende o vero compagnia aveva col Castellano di Castel Sant'Agnolo, che morì. Non sarà qui insino a otto dì di

hasn't arrived yet. Nothing more for now; may God keep you from all harm. From your Allesandra in Florence.

Without a doubt Francesco's[2] death has damaged the family[3] greatly. May God pardon his sins. And Antonio being drawn for the Signoria has been very useful.[4] May God be praised for everything.

7

Alessandra had arranged a marriage for her younger daughter, Lessandra, and she describes the match rather perfunctorily to Filippo. She seems more immediately concerned with the arrival in Florence of various commodities which he had sent her, and with Matteo's safe arrival in Naples.

In the name of God. 10 April 1451.

The last letter I wrote you was on the 11th of December; I haven't written to you since then because I've had a stomach complaint and haven't been able to bend over to write. I've been taking medicine for a month and I'm a lot better; if it weren't Lent[1] I think I'd be completely cured. Easter will come, God willing, and I'll get better.

You've heard from Antonio Strozzi how last month we married Lesandra to Giovanni di Donato Bonsi,[2] who is a respectable, well-behaved young man, and quite acceptable; he has so many good qualities, I'm sure she'll be as well [placed in marriage] as I was. Judging by what I've heard about him, and what I saw last summer, [which I] spent in Riccardo Macinghi's country house, I'm very pleased with him. Although there are seven brothers [in his family] he lives by himself, separate from the rest. He's in Rome at present on business, or rather [about] a company he had with Castellano di Castel Sant' Agnolo, who has died. He won't be here until the 8th of May. She [Le-

maggio. Ha di dota, tra danari e donora, fiorini mille. So che d'Antonio se' avvisato di tutto, di questa materia.

Pel Favilla ebbi la cesta, drentovi libbre 36 di lino e un sacchetto di libbre 51 di mandorle, libbre 24 di capperi, 3 alberegli di confezioni; ogni cosa buono e bello. Vennono a tempo rispetto il mal mio, che te ne fo onore. Mandai delle mandorle e de' capperi alla Caterina la suo' parte; e così Antonio Strozzi, parecchi; che non potevo far di meno: che molto caro l'hanno avute, chè non n'è stato qua quest'anno. E più, pel detto, mandasti a Marco cento dieci libbre di lino. Dissemi detto Favilla ch'era rimaso daccordo teco avere di vettura, di tutto, lire quattordici, e che da te aveva un ducato e mezzo, ch'erano, secondo disse lui, lire 6 e soldi 18. Restò avere lire 7, soldi 2: volli ritenègli queste lire 7: pregommi che pel caso suo, ch'io gli dessi lire 4; e lire 3 soldi 2 iscontassi: e così feci. Ho posto a suo conto lire 3, soldi 2; che tanti gli ho ritenuti. Marco mi die' la suo' parte della vettura, cioè lire 7; che tanti gliene toccava. Di nuovo ho 'vuto 12 coppie di buttarage, molte belle. Fa' bene a ricordarti di me, che oggimai ho bisogno di vezzi da voi: ma vorrei fussi presso a me! Priego Iddio ci die grazia siàno sì presso, che insieme abbiàno consolazione, come desidero.

Della giunta costì di Niccolò e Matteo sono allegra: chè non ti potre' dire la maninconia ho 'uto già duo mesi, non sentendo niuna novella di loro, e sempre mi die' a 'ntendere che qualche fortuna gli avessi fatti mal capitare: sempre ne domandavo Antonio o Marco, se di loro sentivano nulla: dicevammi di no. Ora sentendo son giunti sani e a salvamento, m'hanno detto il caso intervenne loro; che Iddio sia ringraziato, che gli liberò di tanto pericolo. E fece bene Antonio a non mel dire: tra ch' io avevo male, credo di dolore sare' morta. Fa' lor vezzi, e massim' a Matteo, che non se ne sa fare da sè; che debba esser con-

sandra] has a dowry of 1000 florins, made up of cash and trousseau. I know Antonio has told you all about this.

Favilla brought me the wicker cart and inside [were] 36 pounds of flax and a sack of 51 pounds of almonds, 24 pounds of capers and 3 jars of sweetmeats, all of it good and fine. They came at the right time since I've been sick, and I congratulate you on that. I sent Caterina her share of the almonds and capers and a similar amount to Antonio Strozzi. I couldn't do less; they [almonds] have been very dear because there hasn't been any harvested here this year. On the same subject, you sent one hundred and ten pounds of flax to Marco. Favilla told me he'd arranged with you that altogether the cartage would be fourteen lire and you'd given him a ducat and a half, which according to him was [worth] 6 lire and 18 soldi,[3] so he was owed seven lire and 2 soldi. He asked me to give him 4 soldi straight away because he needed the money, and to pay the 3 lire and 2 soldi later, so I did. I've credited the 3 lire and 2 soldi which I didn't pay to his account. Marco gave me his share of the cartage, which was 7 lire because so much of it was his. I've just received the 12 pairs of botargo[4] [which are] very fine. It's good of you to remember me because these days I need your kind thoughts, but I'd like to have you near me even more. May God give us the grace of being near each other and a comfort to each other, as I wish.

I'm glad Niccolò and Matteo have arrived there, because I've been so sad and worried for the last two months, not hearing any news of them. I kept thinking to myself that they'd had bad luck and things had turned out badly for them. I kept asking Antonio and Marco if they'd heard anything, but they kept saying no. Now, having heard they've arrived safe and well, they've told me about the accident. May God be praised for keeping them from harm. Antonio did the right thing not to tell me while I was ill; I think I would have died of grief. Embrace them for me and most of all Matteo. He doesn't know how to

sumato: e se vedi abbia bisogno d'alcuna cosa di qua, avvisami e manderò tutto; che Iddio vi dia della suo' grazia.
Fa' che mi scriva ispesso. Arei ora gran bisogno di lui,
rispetto e bisogni della Lesandra, e del rispondere alle lettere, che non posso tanto iscrivere. Non guardare ch'io
non risponda a tutte le tue: fate pure di scrivermi ispesso;
e ora che v'è Niccolò, attiemmi la promessa del venire in
sin qua: e se possibile fussi ci venissi innanzi la Lesandra
andassi a marito, ci sarebbe a tutti una gran consolazione
tu ti ci trovassi: che Iddio te ne dia la grazia, se debb'essere
il meglio.

Per ancora non ho preso partito nè diliberato nulla
della Cateruccia, che poi ci venne quella ischiavetta da
Barzalona è migliorata, e sta assai in pace. Di quella di
Iacopo, fo pensiero tenella tanto la Lesandra vada a marito: poi se ne piglierà partito: di tutto sarai avvisato. Nè
altro per questa. Raccomandaci a Niccolò, e a te raccomando Matteo. Che Iddio di male vi guardi. Per la tua, in
fretta, Allesandra, in Firenze.

8

Al nome di Dio. A dì 27 di febbraio 1452.

A questi dì passati, per Piero Borromei, ebbi una tua
de' 31 di dicembre, e prima una de' 14 di detto; poi, per

look after himself and he must have been worn out. If you think he needs anything from here let me know and I'll send it. May God give him grace. Make sure he writes to me often. I have great need of him now because of the business with Lesandra, to answer letters, because I can't write that much. Don't pay any attention when I don't answer all your letters and do write to me often all the same. And now that Niccolò is back you must keep your promise to come here, and if possible you should come before Lesandra goes to her husband. It would be a great comfort to us to have you here. May God give you the grace to do so if it's for the best.

So far I haven't made up my mind or even thought about Cateruccia;[5] since that little slave from Barcelona[6] came, she's been better and behaves more peacefully. So far as Jacopo's slave is concerned, I'm thinking of keeping her until Lesandra goes to her husband and then she can leave. I'll keep you informed about everything. Nothing more for now; remember us to Niccolò and do look after Matteo. May God keep you from all harm. From your Allesandra in Florence, in a hurry.

8

This letter was written to Alessandra's middle son, Lorenzo. At this time he worked for Jacopo Strozzi in Bruges and it appears to have been a severe trial to him. Lorenzo had asked his mother for assistance with some frivolous and expensive scheme, and instead received a severe lecture about the necessity of mending his ways.

In the name of God. 27 February 1453.

I received your letter of the 31st of December a few days ago from Piero Borromei, and before that one of the

Bagnacavallo, una de' 9 di gennaio. A tutte per questa risposta.

Delle ragne non ho fatto nulla, però che me ne sono informata, e truovo che volere una da uccellini, bella come vorrebbe essere, a mandarla costà non costerà manco di sei fiorini. E per questo mi sono istata; che mi par tempo da non ispendere i danari in simile cose, che se n' ha a fare cose di maggiore bisogno: però che ci è il Comune che m'ha a consumare, che già hanno posto su questa gravezza nuova, che si scoperse a dì 20 di questo, gravezze 32, che m' hanno posto fiorini 5, soldi 16, denari 10 a oro: sicchè fa' tu il conto, quello me ne tocca a pagare; che puo' fare sieno, tra spese di partite, altri fiorini sei per gravezza. Fa' il conto, se' vie trentadua, quante sono: e questi s' hanno a pagare in pochi mesi, che di marzo se n' ha pagar sei, e così mese per mese; e già è passato el termine di sei gravezze. Sicchè avendo a pagare il Comune, e piatire co Niccolò Soderini, mi pare dovere lasciare indrieto le ragne. Abbi il capo alle cose che sono di maggiore importanza, che per te si farà.

L'età di Filippo è anni ventiquattro, compiè a dì 4 di luglio passato; e a dì 7 di marzo che viene, farà anni dodici che si partì di Firenze. E tu avesti a dì 21 d'agosto che passò, anni venti; e fa ora di questo mese anni sette ti partisti di Firenze. E Matteo arà il primo dì di marzo anni diciassette, e a dì 7 di questo fece anni tre si partì di qua. La Caterina ha anni ventidue a maggio che viene: la Le-

14th of December; then, from Bagnacavallo, [I received] one of the 9th of January. I will answer them all in this letter.

One paragraph: she hoped Filippo would be able to come to Florence to help her with legal difficulties, as her ownership of the farm at Antella, which she had inherited from her brother Zanobi, was being contested by her half brother Antonio Macinghi and brother-in-law Niccolò Soderini.

I've done nothing about the bird-catcher's snares since I found out about them and discovered that [if you] want one of these little birds, beautiful as they are, sending it there [to Bruges] would cost at least 6 florins. And because of this I haven't done anything about it. It isn't the right time to spend money on this sort of thing, because there are more important things to do with it. The Commune is ruining me as they've already imposed this new tax, announced on the 20th of this month, 32 times. They've assessed me at 5 florins, 16 soldi, [and] 10 denari, in gold, so you can work it out, how much I have to pay. So that you can do it, we'll say there are six florins for each tax. Work out the bill, if there are thirty-two [taxes], how much it is. And this has to be paid in a few months. We have to pay the tax six times for March and so on, month by month, and the payment for six taxes has already passed. So what with having to pay the Commune and starting legal proceedings against Niccolò Soderini, we have to forget about the nets. Put your mind on more important things so they really seem important to you.

Filippo was twenty-four years old on the fourth of July last year and on the 7th of next March it's twelve years since he left Florence. You were twenty on the 21st of August last year and this month it's seven years since you left Florence. Matteo is seventeen on the first day of March and on the seventh of this month it was three years since he left. Caterina will be twenty-two this May; Le-

sandra compiè diciotto d'agosto che passò. Sicchè se' avvisato di tutti.

E torniàno al fatto tuo. Che se' d'età da governarti in altra maniera non fai, e oggimai doverresti correggerti, e dirizzare l'animo tuo al ben vivere; che insino a qui è stato da riputar fanciullo: ma ora non è così, e sì pell'età e sì perchè non si può mettere gli error tuoi per ignoranza, e perchè non conosca quello che tu fai; che se' di tale intelletto, che conosci il male e 'l bene, e massimamente quando ne se' ripreso da' tua maggiori. Io intendo che tu non fai e portamenti ch'io vorrei; che n'ho dispiacere assai, e con gran paura istò, che tu non abbia un dì una gran rovina di capitare meno che bene: chè chi non fa quel che debbe, riceve quello non crede. Che oltre agli altri affanni ch' i' ho, m'è il tuo il maggiore. E avevo fatto pensiero che per uscire di spesa e di noia, e ancora per aiutarvi far bene, di vendere il podere dell'Antella; che, pagato gli obrighi che vi sono, ne traessi fiorini ottocento netti; e trecento n' ha Filippo: e facevo conto tra tu e Filippo gli avessi a trafficare, acciò voi cominciassi avanzare l'anno qualche cosa. E per quello senta di te, comprendo se' più tosto da sapere gittar via, che avanzare un grosso: ch'è il contradio del bisogno tuo. E veggo certamente ha' far danno e vergogna a te e a noi; che intendo tu hai costumi che non sono buoni; e riprenderti non giova nulla: che mi dà mal segno, e fammi tirare indrieto d'ogni buono pensiero che mi viene inverso di te. E non so perchè tu seguiti le tue volontà; conoscendo, prima ne fai dispiacere a Dio, ch'è sopra tutto; poi a me, che gran passione mi s'è a sentire e mancamenti tuoi; e 'l danno e la vergogna che ne seguita, lascio considerare a te: e dispiacere ne fai a Iacopo, e grande. E se tu cominciassi ora, sarebbe d'averne isperanza; ma egli è anni che tu cominciasti a fare delle cose non ben fatte, e per amore di me se' stato sopportato. Ma i' credo che se tu non rimuti e modi tua, ch'e prieghi

sandra was eighteen last August. So now you have all the details.[1]

To come back to what concerns you, you're old enough to behave in a different sort of way from how you have been; you've got to sort yourself out and concentrate on living properly. Up till now you've been thought of as a boy, but that's no longer the case, both because of your age and because your mistakes can't be put down to ignorance or to not knowing what you're doing. You've got the intelligence to know right from wrong, particularly when you've been told by your elders and betters. I gather you don't behave yourself as I'd like you to, and this has made me very unhappy. I'm afraid you'll take a tumble one day and come out badly, because he who doesn't do his duty gets a nasty surprise. Your troubles are the worst I have, worse than all the rest. I'd been thinking of selling the farm at Antella to get rid of a lot of expense and aggravation and to help you [all] get on. Once what's owing on it has been paid it would bring in a clear eight hundred florins. Filippo has another three hundred and I'd thought of you and Filippo using the money for business ventures so you could start to accumulate some capital. [But] from all I hear you know more about throwing money away than about saving a penny, and it should be the opposite. I can see you've done us harm and brought us shame, and yourself too. I gather you've got some bad habits and lecturing you does no good at all. It looks like a bad sign to me and makes me take back all my good feelings for you. I don't know why you go your own way, knowing you're displeasing God, which matters more than anything else, and me as well, as it makes me very unhappy to hear about your failings. I leave it to you to consider the harm and shame that come from it. And you're really upsetting Jacopo; if you'd just started he could hope for better, but it's years since you started behaving so badly and he's put up with it for my sake. But if you don't mend your ways I

mia non faranno più frutto per te. E bastiti questo. Sie savio, chè ti bisogna, e farà per te.

Ricordoti non ti getti drieto alle spalle le mie riprensioni, che sono con amore e con lagrime. E priego Iddio che ti disponga a fare quello ch'io disidero. Nè altro per questa m'accade dirti. Iddio di male ti guardi. Per la tua Allesandra fu di Matteo Strozzi, in Firenze.

9

Al nome di Dio. A dì 9 di settembre 1458.

I'ho ricevuto più tue, ed è parecchi mesi non ho scritto nè a te nè a Filippo. Sodisfarò a parte per questa, non ci si

won't be able to help any more. Let this be enough warning for you. Be wise because you need to be, and then it will be enough.

Four short paragraphs: the pins have arrived, and Caterina and Lessandra have been given their share; old tax debts; Alessandra had sent a wax devotional image to Santa Maria Annunziata on Lorenzo's behalf;[2] she had seen a messenger, Tedeschino, from Jacopo Strozzi's household in Bruges.

I must remind you not to shrug off my reprimands, which [are written] with love and tears; may God make you do as I wish. Nothing else occurs to me for now; may God keep you from harm. From your Allesandra, widow of Matteo Strozzi, in Florence.

A short postscript about the tax assessments of various relations.

9

There is a gap of five years in Alessandra Strozzi's surviving correspondence at this point. Matteo, to whom this letter is addressed, was temporarily in Rome but was based in Naples with Filippo, who had begun his first company there (on his own and his brothers' behalf) two years earlier, operating a bank and a wholesale cloth warehouse.[1] Lorenzo was still working for Jacopo Strozzi in Bruges, but no more is ever said about his youthful shortcomings; he had just visited Alessandra in Florence.

In the name of God. 9 September 1458.

I've had a lot of letters from you and it's a good many months since I've written to either you or Filippo. I'll even things up a bit with this letter. Lorenzo is no longer

trovando Lorenzo; che ho una tua a lui de' 2 di questo. Risposta.

I'ho messo in ordine le camice, cioè sei; e braccia quattro di panno lino pelle mutande, che a tuo modo le fara' fare; e mazzi cento o più, se quello vuogli, di finocchio, e bello: e come arò persona fidata, lo manderò.

Lorenzo si partì di qui a dì due, e andò a stare duo dì en Mugello colla Caterina: e di là si partì a dì 4 per la via di Bologna. Honne assa' pena; più perchè none stava della persona come vorrei. Da altra parte, sono rimasa molto sola. Priego Iddio che l'accompagni, e conducalo sano e salvo.

Veggo che da Filippo non hai mai auto il tuo dovere: hogli scritto che non ha fatto bene, e che ti provvegga di tuo dovere più presto può, acciò non abbi da dolerti di me nè di lui. I' gli fo ritenere fiorini 200 per mia bisogni; che n' ho auti parte, e del resto ciascuno abbi rerrata sua. Così gli ho scritto: vedrèno che farà. Di' che per tutto questo 'avere Filippo costì, e forse che farà un passo insin qua: sia alla buon'ora. Da lui ho, per una scrive a Lorenzo, che se s' ha abboccare co' Niccolò, forse si distenderà insin qua. Iddio gli dia a pigliare quel partito che sia el meglio.

Ara' sentito come a dì 7 morì Benedetto Strozzi, dal martedì sera al giovedì, a ore 17. Benchè alcun dì prima avessi chiocciato, non era in modo, che sempre andò per casa, e non pareva che avessi male. Dicono che aveva una posta nel corpo; ma pe' segni che ebbe, si tiene morissi di pistolenzia. Non se ne fa guardia, e tutti v'andiàno. Ène stato grandissimo danno, prima alla sua brigata, poi a noi e a tutta la Casa; che era il ricorso d'ognuno, e non è in Casa uomo, che tanto danno gittassi la morte sua, quanto

here and I have one of your letters to him, of the 2nd of this month. Here is my reply.

I've ordered the shirts, six of them, and four *braccia*[2] of linen cloth for the underpants, which I'll have made up the way you like them. And [there are] one hundred heads of fennel or more if you want it; it's good and I'll send it by someone trustworthy when the opportunity arises.

Lorenzo left here on the 2nd and went to stay with Caterina in the Mugello. He left there on the 4th [to return to Bruges] via Bologna. I've been very upset about it, even more because he's not as well as I'd like and now I've been left too much alone again. I pray God goes with him and brings him home safe and sound.

I see Filippo hasn't paid you what he owes you yet. I've written and told him he hasn't done the right thing and that he should arrange for you to get your due as soon as he can, so you'll have no reason to complain about either of us. I'm keeping back 200 florins for my own needs, so I've got part of it, and everyone else should have their share of the rest.[3] I've told him this, so we'll see what he does. You talk about Filippo going there [to Rome] and that he may come here as well. It's certainly time he did. In a letter he wrote to Lorenzo, he said he might come on as far as here if he needs to go [to Rome] to see Niccolò. May God let him make whatever decision is for the best.

You'll have heard how Benedetto Strozzi[4] died on the 7th [of September]; [he was sick] from Tuesday evening till Thursday at [about] 12 midday. Although he'd been feeling ill for some days, he wasn't in a bad way and he was always going out and didn't seem really sick. They say he had a tumor on his body, but from the symptoms they think he died of the plague. There's nothing you can do to prevent it and we all seem to go that way. It's been a great loss, first to his immediate family and then to us and to all the Strozzi. Everyone turned to him for help and there's no one else in the family who would be missed as

di lui. Bisogna avere pazienza; e che Iddio abbia dell'anima misericordia. A dì 12 si fanno le messe. L'ha tre fanciulle e duo maschi, e la donna grossa di mesi sette.

Giovanni Bonsi è stato anche lui a gran pericolo di morire, che cadde della mula: vogliendo salire a cavallo, la mula lo scagliò a terra; ebbe una gran picchiata nell'anca. Pure, per grazia di Dio, è migliorato; non però che se ne possa andare in villa, che v'ha la brigata: sicchè ho sempre che fare.

La mia ischiavetta feci tornare, e non ebbe di quelle cose: lo 'nfiato tornò adrieto: dicono era esciesa. Iddio lodato. Gran paura avemmo tutti. Nè altro per questa. Siàno al presente sani: e così spero sentire di voi. Che Iddio sia ringraziato di tutto, e mantengavi sani come disidero. Per la tua Allesandra, in Firenze.

Manda la sua a Filippo, che fia in questa.

10

Al nome di Dio. A dì 19 di febbraio 1458.

A dì 20 passato fu l'utima mia; ho dipoi la tūa de' 19 dicembre, che m'è suta di consolazione, veduto che del

much as he will be. But what can't be cured must be endured; may God have mercy on his soul. The mass is on the 12th. He had three daughters and two sons and his wife is seven months pregnant.

Giovanni Bonsi has also been in great danger of dying, from falling off a mule. The mule threw him to the ground while he was trying to jump on, and he hit his hip heavily. Still he's better, by the grace of God. But he hasn't been able to go to the country with the rest of his household, so I've still had plenty to do.

I pulled my little slave through [her illness], and she didn't have those things [I mentioned previously]. The swelling went away slowly and they say it was a cold, God be praised. We were all very afraid. Nothing more for now. We're all well at the moment and we hope to hear the same from you. May God be praised for everything and keep you well, as I wish. From your Allesandra in Florence.

Do send the letter to Filippo, enclosed in this one, on to him.

10

The Medici regime had now moved to enforce by law the exile of Alessandra's sons from Florence, and she begins this letter to Lorenzo by discussing this development. She then describes the marriage arranged for Isabella, Jacopo Strozzi's illegitimate daughter, who had been sent to Florence so that a suitable husband could be found for her.

In the name of God. 19 February 1459.

My last letter to you was on the 20th of last month, and since then I've had yours of the 19th of December. It's

caso occorsovi pigli tutto per lo meglio: che ha' preso buon partito, chè non ci ha rimedio. Di poi hanno appressato e confini miglia 50, e abbiamo auto licenza di potere iscrivere sanza mostrare le lettere agli Otto, le vostre e le mie. E così ha 'vuto Batista, e degli altri, di potere scrivere, da' fatti di stato in fuori, ciò che l'uom vuole.

Avvisoti come a dì 9 si maritò l'Isabella a Marco di Giovanni di Marco, setaiuolo e merciaio e setaiuolo minuto: e non ha più, el padre, de' maschi, ma ha sette fanciulle; una maritata, e sei en casa, che cinque hanno la dota al Monte: ècci detto che stanno bene di roba, e sono le migliori persone; che temono Iddio, che è buona parte. Abbiamo fatto le nozze; e per quello vegga di loro, mi pare ch'ell'abbia auto una gran ventura: essendo della qualità ch'ell' è, e'l mancamento della vista corta ch' ell' ha, come tu sai; che nell' allogarla non abbiàno guatato tanto a metterla in roba, quanto a metterla en luogo sia amata e ben trattata: che è questo el bisogno suo, secondo si vede. El garzone ha ventun anno; e Pierotto, che fia apportatore di questa, ti dirà com'egli è fatto, che iarsera lo vide in casa di Francesco Strozzi a cena. Abbiàgli fatto più onore che non si fece alla mia, per amore d'Iacopo: e così farò per l'avvenire. So che Batista avviserà Iacopo di tutto, e de' danari ch' i' ho auti da lui, e di quegli torrò per bisogno suo; chè voglio fornirla delle cose ha di nicistà, ch'ella paia fanciulla da bene, chè tanto più sarà riguardata. Non ho tempo di scrivere a Iacopo, ma so che da quest'altri sarà avvisato.

L'alberello dello arimatico ti manderò: ma la migliore medicina che sia allo stomaco è il guardarsi della bocca.

been a comfort to me, seeing you've taken what has happened [1] as well as you possibly could. You've made the right decision, because there's nothing we can do about it. Since then they have brought the limits closer, to 50 miles, and we have been given permission to write letters without showing them to the Eight, [2] either yours or mine. And Batista [sic] [3] and the others have also been given permission to write [to those exiled], except about political matters, which is what a man wants.

Two paragraphs about money, property, and a power of attorney which Lorenzo should send.

I must tell you how on the 9th we married Isabella to Marco di Giovanni di Marco, a silk weaver and mercer and a silk merchant in a small way. His father has no other sons, but seven girls, one married and six still at home; five of them have dowries in the Fund. People say they're well off and good people and God-fearing, which is the main thing. We've had the wedding and from what I saw of them I think she's been lucky. Considering her status [4] and that she's longsighted, as you know, we weren't looking to put her in a wealthy household so much as one where she'll be loved and well looked after. That's what she needs, as we saw it. The young man is twenty-one, and Pierotto, who will carry this letter, will tell you what he looks like because last night he saw him at supper at Francesco Strozzi's [5] house. He was treated with more honor there, out of love for Jacopo, than he was in mine, but I'll do the same in future. I know Batista will tell Jacopo all about it and about the money he sent me and how much I used for the things she needed, because if she looks like a girl from a good family they're more likely to think of her that way. [6] I don't have time to write to Jacopo but I know the others will tell him all about it.

I'll send you the jar of aromatic [herbs], but the best medicine for your stomach is to watch what you put in

Così ti ricordo: e così, poichè abbiamo licenza di scrivere l'uno all'altro, fa' di scrivere ispesso, e come tu stai della persona; che n'arò piacere. Nè altro. Raccomandaci a Iacopo: che Iddio di male ti guardi. Per la tua Allesandra, in Firenze.

I I

Al nome di Dio. A dì 6 di settembre 1459.

Figliuol mio dolce. Ensino a dì 11 del pasato ebbi una tua de' 29 di luglio, come el mio figliuolo caro e diletto Matteo s'era posto giù ammalato: e non avendo da te che male si fussi, senti' per quella una gran doglia, dubitando forte di lui. Chiama' Francesco, e mandai per Matteo di Giorgio; e intesi d'amendue come el mal suo era terzana: che assai mi confortai, però che delle terzane, non s'arogendo altra malattia, non se ne perisce. Di poi, al continovo da te son suta avvisata come la malattia sua andava assottigliando; che pur l'animo, ben che avessi sospetto, mi s'allegierava un poco. Dipoi ho come addì 23 piacque a Chi me lo diè di chiamallo a sè, con buon conoscimento e con buona grazia e con tutti e sagramenti che si richiede al buono e fedele cristiano. Per la qual cosa ho auto un' amaritudine grandissima dell'esser privata di tale figliuolo; e gran danno mi pare ricevere, oltre all'amore filiale, della morte sua; e simile voi due altri mia, che a piccolo numero sete ridotti. Lodo e ringrazio Nostro Signore di

your mouth. Do write often as we're allowed to, and [let me know] how you are in yourself; that will make me happy. Nothing more [for now]; remember me to Jacopo. May God keep you from all harm. From your Allesandra in Florence.

I I

Matteo died in Naples in August 1459 at the age of twenty-three, and his death grieved Alessandra deeply. In this letter to Filippo she emphasizes how important it was to her that Matteo had had time to receive all the last rites of the Church, rather than dying suddenly.

In the name of God. 6 September 1459.

My sweet son, on the 11th of last month I had your letter of the 29th of July, saying how my dear and beloved son Matteo had fallen ill. And as you didn't say what he was suffering from I was extremely upset and worried a great deal about him. I sent for Francesco[1] and for Matteo di Giorgio[2] and heard from both of them that he was suffering from tertian fever,[3] which was a great comfort because with tertian fevers you don't die unless you get something else as well. After that you let me know how he was getting better, so although I was still worried my heart was a bit lighter. But since then I've heard how on the 23rd [of August] it pleased Him who gave him to me to take him back. [He was] fully aware and in a state of grace and with all the sacraments a good and faithful Christian needs. Being deprived of my son has given me the greatest grief and while I've lost a son's love it seems as if I've suffered an even greater loss through his death; and you as well, my other two sons, who are now reduced

tutto quello ch'è sua volontà; chè son certa Iddio ha veduto che ora era la salute dell'anima sua: e la sperienza ne
veggo per quanto tu mi scrivi, che così bene s'accordassi a
questa aspra e dura morte: e così ho 'nteso per lettere, che
ci sono in altri, di costà. E bene ch'io abbia sentito tal
doglia nel cuore mio, che mai la senti' tale, ho preso conforto di tal pena di due cose. La prima, che egli era presso
a di te; che son certa che medici e medicine e tutto quello
è stato possibile di fare per la salute sua, con quegli rimedi
si sono potuti fare, si sono fatti, e che nulla s'è lasciato
indrieto per mantenergli la vita; e nulla gli è giovato: chè
era volontà di Dio che così fussi. L'altra, di che ho preso
quieta, si è della grazia e dell'arme che Nostro Signore gli
diè a quel punto della morte, di rendersi in colpa, di
chiedere la confessione e comunione e la strema unzione:
e tutto intendo che fece con divozione; che sono segni
tutti da sperare che Iddio gli abbia apparecchiato buon
luogo. E pertanto, sapendo che tutti abbiàno a fare questo
passo, e non sappiàno come, e non siàno certi di farlo in
quel modo che ha fatto el mio grazioso figliuolo Matteo
(chè chi muore di morte sùbita, chi è tagliato a pezzi; e
così dimolte morte si fanno, che si perde l'anima e 'l
corpo), mi do pace, considerando che Iddio mi può far
peggio: e se per sua grazia e misericordia mi conserva
amendua voi mia figliuoli, non mi dorrò d'alcun' altra afrizione. Tutto el mio pensiero è di sentire che questo caso
tu lo pigli pel verso suo: chè sanza dubbio so che t'è doluto; ma fa' che non sia en modo che t'abbia a nuocere, e
che non gittiàno el manico dirieto alla scure: chè non ci è
ripitío niuno nel suo governo: anzi è suto di volontà di
Dio ch'egli esca delle sollecitudine di questo mondo pieno
d'affanni. E perchè veggo, per la tua de' 26 detto, avere di
questo caso tanta afrizione nell'animo tuo e nella persona;
che m'è suto, ed è, e sarà insino ch'io non ho tue lettere
che tu pigli conforto, tal pena, che m' ha a nuocere assai.

to such a small number. I praise and thank our Lord for everything which is His will, because I'm sure God took him when He saw his soul was healthy. I see from what you've written that you've resigned yourself to this trial and this hard and bitter death. I've heard this too from letters other people have had from there. And although the pain in my heart is like nothing I ever felt before, I've taken comfort from two things. First, he was with you so I'm certain he had doctors and medicines and everything was done for his well-being, and any remedies which could be used were used and nothing was neglected to keep him alive, but that nothing was any help to him and it was the will of God that it should be so. The other thing which has comforted me is that Our Lord gave him the opportunity while he was dying to free himself of sin, to ask for confession and communion and extreme unction, and all of this, I gather, he did with piety. We can hope from these signs that God has prepared a good place for him. And knowing we must all take this journey and not knowing how and not being sure of doing so in the way my beautiful son Matteo has (having achieved a state of grace) gives me peace, keeping in mind that God could have done far worse to me, because those who die suddenly, who are cut to pieces (and this happens to many of the dead), they lose their body and soul together.[4] And if by His grace and mercy He leaves me both of you my sons, he won't give me any more suffering. Now my only thought is to hear that you've taken what has happened in the right way, because I know you're grieving, but make sure it's not in a way which does you harm, so we don't throw the handle out after the axe blade. Nothing was lacking in the care he received, on the contrary it was God's will that he escape the cares of this world, which is so full of troubles. From your letter of the 26th I saw how you're suffering in mind and body and this has upset me greatly and will until I hear that you've consoled yourself.

E non piaccia a Dio che i' viva tanto ch'i' abbia aver più di queste! Considero che avendo auto el disagio delle male notti, e la maninconia della morte e dell'altre cose, che la persona tua non de' stare troppo bene: e tanto mi s'avviluppa questo pensiero el dì e la notte pel capo, che non sento riposo. E vorrei non avere chiesto consiglio a persona; anzi, aver fatto quello che mi pareva, e volevo fare: chè sarei giunta a tempo ch'io arei veduto e tocco el mio dolce figliuolo vivo, e are' preso conforto, e datone a lui e a te. Voglio riputare tutto pello meglio. Vo'ti pregare (s'e mia prieghi possono in te, come i' credo) che tu ti conforti avere pazienza per amore di me; e attendi a tutta la salute della tua persona, e poni un poco da parte le faccende della compagnia. E sare' buono a purgarti un poco, pure con cose leggeri, e massimo con qualche argomento; e poi pigliare un po' d'aria, se per niun modo potessi: ricordandoti, che abbi più caro la tua persona che la roba; chè, vedi, tutto si lascia! Ed io, madre piena d'affanni, che ho a fare sanza voi? Ch'è a me sentire facciate della roba assai, e per essa vi maceriate la persona vostra con tanti disagi e sollecitudine? Duolmi, figliuol mio, ch' i' non sono presso a te, che ti possa levare la fatica di molte cose, che aresti di bisogno: che dovevi, el primo dì che Matteo malò, dirmi en modo ch' i' fussi salita a cavallo, che 'n pochi dì sarei suta costì. Ma i' so che per paura ch'io non ammalassi e non avessi disagio, nollo facesti: e i' n'ho più nell'animo, ch'io no n'arei auto nella persona. Ora di tutto sia Iddio lodato, chè per lo meglio ripiglio tutto.

Dello onore che ha' fatto nel seppellire el mio figliuolo, ho 'nteso che ha' fatto onore a te e a lui: e tanto più ha' fatto bene a onorallo costì, chè di qua non si costuma, di quegli che sono nel grado vostro, farne alcuna cosa. E così ne sono contenta che abbi fatto. Io di qua, con queste due esconsolate figliuole, della morte del lor fratello ci siàno vestite: e perch'io non avevo ancora levato el panno

I hope God doesn't let me live long enough to go through this again. I've been thinking that what with sleepless nights, the grief caused by death, and other things, you're probably not too well yourself. I've been worrying about this day and night and I can't get any rest. I wish I hadn't taken anyone's advice and had done what seemed right to me instead, what I wanted to do, because then I would have got there in time to see and touch my sweet living son, and that would have comforted me and him and you. I want to believe everything is for the best. I want to ask you, if my prayers can persuade you and I hope they can, to resign yourself to this for my sake and look after yourself and put your business affairs to one side for a little while. You should purge yourself a little with something mild, by one means or another. And then you should get some fresh air if you can manage it, remembering to look after yourself better than your property, because in the end you leave it all behind. And what would I, your grieving mother, do without you? I gather you're making a lot of money and letting your body waste away while you do so, with all your cares and discomforts. I'm sorry I'm not there with you so I could help share your load, which is what you need. You should have told me the first day Matteo was sick and I could have jumped on a horse and been there in a few days. But I know you didn't do it because you were afraid I'd make myself sick or suffer discomfort, and so I've suffered in mind instead of body. Now God be praised for everything, because I'm taking it all for the best.

About the honors you gave my son when you buried him, I believe you honored yourself as well as him. You've done all the better in honoring him there because it isn't the custom here to do anything for those who die in your circumstances,[5] so I'm glad you've done so. I'm here with these two unhappy girls who are wearing mourning for their brother. And because I hadn't cut out the cloth to

per farmi el mantello, l'ho fatto levare ora; e questo pagherò io. E braccia tredici di panno do per una di loro; che costa, a danari contanti, fiorini quattro e un quarto la canna; che sono in tutto canne sei e mezzo. Questo farò pagare a Matteo di Giorgio, e da lui ne sara' avvisato.

La copia della sua volontà ho veduta; e così si vuole mettere in asseguzione, più presto che si può, quello che è per soddisfacimento dell'anima sua. L'altre parti più a bell'agio si possono fare; e di così ti priego che faccia, e me avvisa se nulla posso far qua; che ci è una sorella del tuo ragazzo che avesti di qua, che è maritata, e none può andare a marito, che è una gran povertà la sua. Per altre te l'ho raccomandata, e mai n'ebbi risposta. Ora essendo questo caso, si vuole aiutarla: che sono in tutto fiorini quindici: e non voler mancare. E in caso che del suo non vi fussi tanto, che si potessi fare quello che lascia e questo, vo'lo fare di mio, o vo' fare del tuo; chè tanto è una medesima cosa. Sieti avviso, e avvisa come sta, e quello si può fare.

Veggo Niccolò era malato di terzana; che, oltre alla pena mia, ho auto dispiacere per più rispetti. A Dio piaccia per sua misericordia liberarlo.

Da messer Giannozzo ho per sua benignità una lettera, che n' ho preso assa' conforto, veduto l'affezione e amore ti porta, e con quanta carità e con quanti assempri m'induce aver pazienza. Che Iddio gliene renda merito. E perch'io non mi sento di tale virtù, ch'io sapessi e potessi fare risposta a un tanto uomo quanto è lui, me ne starò; ma tu per mia parte gli fa' quel ringraziamento che t'è possibile. E me avvisa, e spesso, come ti senti: che Iddio me ne mandi quello disidero; chè, perch'io sia usa avere delle avversità pe' tempi passati, queste mi fanno più sentire. Ancora ringrazia per lettera Bernardo de' Medici; chè non ti potre' dire con quanto amore mi venne a vicitare e confortare, e quanto si duole del caso e della passione nostra. Non dirò più per questa, per non ti dar tedio a leggere; se no ch'io aspetto tue lettere che ti conforti, e di sentire che

make myself a cloak, I've had it done now and I'll pay for it myself. There are thirteen *braccia* of cloth in [each] one of them, which costs in ready money four florins and a quarter the rod; [6] in all there are six and a half rods. I'll pay this through Matteo di Giorgio [Brandolini] and he'll let you know about it.

I've seen the copy of his will and I'd like you to act as quickly as possible to carry out those parts which are for the good of his soul. The rest can be dealt with at greater leisure. I ask you to do this and let me know if there's anything I can do here. Your boy [7] has a sister here who's married but can't go to live with her husband because she's so poor. I suggested you help her in other letters, but you've never replied. Now given what's happened I'd like to help her; [8] it's a matter of fifteen florins in all and it's something we shouldn't fail to do. If there isn't enough of his money to do what he asked I'd like to do it with my money or yours, which is all the same thing. So I'm letting you know about it. You should let me know how things stand and what we can do.

Messer Giannozzo [9] has kindly sent me a letter which has been a great comfort, seeing how fond he is of you and how he's tried so kindly to persuade me to resign myself, with so many good examples. [10] May God hold this in his favor. And as I don't have the knowledge or ability to write an answer to a man like him, I'll delay and you can thank him on my behalf as well as you can. Do let me know as often as you can how you're feeling. May God grant me what I want, because although I've been used to troubles in the past I'm feeling this more. You should also thank Bernardo de' Medici [11] by letter; I can't tell you how much love he's shown, coming to see me and comfort me, and how he's sympathized with us in what has happened and how we've suffered. I won't say anything else for now so as not to try your patience, but only that I'm waiting for your letters [to hear] you've consoled yourself and that

tu sia sano: che Gesù benedetto ce ne conceda la grazia, come disidero. Per la tua poverella Madre, in Firenze.

I 2

Al nome di Dio. A dì 13 di settembre 1459.

A dì 6 fu l'utima mia; e benchè gran doglia fussi nel cuor mio a fare risposta a tal novella, pure mi feci forza a farti que' parecchi versi: chè, oltre al dolore e la grande passione ch'i' avevo della morte del mio dolce figliuolo, avevo ancora gran pena di te; chè consideravo, e considero al continovo, come la tua persona debba stare 'avere sopportato tanti affanni nell'animo e nella persona, come tu hai. Dipoi ho la tua de' 30 passato, che mi fu un poco di rifrigiero alla mia passione. Risposta per questa.

Non dubitar punto che i' ho sentito un gran duolo; e son certa che se tu avessi per alcun modo potuto fare ch'io non avessi per lungo tempo sentita questa novella, l'aresti fatto; ma non era possibile a farlo, e però fu di bisogno la sentissi prima da te che da altri. E non è dubbio, a mio parere, che ne ricevi danno assai, e più ancora di me: però che a me è danno per l'amore materno, che è grande quanto dir si può; e a te è l'amore dell'esserti fratello, e al modo tuo ne traevi frutto, ed era presso a te a poterti aiutare della sua possibilità, e confortare l'un l'altro al bisogno: chè è gran consolazione, quando l'uomo ha delle fortune, avere de' sua presso a sè; ed io ne so ragionare, che sono escussa d'ogni consolazione; e credo che più te

you're well. May blessed Jesus give you grace, as I wish. From your poor little mother in Florence.

12

In this letter to Filippo, Alessandra again writes about Matteo's death and her anxiety about Filippo's health and state of mind. She also tells him how difficult it was for her to bear her grief while separated from both him and Lorenzo.

In the name of God. 13 September 1459.

My last letter was on the 6th, and although it broke my heart to write an answer to that news I forced myself to be strong and write you those few lines. Apart from how I've suffered from my sweet son's death I've also been very upset on your behalf, because I've been thinking and I still am, about how you're bearing up under all the suffering you've had, both in mind and body. Since then I've had your letter of the 30th of last month, which made my grief feel new again for a little while. I'll answer in this letter.

This has been a terrible grief to me without a doubt and I'm sure if you could have, you would have arranged it so I didn't hear the news for a long time. But that wasn't possible and I had to hear it from you instead of from someone else. I don't doubt this has hurt you more than me; it has hurt me through my love as a mother and no one can say how great that is, but you loved him as your brother who was useful to you. He was there with you and could help you as much as he could, and you could give one another advice when you needed it. It's a great comfort when you have troubles in life to have your nearest and dearest with you. I know what I'm talking about as I've had all that comfort taken away from me. I think

n'avvedrai di qui a un anno che ora, chè di più in più
t'arebbe levato della fatica assai. Ora questa è materia che
quanto più se ne ragiona, tanto è di più pena a chi tocca;
e pertanto ti priego pigli buon conforto; chè, secondo tu
di', non gli è mancato alcuna cosa, nè per l'anima nè per
el corpo: ch'è da starne paziente, considerato ch'è suto
volere di Dio chiamarlo a sè così giovane: chè quanto a
migliore otta ci partiàno di questa misera vita, minore fa-
stello di peccati ne portiàno. E così io mi conforto a pazienza; che non ci è rimedio a questa morte; e veduto el
governo che ha 'uto, per una lettera tanto dolce e confor-
tativa, che ho auta da Fra Domenico di Santa Maria di
Monte Uliveto, che lo confessò, e di passo in passo mi
dice come si governò a quello istremo punto; che è quello
che mi fa dar pace e mitica un poco el mio duolo. Ora si
vuole porre questo da canto; e la prima cosa, che si sodis-
faccia agli obrighi che ha lasciato per l'anima sua; e quello
che tu ha' promesso tu, ancora si soddisfaccia. Di' che lo
botasti qua all'Annunziata, di porlo di cera: avvisami se
s'ha a fare più in un modo che 'n altro, che la farò fare. La
pianeta non so dove ti botasti di farla; e non sendo obrigato di porla più in un luogo che 'n un altro, mi parrebbe,
e così mi contenterei, la facessi costà, acciò che di lui vi
fussi qualche memoria. E 'ntorno all'onore del corpo, per
la mia de' sei dì t'avvisai di quanto aveva seguìto, di vestire
queste due fanciulle, che altro di casa loro non hanno
avere. Iddio lodato.

Tu di' che ti pare necessario di fare pensiero d'accos-
tare Lorenzo in qua più presso a noi. A questo ti dico, che
tu sai che la voglia mia era questa, e scrissitene duo versi:
rispondestimi cota' ragioni, ch' io restai paziente; sì che a

you'll realize this more in a year's time than you do now, because he would have taken more and more of the load from your shoulders. Now this is a topic which is more upsetting the more you discuss it, so I do ask you to console yourself, because from what you say he lacked nothing either for body or soul. We must resign ourselves because it was the will of God to call him back so soon. The sooner we leave this miserable life, the lighter the burden of sins we carry out of it. I have to resign myself to what's happened as there is no cure for this life. And considering the spiritual guidance he had (I've had a very sweet and comforting letter from Fra Domenico di Santa Maria di Monte Oliveto,[1] telling me how Matteo confessed to him, and how he acted, step-by-step, in his last moments) has given me peace and eased my grief a little. I want to put this to one side as soon as we've done what he asked of us, for the good of his soul. As far as that's concerned, you must do what you promised. You say we should consecrate him here at the Annunziata by placing his image there in wax.[2] Let me know if there's a right way of doing this and I'll do it. About the chasuble,[3] I don't know where you've decided to have it made or whether it would be better done in one place or another, so it seemed to me best to have it made here. I'd be happy with that, so that he'd have some memorial. Talking about what we've done to honor him, in my letter of the sixth I told you about my arrangements to provide mourning for the two girls, as apart from their house [4] he hasn't left them anything.

One paragraph: discusses whether she will accept the inheritance of Matteo's estate.[5]

You say we should think about getting Lorenzo closer to us. My answer is that you already know I want that and I wrote you a few lines about it. You argued so much

questa parte lascerò pigliare el partito a te: chè non avendo io a stare dove voi, tanto mi fa che istia a Brugia, quanto a Napoli o in Catalogna; chè a un modo ne arò consolazione: sì che a te tocca a pigliare partito di quello s'ha a fare; e conosci meglio el bisogno di questo, che non fo io; però che l'amore e la passione mi vince tanto, che forse non vederei così tutto. E pertanto non dirò altro sopra di ciò.

Non bisogna raccomandare la vita mia a me per vostro amore, ma a voi bisogna raccomandarvi la vita vostra per amore di me, che vivo della vita e sanità vostra: che a Dio piaccia per sua misericordia mantenervi amendua lungo tempo con quella sanità ch'io disidero per l'anima e per el corpo.

Fra Domenico ringrazia; che s'io arò tempo gli risponderò; e se pure non gli facessi risposta alla sua, farai tu el bisogno e mia scusa. Per la tua madre Allesandra, in Firenze.

Tenuta a' dì 15. Perchè non pigli ammirazione dello scriver mio in questa, che dico, *s'io non ho a stare dove voi;* per tuo avviso, i' non dico questo perch'io non disideri con tutto el cuore e l'anima mia di stare sempre ch' i' vivo dove voi, e non ho altra paura se non di non morire prima ch'io ne rivegga niuno di voi; e perchè està a te el diliberare l'andar mio e lo stare, dissi così: che veggo per quest' utima tua el pensiero avate fatto, che in questa quaresima venissi a Roma, e voi ne saresti venuti per duo mesi; chè mi stimo che a quelle parole non fussi tuo pensiero ch' i' venissi a stare con voi: sì che, figliuol mio, avvisa se l'animo tuo è ch' i' venga o ch' i' stia, chè sappia el certo della tua volontà; che così seguirò. Che Iddio ti dimostri quello debb' essere el meglio per voi e per me. La Checca è dipoi meglio.

[against it] that I resigned myself [to Lorenzo being in Bruges]. So at this stage I'll leave the decision to you. As I don't happen to be living with either of you I could just as easily bring myself to live in Bruges as in Naples or Catalonia,[6] because that would comfort me. So it's up to you to decide what he should do, and you know what's needed better than I do. My love and grief have made me lose control of myself to such an extent that I mightn't take everything into account.

One paragraph: Filippo should tell her if Niccolò is better; Checca[7] *is also ill.*

There's no need to tell me to look after myself for your sake but I do need to ask you to look after yourselves for my sake, because I only live for you and your health and well-being. May God in his mercy keep you both well for a long time and healthy in body and soul as I wish.

Thank Fra Domenico, I'll answer him if I have time but if I don't reply to his letter, you'll do what's needed and make my excuses. From your mother Allesandra in Florence.

Held until the 15th. You won't think much of what I've written in this letter, when I say "as I don't happen to be living with [either of] you." So that you'll know, I'm not saying this because I don't want with all my heart and soul to live where you are, and my greatest fear is that I'll die before I can see either of you again. And because it's up to you to decide whether I should go or stay, I say this: I see from your last letter you're thinking I might come to Rome and that you'd also come for two months. It seems to me that as you say this, you're not thinking of me coming to live with you. So my son, let me know whether you want me to come or stay, so I know for certain what you want and I'll do it. May God show you what's for the best for you and me. Checca is better now.

I 3

Al nome di Dio. A dì 2 di novembre 1459.

A dì 24 di settembre fu l'utima mia. Ho dipoi la tua per Gherardo; che piacere ebbi della sua venuta, che a bocca mi disse buone novelle di te, e come stavi benissimo della persona, e che eri ritornato nell'esser tuo di prima innanzi che avessi male: che ringraziato sia Iddio che t' ha renduto buona sanità. Risposta per questa alla tua.

Veggo che poco ha' da fare costì; e la pratica di Niccolò è tornata in acqua: che tutto si vole pigliare per lo meglio. Ho più lettere da Filippo poi che fu el caso del mio Matteo; e sì gli parrebbe ch' io t'avessi escritto che ti dovessi

I 3

Here Alessandra discusses with Lorenzo whether or not he should move to Naples. She doubted whether he would get on well with his brother. While it is not clear here, Filippo's proposal was that if Lorenzo joined him in Naples, Alessandra should come too, at least for a trial period of six months. This may have been intended to make it difficult for Lorenzo to refuse, but he nevertheless remained in Bruges until 1462.

In the name of God. 2 November 1459.

My last letter was on the 24th of September, and since then Gherardo has brought your letter. I was very pleased to see him because he gave me good news of you, how you were very well in yourself and as well as you were before you were taken ill, God be praised. This is in answer to your letter.

Eight paragraphs: Lorenzo has heard about Matteo's death in many letters and Filippo will have told him how Matteo's affairs were left; Antonio Macinghi has had tertian fever, and the inheritance disputes were continuing among Alessandra's siblings and herself; she has done nothing yet about selling their property at Quaracchi; her heavy taxes; the candlesticks have not yet been bought; she is glad the hamper arrived in Bruges in good order and she is sending another one, containing chickpeas, cheeses, raisins, fennel, and an aromatic ointment; a reference to cloth and cushions; Pagolo [1] *has gone to Santa Maria Impruneta,* [2] *taking a one-pound wax candle on Lorenzo's behalf.*

I can see you have little to do there, and that Niccolò's advice has turned to water. I hope everything turns out for the best. I've had many letters from Filippo since my Matteo died and he thinks I should write to you [to say]

ritrarre di costà, e venissi a Napoli. E ancora gli parrebbe ch' io lo dovesse iscrivere a Iacopo, acciò che se si volessi provvedere d'un giovane, che possa. Non te n' ho mai voluto dire alcuna cosa, perchè essendo la guerra nel Reame, come v'è, e ancora s'aspetta maggiore per mare e per terra, non mi pareva che per nessun modo ti parta per ora di costì; che ho pena che lui vi si truova. Da altra parte conosco la natura di te e di lui, e non so come v'accordassi ensieme. Sicchè per questo non te n' ho iscritto. Ora i' t' ho avvisato di quanto mi scrive ch'è suo pensiero: avvisandoti ch'io non so come l'aria di là ti comportassi; che per Matteo v'è stata cattiva, e sì me lo menò. Sicchè fa' tuo pensiero, e tieni questo a te, nè a Filippo no ne dire nulla: chè se lo diliberrà, te n'avviserà: che gli ho detto, ch'io non te ne voglio scrivere nulla. E pensaviti su coll'animo riposato prima che pigli partito: e tieni tutto a te.

Niccolò è guarito, e per tutto el passato doveva tornare a Roma.

Questa mattina ho lettere da Filippo; e mi dice ch' io ti scriva che ti ritragga in qua; e che i' lo scriva a Iacopo: e che ha scritto a te e a Iacopo quello gli pare che tu facci. Sì che da lui intenderai, e sarai avvisato del suo pensiero; ed io sarò contenta a quello farete. Pensa pure a quello che fai, ennanzi che pigli partito: che Iddio ti metta innanzi quello che debb'essere el meglio. A me escrive che in questo verno pigli partito delle possissioni e d'alcune masserizie; e che passando tu in qua, o per mare o per terra, ch' i' fussi in luogo atto a venirne teco. Ora el tempo mi consiglierà; e se diliberrai passare di qua, me ne darai avviso: e io alsì a te di mio pensiero. Nè altro per questa. Iddio vi mantenga sani e 'n suo' grazia, come disidero. Per la tu' Allesandra, Firenze.

you should leave there and come to Naples. He also thinks I should write to Jacopo to say that if he'd like us to find him a young man,[3] he [Filippo] can do so. I haven't wanted to say anything to you about this, as the Kingdom [of Naples] is at war[4] and it's expected to get worse, both on land and at sea, and I didn't think you should leave there at the present time and I'm worried because he's there. I also know what you're like and what he's like and I don't know how you'd get on together. That's why I haven't mentioned it to you. Now I've let you know what he's told me he's thinking about this, and I also wanted to say that I'm not sure the air there would agree with you. It was bad for Matteo and took him away from me. So think about it and keep your thoughts to yourself; don't say anything about it to Filippo. If he makes up his mind he'll tell you about it; I've told him I don't want to say anything about it to you. Take your time and think about it before you decide, and keep your thoughts to yourself.

Niccolò's better and should have been back in Rome for the past month.

This morning[5] I've had a letter from Filippo. He says I should write to you and to Jacopo, saying you should come back here,[6] and he says he's written to you and to Jacopo saying what he thinks you should do. So you'll hear it from him and he'll tell you what he's thinking, and I'll be happy with what you do. But do think about it before you make a decision; may God show you what's for the best. He told me you might be buying some goods and household furnishings this winter and that [if you] come this way, either by land or sea, I should meet you somewhere and go there [to Naples] with you. Time will tell, and if you decide to come this way you'll let me know and I'll tell you my thoughts on the subject. Nothing more for now. May God keep you well and in His grace, as I wish. From your Allesandra in Florence.

14

Al nome di Dio. A dì 28 di febbraio 1460.

Del mese passato fu l'utima mia. Ho poi dua tue de' 3 e 24 passato. Risposta al bisogno.

Io disiderrei che tu non t'obrigassi a partito nessuno in coteste parti per verun modo; però che l'utile e 'l ben vostro mi pare sia di stare presso l'uno all'altro; e che di più consolazione sarebbe a voi e a me l'essere in luogo di potere dare aiuto e favore l'uno all'altro, per molti casi che possono avvenire: che stando tu in coteste parti, mi pare averti mezzo perduto. Sete ridotti a sì piccolo numero, che a ogni modo e per molti rispetti mi piacerà che tu pigli partito d'andare a trovar Filippo, e di far quel che per più sue t' ha detto. I' non mi distenderò sopra di ciò in altro dirti, perchè nostre faccende non si sentan per tutto: chè istimo le lettere mie ne sia fatto el servigio che delle tue, che poche n'ho che no sieno istate aperte. Donde si venga el difetto, non so. Insino alle tue che vanno a Filippo, sono trassinate. Sicchè cose che fussino d'importanza non mi scrivere, se no per persona fidata: e così farò

Two postscripts: Esmeraldo Boni will bring him the hamper; some news Filippo had told her about the progress of the war in the Kingdom of Naples.

14

Here Alessandra tells Lorenzo of her belief that their letters were being opened and read in transit.

In the name of God. 28 February 1461.

I wrote to you last month and since then I've had two letters from you, of the 3rd and the 24th of last month. I'll answer them as I need to.

Three paragraphs: she has still not sold all their property in the Florentine countryside; the wall hangings arrived two months ago; there had been a legal judgment against her in the inheritance dispute with her nephews.

I wouldn't want you to get involved in anything over there because it seems to me your best interests are served by staying close to one another and that you'd both get more comfort from being where you could help each another in any circumstances which might arise, and so would I. So long as you're over there it seems like I've half lost you. There's now so few of you and I'd be really pleased if you decided to go and find Filippo and do what he's asked of you so many times. I won't say anything more about this, so we won't have everyone hearing about our business, because I think my letters are being treated the same way yours are and I seldom get one which hasn't been opened. I don't know who's doing this. Even the letters you send Filippo have been opened. So don't write anything important to me unless it comes by someone

a te. Filippo mi se n'è doluto più volte, che le sono state aperte. È gran mancamento di chi lo fa: e bench' e nostri fatti no sono di troppa importanza, pur è mal fatto.

Non m'accade altro per ora. Filippo e le nostre fanciulle sono sane per ora; Iddio lodato. I' mi sto pure chioccia; che sono nel tempo che ci appressiamo al nostro fine: che Iddio me lo dia con salute dell'anima. La Checca ti manda mille salute. Che Iddio t'allumini del meglio dell'anima e del corpo: e fa' di star sano. Per la tua Allesandra, in Firenze.

15

Al nome di Dio. A dì 11 d'aprile 1461.

A dì 25 passato fu l'utima mia. Non ho da poi tua, che quella de' 8 di febraio, che ne fu apportatore Coppino. Per quella tua intesi della malattia di Iacopo: el simile mi disse Coppino; ma poselo fuori di pericolo della morte. Dipoi ho sentito da molte persone come a dì 13 di marzo egli era piggiorato en modo che, rispetto la malattia aveva, pochi dì, poteva durare: per la qual cosa ho 'uto gran dispiacere per molti rispetti, e massime per la sua famiglia; che sono e primi che ne ricevono danno. Iddio sa el bisogno nostro; e non fa se non bene, e per salute dell'anima

trustworthy and I'll do the same. Filippo is always complaining to me that they've been opened. It's very wrong of whoever is doing it, even though our affairs aren't of great importance.

One paragraph: she is glad to hear that Jacopo is better.

Nothing else occurs to me for the moment. Filippo and our girls are well at present, God be praised. But I'm an old bird now and I'm getting near the end. May God let me die with a healthy soul. Checca sends you her best regards. May God give light to your body and soul. Do stay well. From your Allesandra in Florence.

---

1 5

Alessandra had heard that Jacopo Strozzi was about to die,[1] and in this letter she warns Lorenzo to avoid becoming involved in the administration of the estate because it was likely to bring him nothing but trouble. He did not take his mother's advice on this matter, which turned out very much as she predicted.

In the name of God. 11 April 1461.

My last letter was on the 25th of last month. I haven't had a letter from you since the one you wrote on the 8th of February, which Coppino brought. You told me how Jacopo was sick and Coppino said the same thing, but he said there was no danger of him dying. Since then I've heard from several people how he got much worse on the 13th of March and that he was unlikely to live more than a few days longer. I was very upset about it for a number of reasons, and most of all for his family's sake, because they will be the ones to suffer. God knows what they need and He always does the right thing for our souls, so this

nostra: così arà fatto per salute dell'anima sua, se l'arà chiamato a sè, ed arà fatto el passo suo: che così abbiàno a far noi. Estimo che arà acconci e fatti sua: e trovandosi fuori di casa sua, e fuor di sua parenti; da voi en fuori, non so a chi si lasci carico di suo' fatti. Se a te avessi lasciato a nulla, per mio consiglio nollo accettare, e rinunzia a ogni governo che t'avesse lasciato; perch' e fatti delle redità sono di gran pericolo, e di noie e briga assai, e non farebbe per te; e sopra tutto fa' che non t'obrighi a nulla, nè a persona, e sia chi si vuole; chè sai non puoi obrigare se no la persona. E a questo sia savio, e ti sia detto per tutte le volte. Non dico che, mentre istai costà, non facci quel buono che puoi; ma sanza obrigo niuno. E questo ti basti intorno a di ciò. Ricordoti che di que' pochi danari ha' di mio, che tu, non avendo ritratto, gli ritragga, e facci quanto per altra ti dissi. Ho da Filippo che Niccolò scrive che, seguendo la morte di Iacopo, Lionardo si mandi a lui a Roma; sicchè non potrebbe avere miglior compagnia che la tua. L'apportatore di questa sarà Batista Strozzi: sara' co lui. Che Iddio vi dia a pigliare il partito debb'essere el meglio; che Iddio lo conduca a salvamento. Nè altro per questa. Iddio di male ti guardi. Per la tua Allesandra Strozzi, in Firenze.

must have been for the good of his soul, if He has taken him now. So he will have completed his journey, as we all must. I'm sure he will have put his affairs in order, and being away from his family and relations, I don't know who he'd leave in charge of his affairs, if not you. If he hasn't left you anything, take my advice and don't accept anything [offered by anyone else], and if he has left you in charge you should refuse to do it. Things to do with in-heritance are very risky and can lead to a lot of trouble and aggravation and you don't want to get involved in that. Above all make sure you don't let yourself become legally liable for anything or to anyone, no matter who wants it, because you know if you accept liability you do so personally. Do the clever thing where this is concerned and let this warning be enough. I'm not saying that you shouldn't do what you can while you're there, but don't let yourself get legally involved. This should be enough for you on that subject. I must remind you about that bit of money you have of mine; if you haven't yet withdrawn it [from Jacopo's business] you should do so and do what I told you to do with it, in my other letter. Filippo tells me Niccolò has written to him to say he is sending for Lionardo[2] to come and see him in Rome, because of Ja-copo's death, so he couldn't have better company on the way than you. Batista Strozzi will bring you this letter; he will be staying with you. May God let you make whatever decision is for the best and bring him there safely. Noth-ing else for now; may God keep you from harm. From your Allesandra in Florence.

16

No letters written by Alessandra survive for the period between March 1462 and December 1463. During this time Lorenzo fi-nally moved to Naples to join Filippo in running their business.

16

Al nome di Dio. A dì 22 di marzo 1463.

A dì 15, per Francesco di Sandro Strozzi, ti scrissi, e per non aver tempo, non feci risposta alla tua de' dì 6 di detto: farolla per questa.

Sarà di poi arrivato costì el detto Francesco, e vedrai la vista sua, se somiglia Nofri; che a me non pare. Hogli detto che io sono quella che te l' ho dato, e che l'onore di lui ha esser mio; chè t' ho pregato lo tolga: e così l'opposito; che non si portando bene, i' n'arò il carico da voi; e lui n'arà danno e vergogna, e che in qua sarà rimandato. Risposemi, che aveva pensiero di farmi onore, e simile a tutti gli altri. Così mi piacerà che faccia.

Raccomandotelo; chè 'l padre l' ha dato a mie' caldo, e raccomandato a me: dissi, che l'opere sue, essendo buone, si farebbono essere raccomandate per loro medesime: sicchè, poi che se l'arrecano da me d'averlo mandato, quando ti paressi ch' io avessi a ricordàgli più una cosa che un'

There are two main topics discussed in this letter to Filippo. The first is Francesco Strozzi's arrival in Naples to work for Filippo. He was about fourteen and came from a very impoverished branch of the lineage; Alessandra believed it was an act of mercy to help such poor relations. (Francesco's brother Nofri already worked for Filippo.) The letter then refers to an allegation which had been made against Filippo. Although its precise nature is not clear, it would seem to have involved a dubious financial arrangement. Alessandra expressed her readiness to believe that it was untrue, but she also gave Filippo a short lecture on the theme that Christian conduct was more important than money.

In the name of God. 22 March 1464.

I wrote to you on the 15th, by Francesco di Sandro Strozzi. I didn't answer yours of the 6th because I didn't have the time; I'll answer in this letter.

Francesco will have arrived there by now, and you'll get a good look at him and see whether he looks like Nofri, which I don't think he does. I've told him he has me to thank for his position with you and that if he does well, I will get the credit because I asked you to take him on. And if he doesn't behave well, I told him you will blame me but that it would be his loss and shame and he would be sent back here. He told me he meant to do me credit, and all the others as well. I'll be more than pleased if he does.

One paragraph: she has withdrawn four florins from their account for Francesco's expenses on his journey to Naples; he would explain how he had spent this money when he got there.

I do ask you to look after him, because his father has entrusted him to me; I said if he does well his deeds will speak for themselves. Since I persuaded them to send him, you should let me know when you think it might be a good idea for me to remind him about something or

altra, avvisamene, e gli farò duo versi, e riprendendolo del mancamento; e alle volte gli farò un verso, ricordandogli che mi faccia onore. Così gliene dia Iddio la grazia.

Veggo, sopra il carico ch'io ti scrissi che t'era dato, e simile Matteo te ne scrisse, puossi considerare en buona parte donde viene; ed ho molto caro che le sieno bugie, più che l'opposito. Iddio rallumini la mente a chi dice quello che non è; ed è d'avere compassione a tali nature. La verità ha sempre suo luogo. Attendete pure a far bene; e guardatevi, come tu di', di non fare torto a persona; chè facendolo, offenderesti Iddio e l'anima vostra, ch' è il tutto. Ennanzi men roba, che offendere quel Signore che ci ha a giudicare l'opere nostre. E in questo mondo è brieve questa nostra vita; e ci bisogna adoperare che nell'altra vita, che non ha fine, viviàno co riposo. E una delle cose che ci dannano, si è il non fare il debito al prossimo; chè lo dice il Vangelo: Fa' al prossimo tuo come vorresti fussi fatto a te. E questo ti scrivo, so che lo sai; ma ve lo ricordo, perchè sete della mia carne e sangue, e grande amore ne porto all'anima e al corpo; ed è mio debito ricordarvi el ben vostro. Sono molto contenta della buona fama e dell'esser tuo, e honne gran consolazione e piacere, che per le parole de' maldicenti sempre vada diritto, sempre con salute dell'anima. Così priego Iddio che ve ne dia la grazia. Di Tommaso Lottieri, mi disse Giovanni che a lui l'aveva detto, e che si lodava così di te; e che tu avevi una schiava che sapeva così ben fare, e ne disse molto bene; e del desinare che tu gli avevi fatto così alla sprovveduta, che sare' bastato a molti forestieri: sì che ne disse bene a Giovanni. Se ad altri ti diè carico, non so: questo mi disse Giovanni aver da lui. Non è in questo fatto

other, and I'll write him a few lines telling him he has to do the right thing for my sake.

One paragraph: she has had a letter from Lorenzo, who was in Sicily, and he is well.

About the accusation I said had been made about you, and that Matteo[1] also wrote to you about, we have to keep in mind where it comes from, and I certainly hope that it's all lies, rather than the truth. If anyone says something which isn't true, may God let them see the light; we should be sorry for anyone like that. The truth always has its place. Do try to do the right thing and as you say, be sure of not doing wrong by anyone because you'll offend God and do harm to your soul, which is the only thing that matters. It's better to have less money than to offend God, who sits in judgment over us. Our life in this world is so short we have to try to make sure we live in peace in the next life, which lasts forever. And not doing our duty by our neighbor is one of the things which damns us, because the Bible says: "do unto others as you would have them do unto you." I know you already know what I'm telling you, but I'm reminding you about it because you're my flesh and blood. I love your soul as well as your body and it's my duty to remind you for your own good. Your good reputation and well-being make me happy and give me great pleasure and comfort and you should always do the right thing, in spite of the words of slanderers, and look after your immortal soul. I pray God may give you that grace. About Tommaso Lottieri, Giovanni told me he had spoken to him and that he sang your praises; he said you had a slave[2] who had a very good idea of what to do, and [he] spoke to Giovanni in glowing terms about the lunch which luckily you'd had prepared and which was enough for several visitors. If you've offended anyone else I don't know about it; Giovanni told me about this and it came straight from him [Tommaso]. You shouldn't make any more of this than you need to, if you feel you're

farne più caso si bisogni, sentendoti netto. E così di quello de' Mannegli, non è da por mente a sue parole.

La morìa ci è pure un poco ritocca, ma in gente manuali: ma ci si fa una gran guardia, e sta alle volte dì quindici nulla si sente: poi ritocca, pure in gente di bassa mano. E non ci si sta sanza sospetto: per ancora e cittadini ci si stanno. Credo bene che fatto pasqua, chi arà villa che vi sia buona istanza, vi s'andrà a stare, tanto si vegga quello che fa. Giovanni quest'anno s'è stato colla brigata in villa, e starà mentre che v'è sano. Lui ci viene alle volte, o per mia fatti o per sua; e sta duo dì per volta, secondo el bisogno suo e mio. Marco ha comperato un podere in Mugello presso al suo, con un poco di ceppo di casa; che sendoci morìa, e là fussi sano, forse vi s'assetterebbe. Ha speso fiorini 400. Di' che per ogni via faccia pensiero di partirmi, essendoci morìa: farèno quello crederrò che ben sia. Che Iddio m'ammaestri del meglio.

Sono a dì 23, ed ho la tua de' dì 10. Risposta al bisogno. Se' avvisato della vendita de' duo pezzi di terra, e de' danari rimessi a Niccolò; e questo dì ho lettere da Roma, come e danari se ne farà la tua volontà; e di già dice Niccolò avertene iscritto. Di' che teco non bisogna pigli escusa del pigliare il danaio ho di bisogno, ma ch'io gli spenda pure utilemente. A che ti dico, che i' ti scrissi bene

not to blame in the matter. So far as that Mannegli[3] is concerned, there's no need to pay any attention to what he said.

One paragraph: there were only two pieces of land remaining at Quaracchi to be sold.

The plague has started up again here, but only a little and only among the laboring people. We keep a close eye on it and don't hear anything about it for about fifteen days or so, but then it starts up again among the lower-class people. And while there's some risk involved in staying here, the citizens are staying, all the same. After Easter I'm sure everyone who has a country house in a healthy district will go and stay there. So we'll see what happens. Giovanni [Bonsi] has been with his family in the country this year, and will stay there so long as it's healthy. He comes here sometimes either on his business or mine and stays for two days at a time, depending on what he needs to do or on what I need done. Marco has bought another farm in the Mugello close to his, with a little alms-box of a house on it, so if there was plague here and it was healthy there perhaps I could stay there for a while. It cost him 400 florins. You say I should think about leaving any way I can, if there's plague here. We'll do what I think is best; may God show us what that is.

One paragraph: Marietta di Lorenzo Strozzi[4] was waiting in Florence to be joined by her mother; Lorenzo is thinking of waiting for a year or so before marrying.[5]

It is the 23rd [of March] now, and your letter of the 10th has arrived. I will answer it as I need to. You heard about the sale of the two pieces of land and about the money I sent back to Niccolò: well today I've had a letter from Rome saying that he'll do whatever you want with the money, and Niccolò says he's already written to you about it. You say I don't have to make excuses for taking whatever money I need but that I should spend it more

per avere materia di darti che leggere: ma più lo feci perchè sapessi quello che volevo fare de' danari, perchè non crediate ch'io me gli spenda in altro. E s'io mancassi, voglio che sappiate ch' i' non ho danari nella cassa; ma questi s'hanno a spendere nella più utile cosa ch'i'abbia, ch'è l'anima mia. E delle male ispese mi guardo, e di spendere inutilemente. E sopra di ciò non n'accade altro dirne. Farò sempre quello crederrò sia bene per me e per voi.

Questo dì si comperorno gli occhiali, e ti si mandano sotto lettere di Niccolò Strozzi a Roma pel fante: sì che fa' d'avergli. Nè altro per questa m'accade. Raccomandomi a te; che Iddio di male ti guardi. Per la tua Allesandra Strozzi, in Firenze.

17

usefully. To which I say that I wrote to you at the very least to give you something to read, but in particular to tell you what I wanted to do with the money, so you wouldn't think I'd spent it on something else. I want you to know that if I die I won't have any cash in my coffers,[6] because I will have spent it on my soul instead, which is the most useful thing I have. I'm careful not to spend money badly or uselessly, so there's nothing else to be said about it. I'll go on doing what I think is best, both for me and you.

Five short paragraphs: she is glad Filippo has carried out the terms of Matteo's will; she has heard that Niccolò Magalotti is out of town on Filippo's business; brief comments on Battista Strozzi and Niccolò Ardinghelli;[7] she gathers that Filippo has Caterina's flax and will send it by road; she will buy the spectacles[8] through Giovanni Bonsi.

They bought the spectacles today, and they're sending them to you in Rome by the servant who takes Niccolò Strozzi's letters, so do be sure to collect them. Nothing else occurs to me for now. Do keep me in your thoughts; may God keep you from all harm. From your Allesandra Strozzi in Florence.

Postscript: she has had news of Lorenzo from Ruberto Mannelli, who has just arrived in Florence from the Levant; he didn't bring her any sugar, so she cannot send Filippo any.

17

This letter to Filippo follows on directly from the last, and it shows that Alessandra was quite tolerant of the fact that Filippo's slave Marina was his mistress. She disapproved initially of his gift to Caterina of a large quantity of flax which, as she comments, Marco Parenti could have well afforded to pay for, but later changed her mind.

Al nome di Dio. A dì 7 d'aprile 1464.

Ancora di' che se' contento, che quello mandi alla Caterina nolli costi danaio. Questo voglio detto, perchè mi par troppo lino a donare a Marco, che ha el modo a pagare; e quando gliene donassi dieci mazzi per volta, era assai, e innanzi, tra duo volte. Quando volessi donargliele, i' no gli dirò altro ensino non ho risposta da te; e auta, ne seguirò la tua volontà.

Per una tua a Giovanni Bonsi di' che 'l fanciullo di Sandro era a dì 25 giunto costì; che Iddio lodato. Arai dipoi veduto se l'aria sua ti piace, e me ne di' quello te ne pare. Avete costì Andrea, che se ne dice miracoli della virtù sua, e massimo Tommaso Ginori, che venne el dì della pasqua, e me n' ha detto molte cose delle virtù ch'egli ha: e così della Marina, de' vezzi ch'ella ti fa. E sentendo tante cose, non mi maraviglio che vogli endugiare ancora un anno, e che si vada adagio al darti donna. Fai come colui che voleva endugiare la morte e 'l pagamento el più che poteva. Non hai più ch'una femmina per casa, e se' ben governato; e se to' donna, n'arai parecchi, e non sai come ti starai. Sicchè mi pare tu sia savio a pigliar tempo, e del buono, quando lo puoi pigliare. I' ho detto a Tommaso parecchi cose a che avevo el pensiero: non so che si seguirà.

In the name of God. 7 April 1464.

One paragraph: her last letter was on the 23rd of March and she has had one from Filippo of the 20th. Caterina's flax has not yet arrived, but when it does she will not confuse it with what he is giving to his "godmother." [1]

You still say you're happy that [the flax] you're sending Caterina shouldn't cost them anything. I wanted you to say so, because it seems to me too much flax to give Marco because he can afford to pay for it. Giving them ten bundles at one time is a lot and enough for two presents. When I realized you wanted to give it to them I left saying anything about it until I'd heard from you, and now I'll do what you want.

In a letter to Giovanni Bonsi you say that Sandro's boy [2] arrived there on the 25th, may God be praised. Since then you'll have seen whether you like the look of him and you'll let me know how he strikes you. You've got Andrea [3] there, and I've heard amazing things about how clever he is, particularly from Tommaso Ginori, [4] who came [to see me] on Easter Day and told me all about how good he is, and about Marina and how well she looks after you. Hearing such things I find it easy to understand why you want to put off getting married for a year and why they're so slow in finding you a wife. You behave like a man who wants to put off dying or paying his debts for as long as he can. At the moment you've only got one woman in the house and you're well looked after, but when you get married there'll be lots of them and you wonder how you'll get on. So it seems to me you're wise to take your time, as you must make up your mind eventually. I talked to Tommaso about several things which I've had on my mind, but I don't know what will come of it.

Tornò qui Giovan Tornabuoni, e non sento dire nulla della figliuola di Lorenzo. È ben grasso, ed ha presso al 40, al modo tuo. Non credo Giovanni lo facessi: e quando pur volesse, la madre non è di quel volere, se non si rimuta d'animo.

Ara' sentito della galea perduta en Fiandra, che è stato grande scurità: perduto tante persone e la roba. Iddio abbia 'vuto misericordia di loro. Estavo prima co pensiero di Lorenzo quando sento che va in mare: ma ora ne starò con maggiore paura quando saprò abbia andare o tornare per nave: che l'Agnol Rafaello l'accompagni. Avvisa se è tornato, o quando l'aspetti: che di male vi guardi Iddio. Per la tua Allesandra Strozzi, Firenze.

Raccomandoti Francesco: se non è con tante virtù come Andrea, abbi pazienza, e 'nsegnategli, chè ha buon sentimento, e credo apparerà.

18

Al nome di Dio. A dì 21 d'aprile 1464.

A dì 9 per Tommaso Ginori fu l'utima mia: dipoi ho dua tue, de' 4 e 9 detto. Risposta al bisogno.

Three paragraphs: there is plague, but not among the well-to-do, although there have been cases close by; Filippo should have had the 134 florins from Niccolò and the spectacles for his friend; she hasn't written to Lorenzo because she does not know if he is back from Sicily.

Giovanni Tornabuoni[5] has returned, but I haven't heard anything about Lorenzo's daughter [Marietta Strozzi]. He's very fat, and like you he's nearly forty. I don't believe Giovanni would do it[6] and even if he'd wanted to, her mother isn't in favor of it, unless she's changed her mind.

You'll have heard about the galley which was lost off [the coast of] Flanders; not much is known but many people and goods were lost. May God have mercy on them. At first I thought about Lorenzo, when I heard he was going by sea, and I'll still be very afraid when I know he's going or returning by ship; may the Angel Raphael go with him. Let me know if he's back, or when you expect him. From your Allesandra Strozzi, Florence.

Do please look after Francesco; even if he doesn't have as much ability as Andrea, you should be patient and teach him, because he has the right ideas and this should become clear to you.

18

Alessandra adopts her most admonitory style here, lecturing Filippo about how he should treat Francesco, and about his behavior to Caterina. She also reminds him that he must be careful to escape the plague, as death would put an end to all his plans.

In the name of God. 21 April 1464.

My last letter, sent by Tommaso Ginori, was written on the 9th. Since then I've had two from you, of the 4th and the 9th. I'll answer them as I need to.

Condussesi costì Francesco di Sandro; e veggo dipoi l'
ha' provato, e ti pare pure da poco ne' fatti di casa: ed
è vero; chè procede en buona parte da chi gli allieva.
Questo suo padre è buono uomo e favellante, ma non è
secondo la vista che mostra; chè l'ho pratico ora, per
l'amicizia presi di questo fanciullo, e sommi adoperata al
maritare d'una sua figliuola, cioè di confortare e parenti
di chi l'aveva a tòrre, en modo che s'è fatto el parentado:
sicchè non m'è riuscito come credevo. È la donna da più
che non è egli. Hanno gran famiglia, e poca roba, e deb-
bangli allevare grossolanamente. Pure fatene la diligenza
vostra; e tu hai Andrea, che gli doverrà ensegnare: e non
sendo grosso istormento, doverrà pure apparare. Che Iddio ce ne dia onore. E fiorini 4 ebbe qua, io gli ho fatti
buoni a Miraballi per parte.

La Caterina ebbe i' lino: pare a lei e a Marco buono e
bello. No gli ho detto che tu glielo doni. Fagli tu duo
versi, e digliele tu medesimo: che pure parrà che tu ti ricordi di lei; e che poi che Iddio l'ha private di tale consolazione, quanto aspettavano di vedere alla tornata vostra
ennanzi e vostri casi, che faccendogli duo versi e tale dono
di questo lino, n'arà piacere, e no gli parrà in tutto essere
privata dell'amor fraternale: e un poco di caldo gli darai di
te, che da persona non hanno. Avevoti detto per altra, che
Marco aveva el modo a pagare: di poi mi pensai che li è
ben fatto donargliele; che pure arà quello di dire: Me lo
mandò mio fratello!

Francesco di Sandro has arrived there and I gather you've tested him since he came and you think that so far he knows very little about what to do in the business. It's true, and the person who brought him up is mainly to blame. His father is a good man and plausible, but he isn't really as he seems. I know him better now, because since I made friends with the boy I've made myself useful by arranging a marriage for one of his daughters, by advising the relations of the man who was marrying her, so that the match was made. It turns out he's not really the sort of man I thought he was, and his wife is better than he is. They have a large family and little money so they're forced to bring them up in rather a rough way. Still you should apply yourself [to helping Francesco], and Andrea is there and can show him what to do; as he isn't stupid he'll learn. May God hold this in our favor. He got the four florins here; I've repaid Miraballi[1] for them.

Three paragraphs: some financial transactions between them; there was still one piece of land to sell at Quaracchi; Filippo and Lorenzo should send a new power of attorney to Giovanni Bonsi because the old one had expired.

Caterina has got the flax and she and Marco think it's good and fine. I haven't told them you're giving it to her; do write them two lines and tell her so, and it will seem as if you're really thinking of her. That way, although she has lost most of the comfort of having a brother (because they've waited a long time for you to come back, since before your disasters) if you write two lines to her, with that and the gift of the flax it will make her happy and she won't feel she's entirely without a brother's love. It will give them a little bit of affection from you, when they can't get any in person. I said in another letter that Marco was able to pay, but since then I've decided that it's a good thing for you to give it to her; then she can say "my brother sent me this."

La figlia di Lorenzo si sta così: non ho sentito di poi altro. Aspettacisi la madre. Questa morìa dà loro gran noia, alle fanciulle, chè pochi parentadi ci si fa. Veggo che voi di costà n'avete anche sospetto, e di già ve n'è morti alcuni: che n'ho dispiacere assai, più essendo costà che qua, e co più sospetto ne starò. Priegoti quanto so e posso, che tu ti sappi guardare, e non aspettare che la cosa trabocchi prima ti parta: fa' d'essere de' primi: ricordandoti, ch'e nostri passati, tutti sono iti di tale male, da Matteo mio figliuolo in fuori: sicchè stieti a mente. Lorenzo doverrà esservi presto; e di poi pigliate partito, seguitandovi tal male: che Dio e San Bastiano vi scampi di questo e d'ogni altra tribolazione, come disidero. E a campar la vita, è buono a por le faccende e' guadagni da parte. E più rompe e disegni la morte, che altro. Attendete a vivere el più che potete. È morto qui di pesta Piero Piaciti da sabato a ore 22 a lunedì a 20 quattr'ore. Sonsi trovate la madre vecchia, e la moglie col corpo grande, e sei figliuoli, sole e sanza governo d'anima, e male governo del corpo. Non vi si trovò che duo servigiali di Santa Maria Nuova. Non è chi faccia loro un servigio: ensino al pane, non truovano chi lo cuoca loro: ogn'uomo fugge: aveva un ragazzo, e gli Otto l' hanno fatto mandar via. È una iscurità a sentire quello si fa. Iddio ci aiuti.

Two paragraphs: she has seen what Matteo di Giorgio Bran-dolini wrote to Filippo, and it pleased her, but it was unwise to place hope in mere words; she has heard the proposal of Filippo's friend,[2] and the answer which Filippo gave, which have also pleased her.

Lorenzo's daughter [Marietta Strozzi] is still here but I haven't heard anything else about it. She's waiting here for her mother. The plague's a great inconvenience for girls because hardly any marriages are being arranged here. I see there's also some fear of an outbreak there and that some people have died from it already. This has upset me very much, more than the fact that it's here, and I'll go on being afraid of it. I do beg you as much as I can to be wise enough to watch out for it; don't wait until it boils over before you leave. Do be one of the first to go, and remember that everyone who's died in our family has gone of this disease, right up to my son Matteo. So keep this in mind. Lorenzo will be there soon and then you can both decide, if there's still plague there. May God and St. Sebastian save you from this and every other suffering, as I wish. It would be a good idea, so that you can go on making your living, to put business and making money to one side; death has wrecked more plans than anything else. Concentrate on living as well as you can. Piero Piaciti has died of the plague here, between Saturday at 5 p.m. and Monday at a quarter past three. He left an elderly mother and a pregnant wife and six children alone and without any spiritual guidance, and badly looked after in body as well. There was no one there except two nurses' aides from S. Maria Nuova.[3] There was no one to do them a good deed and no one would even cook their bread for them as everyone had run away. He [Piero Piaciti] had a boy,[4] but the Eight[5] had sent him away. It's hard to find out how they're getting on. May God help them.

Non vi sendo Lorenzo, no gli scrivo; chè a te iscrivo a bastanza. Leggi quando non hai troppa faccenda. Che Iddio di male vi guardi. Per la tua Allesandra Strozzi, Firenze; a voi mi raccomando.

19

Al nome di Dio. A dì 15 di settembre 1464.

Duo dì sono ch'i' ebbi dua tua; l'una de' 14 del passato, e l'altra de' 31: risposta al bisogno. Non è dubbio che gli animi d'alquanti cittadini per la morte seguìta non abbino fatto in tra loro nuovi pensieri del governo della terra; ma per ancora non si sente; chè la cosa è fresca, e Dietisalvi è stato ammalato. Non si sente altro, se no che s'attend' a ben vivere: e de' fatti vostri o di niuno che sia in vostro grado, non se ne ragiona; sicchè ha' fatto bene a non escrivere a nessuno di questa materia. E per questo non bisogna ch' i' stia a Firenze; chè non arei guatato per morìa che vi fussi, quando bene ne fussi iti venti per dì, se

Three paragraphs: Giovanni della Luna died three days ago, but not of the plague; she is pleased that Filippo has cancelled Miniato's debt; linen for shirts.

As Lorenzo isn't there I haven't written to him and I've said everything necessary to you instead. Read it when you don't have too much else to do. May God keep you from all harm. From your Allesandra Strozzi in Florence. Do keep me in your thoughts.

19

Political changes were anticipated in Florence following the death of Cosimo de' Medici. In this letter to Filippo, Alessandra's interest centered on whether such changes were likely to lead to the revocation of the sentence of exile against her sons.

In the name of God. 15 September 1464.

One paragraph: her last letter was on the 2nd, and she had also sent him fennel and twelve shirts.

Two days ago two letters of yours came, one of the 14th of last month and the other of the 31st; I'll reply as I need to. There's no doubt that this death[1] has given many of the citizens some new ideas about how the land should be governed, but so far there's nothing much to be heard, partly because it's so recent and partly because Dietisalvi[2] has been sick. I haven't heard anything, except that they[3] are expecting to enjoy themselves. So far as your affairs are concerned and those of others in your position, it's not being discussed, so you've done the right thing not to write to anyone about it. There was no need for me to stay in Florence on that account, because I would have been looking the plague in the face while a good twenty

io avessi inteso un piccolo accennamento di ragionamento di questa materia: ma nulla se ne ragiona. E cittadini sono, rispetto la morìa, per le ville, e non si sente troppo: ma da Ognissanti en là si doverrà sentire qualche cosa. E non dubitare che quando sentissi cosa alcuna, che si favellerà dove e con chi bisognerà: e non si lascerà, nè per danari nè per non volere, adoperare amici e parenti; anzi non si lascerà a far nulla. Ma s'aspetta, prima di sentire qualche cosa che l'uomo abbia da parlarne, qualche movitiva e qualche indizia di loro pensiero, di chi governa. Come ti dico, Dietisalvi è stato ammalato: Bernardetto non è, secondo sento, da farne troppo conto. El tuo messere A. non è però dove tu credi; e stimo bene che sia di buon animo inverso di te: ma, secondo entendo, non è però el principale: e d'uffici o d'ordini di nuovo non sento, se no d'un bel Prioratico, ch'entrò el primo di questo: che quello che v'è di meno riputazione, fuori dell'ufficio, si è Giovanni d'Anton di Salvestro, che è gonfaloniere di giustizia: evvi parecchi de' Signori che sono uomini maturi, e altre volte suti gonfalonieri di giustizia: sì che questo hanno fatto: altro non so. Dissi a Giovanni che ti scrivessi qualche cosa in questa parte, se sapeva altro. Loderei alle volte che tu scrivessi duo versi a Tommaso Davizzi, che è in luogo da sentire; e raccomàndategli: ed io anche lo farò, quando bisognerà: e in questa parte non mi peserà la penna, avvisarvi quando vedrò el bisogno. Che no l' ho fatto da dua mesi en qua di scrivervi espesso, perchè non ci è suto cosa d'importanza. La morte di Cosimo stimai lo sentissi più presto che da me, e però no lo scrissi.

people were dying of it a day. [It would have been worth it] if I'd heard the slightest hint of a discussion of this matter, but no one mentioned it. The citizens are in the country because of the plague, and no one feels like discussing it much. But by All Saints' [1 November] or thereabouts we should hear something. You needn't doubt that when we hear something we'll talk to whoever we need to, wherever we need to, and we won't fail to make use of our friends and relations, either from lack of money or from not wanting to, and we won't forget anything. But first we're waiting to hear what's being said about it and to get some idea what those in charge might be think-ing. As I told you, Dietisalvi has been sick and from all I hear Bernardetto [de' Medici] doesn't carry too much weight. Your Messer A[4] isn't as well placed as you think he is; while I certainly believe he's well disposed toward you, from what I gather he's not the most important man in these matters. I haven't heard about the new offices and positions, except that there's a good Signoria which took office on the first of this month. One of its members doesn't have much of a reputation apart from his office and that's Giovanni d'Anton di Salvestro,[5] who is Gonfa-lonier of Justice. Several of the priors are experienced men who have been Gonfalonier of Justice at other times, so they[6] have done this. I don't know anything else. I told Giovanni [Bonsi] he should write to you about this busi-ness if he knew anything. It might be a good idea if you wrote a few lines to Tommaso Davizzi[7] who's well placed to hear something, and to recommend yourselves to him, and I'll do the same when it's necessary. Where this is con-cerned I won't feel the weight of the pen, and will keep you informed as often as I think is necessary. I haven't written so often during the last two months because there's been noth-ing important going on here, and I knew you'd hear about Cosimo's death more quickly from someone else so I didn't write to you about it. So far as your position is concerned,

E di grado, estimo siate più tosto in migliore che piggiore: e per ora non è da scriverne a persona; quando sarà el tempo, vi si dirà.

Anton di Puccio è quasi guarito; che ha 'uto gran paura: ha dato molti danari per Dio, ha tratti prigioni delle Stinche; e tanto ha fatto, c' ha riceuto grazia di guarire. Per la tua Allesandra Strozzi, alle Selve.

20

Al nome di Dio. A dì 3 di gennaio 1464.

Veggo ti duole el caso di Lodovico; e avete fatto bene a profferervigli: dicesi che renderanno soldi 20 per lira, e che rimarranno ricchi. Hanno di molte case, e possissioni si dice e masserizie per 16 mila fiorini: sicchè in questo

it should get better rather than worse. For the moment there's no point in writing about it to anyone; we'll let you know when the time is right.

Four paragraphs: Agnolo Acciaiuoli has acquired a feudal estate in the Kingdom of Naples and is going there; she will try to send Filippo cheese and fennel on Bernardo Bonsi's galley; she has received Lorenzo's letter; she is glad Filippo and Lorenzo are well.

Antonio di Puccio[8] has nearly recovered. He was very afraid and gave a lot of money to God, rescuing prisoners from the Stinche.[9] He did so much, he was given the grace to recover. From your Allesandra Strozzi at Le Selve.[10]

20

There were many business failures among Florentine companies in the months following the death of Cosimo de' Medici, and among these were two companies owned by members of the Strozzi lineage. In this letter, addressed to Filippo but also intended to be read by Lorenzo, Alessandra discusses these events in Florence.

In the name of God. 3 January 1465.

Two paragraphs: her last letter was on the 29th of December; Filippo and Lorenzo's request was a great one,[1] but they had certainly conducted themselves very well.

I see you're sorry about what's happened to Lodovico,[2] and you've done well to offer to help him. It's said they'll [eventually] be able to pay [their creditors in full], 20 soldi in the lira[3] and that they'll still be rich. It's said they own many houses and properties and a lot of household goods,

caso perdono più di riputazione che altro. E dipoi arete inteso di Giovanfrancesco; ha rifiorito la casa nostra. Hacci debito assai: chi dice che farà il dovere, e chi no: credo per questo la nipote n'arà danno assai. Non se ne sente nulla ragionare di quegli che pel passato si diceva: doverrassi vedere di qui a qualche mese. La cosa di questi falliti per ora pare posata; che da Giovanfrancesco en qua non ho sentito poi d'altri. Hanno fatto ferie tutto questo mese: non so a che fine; che credo sia buono per chi ha debito.

Egli è parecchi mesi che quel pizzicagnolo di Borgo Sa' Lorenzo m' ha istimolata di nove fiorini aveva avere da vostro padre. Credo che altre volte l'abbiate inteso, e massimo Lorenzo, che gli parlò quando e' ci era ammalato. I' l'ho sostenuto quanto m'è stato possibile, e con dire non ho a pagare a debiti di vostro padre. E'n fine, veduto no ne può avere altro, e n'ha fatto ammunizione, e tratta la scomunica: dove a questo parendomi che fussi di nostro danno e vergogna, gli ho fatto parlare al nostro prete, che

worth 16,000 florins altogether, so in this case they'll lose their reputation rather than anything else. And since then you'll have heard about Giovanfrancesco;[4] he has made our house bloom again.[5] He has a great many debts here; some people think he'll do what he should, but others think he won't. I'm sure his niece [Marietta Strozzi] will be greatly damaged by this. No one says anything about those who were discussed in the past;[6] it remains to be seen in the coming months. They have declared a legal moratorium for all of this month; I don't know why, but it will help those who have debts.

Nine paragraphs: she is pleased that the King is so well disposed toward Filippo; the value of Monte [7] *shares had fallen due to recent events, and if Filippo sends his power of attorney she will reinvest in something more secure if the opportunity arises; she thinks the rumors about Niccolò Strozzi's affairs are all lies; she doesn't want to worry herself further about the benefice of Santuccio;* [8] *a short discussion about possible wives for Filippo and Lorenzo; nothing has been heard from Niccolò Ardinghelli since March; she had heard nothing about a certain (unspecified) marriage alliance; some business she had tried to do for Niccolò Strozzi with Piero and Tommaso Capponi; if Giovanfrancesco failed to do his duty by his Florentine creditors he would be declared a rebel of the Commune and might be condemned to death in absentia.*

That pork butcher from San Lorenzo has been trying for several months to get me to pay him 9 florins he was owed by your father. I think you've both heard about it before, and particularly Lorenzo as I talked to him about it when he was here, while he was sick. I've put up with it for as long as possible, telling him I don't have to pay your father's debts.[9] In the end he's warned me that it's a matter for excommunication, seeing he can't get it any other way.[10] That would do us harm and bring us shame,

è un valente e buono uomo; ed egli ha preso tempo uno mese da lui, con dire ch'io vi scriverrò e avviserò di questo fatto, e aspetterò vostra risposta, e di quello s'abbia a seguire. Egli ha una scritta di mano di notaio, dove Matteo s'obriga di dargli questi danari per Agnolo da Vergereto, cavallaro; che Matteo è suo debitore. Rispondete che è da fare; che quanto per me non posso più co lui, nè sostenerlo più colle parole: e per quello truovo al Libro, Matteo è debitore di quest'Agnolo de'fiorini da 20. Sicchè faccendone iscomunica, aremo voi ed io questo peso addosso, che pure abbiàno di quello di Matteo voi ed io: sì che, quando cadessimo in questo, i' non crederre' mai capitar bene di nulla ch'i'avessi a fare. Avvisate di vostro pensiero.

Per altra dissi, le lettere avevo ritenute di Tommaso, e tutte quelle v'erano drento: serberolle bene alla sua tornata. Siàno a ore 23, e ancora non ci è el fante da Roma, che s'aspetta fra tre dì: fomi ennanzi allo scrivere perchè el freddo mi dà noia, e a bell'agio la piglio. Aspetterò a suggellare, e se 'l fante venissi. Di' che scrivi a Tommaso per questa tua de' 18, del fatto de'danari, quello Tommaso n'abbia a fare: non truovo ci sia suo' lettere; estimo Niccolò l'arà ritenute a Roma, sendo venuto in costà. Ed è vero che gran rovina ci è stata. Ora la cosa s'è raccheta: o che sia rispetto le ferie che sono, o quello si sia, la cosa si sta. Nè altro per ora. Iddio di male vi guardi. Per la vostra Allesandra, Firenze.

so I went to talk to our priest about it, as he's a good man and a clever one; he has obtained us a month's grace by saying I'd write and tell you all about it and wait for your answer and whatever might follow. He [the pork butcher] has a document written by a notary [11] which says Matteo committed himself to give him this money on behalf of Agnolo di Vergereto, a horse dealer, and that Matteo was his debtor. You must answer and let me know what should be done, because so far as I'm concerned I can't do anything else or put him off any longer by talking. And according to what I find in the Book [of Accounts] Matteo is this Agnolo's debtor to the tune of 20 florins. If this excommunication is put into effect we'll all have this weight on our shoulders, and we have what was Matteo's, you and I. When we got involved in this I never thought that what I had to do would turn out well. Let me know what you think.

Two paragraphs: there was still a barrel for her at Pisa; she was writing using her spectacles; and they should read the letter more than once to make sure they understood it.

In another letter I told you about the letters for Tommaso [Ginori] that I'd held on to; I will keep them until he comes back. It's 4 p.m. and the servant from Rome still hasn't come; I was early with my writing because the cold worries me and I like to take my time. I'll wait to seal it until I see if the servant is coming. In your letter of the 18th you say you're writing to Tommaso about the money and what he should do about it, but the letter doesn't seem to be here. I think Niccolò must have kept it in Rome, if it went that way. It's true that things are in a terrible state here. It's calming down now, or should do so, with the moratorium they're having, but we'll be left with what has [already] happened. Nothing more for now; may God keep you from harm. From your Allesandra, Florence.

2 I

Al nome di Dio. A'dì 7 di febbraio 1464.

A dì 26 passato fu l'utima mia: ho di poi, sotto lettere di Lorenzo da San Chirico, una tua de' 18 di detto. Accaderà poca risposta: farolla per questa al bisogno. Giunse qui Tommaso a' dì 31 passato, a ore 23, e essofatto diè le lettere recate di costà a chi l'aveva a dare, e da 46 e 54 e dagli altri amici ebbe grate risposte. Dal fratello di 32 assai buona. Dietisalvi t'è grande e buono amico, che n'ha fatto dimostrazione, e così Zanobi, in questa licenza di Lorenzo: chè troppo sete loro obbrigati; e benchè ci sie ito un poco di tempo in averla, e che per gli amici tua si sia durato fatica, pure, per la grazia di Dio, iarsera di notte s'ebbe detta licenza. E perchè la legge dice che niuno confinato possa venirci se no per le 44 fave e pe' Consigli, se non ch'e'caggia in bando di rubbello; e pertanto s'è fatto per via di comandamento che, a pena della alturità loro, che venga qua fuori della porta, dove vuole, per tutto marzo. E questo, secondo m'è detto da chi entende, che

2 1

When Alessandra began this letter to Filippo, Lorenzo was in San Quirico, a small town near the border between Siena and Florence, waiting to receive the safe-conduct which, as an exile, he needed to enter Florentine territory. Alessandra discusses which of the city's influential political figures would be prepared to help Lorenzo obtain it. Because this was a politically sensitive matter and she suspected that her letters were being tampered with, a numerical code is used for some names.

In the name of God. 7 February 1465.

My last letter was on the 26th of last month and since then I've had one from you written on the 18th, which was enclosed in Lorenzo's letters from San Quirico. It doesn't need much of an answer but I'll do so as I need to here. Tommaso [Ginori] came on the 31st [of January] at 5 p.m. and gave the letters he'd brought from there [San Quirico] to the people he was supposed to give them to, and he was given positive answers by 46[1] and 54[2] and your other friends, and a very good answer by 32's[3] brother. Dietisalvi is a great friend of yours, and a good one, and he has shown this, and so has Zanobi,[4] in this business of the permit for Lorenzo, and you owe him a great deal. And although it took a while to get it and your friends had to work hard for it, still by the grace of God the permit was granted yesterday evening. This is because the law says that no exile can come here unless there are 44 votes in favor and [it is agreed to] by the Councils,[5] otherwise he can be condemned as a rebel. And for that reason it has been decided by decree that on pain of such punishment he may come here as far as the gate and stay wherever he wishes [outside the walls] for all of March. And this, ac-

gli sta in buona forma. E per tanto Carlo Guasconi gli
mandò un fante a ore 5 di notte col detto comandamento.
Aspettiàllo a' dì 9. Mandilo Iddio salvo. Non ci pare en-
teramente la chiesta del Re, che lo chiede per drento nella
terra; e ancora el bisogno suo e 'l contento nostro; chè ci
sarà di gran disagio a lui e a me, e di più spesa. Pure non è
cosa da ricusarla, e potrebb'essere che di qui a qualche dì,
che gli amici nostri lo faranno venir drento: che di così
sono confortata. E in questa sua venuta, quando non si
fussi acquistato altro, pure s'è veduto che ci avete degli
amici, e di quegli che vi darebbono aiuto e favore a maggior cosa che questa: sì che del dubbio ch'io ti scrissi per
l'utima ch'i'avevo, mi sono rimossa per le parole ho sen-
tite son ite a torno in questo fatto di Lorenzo; che me ne
conforto. Prechiamo Iddio che per sua misericordia provvegga al nostro bisogno dell'anima e del corpo.

Siàno a' dì 9, e ieri ebbi la tua de' 25 passato. Risposta
per questa. Mandai la sua a Messere, come l'ebbi: Lorenzo
aspettiàno istasera: mandilo Iddio salvo e'n buon punto
per l'anima e pel corpo, e se a Dio piacerà ci vedrèno di
presso, e intenderò di vostro pensiero, e voi el mio: e di
certo questo tempo che ci starà n'arò contento. Così volesse Iddio ch'i' l'avessi d'amendue, benchè tu me ne dia
noia, ch'egli è quello che è da me più amato. Ho caro che
tu dica così, chè quando ti dicessi di lui più una cosa che
un'altra, non te ne maraviglierai, e non mi negherai
quando te lo raccomandassi. Di' che con anima m'allarghi

cording to what was said to me by someone who'd heard about it, is so long as he observes the proper forms. And Carlo Guasconi sent him a messenger at 11 at night with that decree. We expect him on the 9th; may God bring him here safely. This doesn't seem to be everything the King[6] asked for, as he asked for him to be allowed into the city, which was what he needed and what we wanted as well. This way it will be very inconvenient for him and for me, and much more expensive. Still, it's not something we can say no to, and after a few days our friends may be able to bring him in, and I've comforted myself by thinking about that. And his coming here, even if it hasn't gained us anything else, has shown us we have friends who would help us with something more important than this. So while I did tell you in my last letter that I had some doubts, the things that people have said to me during this business of Lorenzo's have put an end to them, which is a comfort. We pray God in His mercy to provide for our needs, both of body and soul.

Two paragraphs: ambassadors have been chosen to go to the courts of Milan and Naples; Filippo must cultivate the favor of the new Florentine ambassadors in Naples by presents and other means.

It is now the 9th, and yesterday I had your letter of the 25th of last month. I sent Messer[7] his letter just as I received it. We expect Lorenzo this evening; may God bring him here in good shape, both in body and soul, and then God willing we'll see one another and be together again, and I'll hear your thoughts and you'll hear mine, and while he's here I'll be happy. It was God's will that I should have him here, of the two of you, but you make me angry by saying he's the one I love most. I don't like you to say so, because when I tell you something or other about him you won't be surprised, and you won't refuse when I ask you to do what you can for him. You say I

di cose sentissi. A che ti dico, che da Tommaso è da guardarvi, che è molto largo nel parlare; e credo che Giovanni Bonsi e Marco abbian 'uto da lui le cose scrivo, perchè i' l' ho da 14 e 13; ed io ancora glien' ho sentito ragionare, ma poco, chè poco tempo ha'uto in questi dì di ragionare: ma dubito che co' sua non ne ragioni; e sino martedì, non credendo che sì tosto Lorenzo avessi licenza, ritornò a San Chirico, e co Lorenzo ne verrà. Ricorderògli espesso che non parli così aperto con ognuno come e' fa, che vi potrebbe nocere assai. Ricordagliele, e non dire averlo da me.

Farò vezzi a Lorenzo quanto i' potrò: così ve ne potessi io fare tramendua insieme; ma posso poco, chè tuttavia crocchio; e ogni dì priego Iddio e fo pregare che Iddio mi conceda grazia che mi possa istare questo poco ci ho a vivere con esso voi con pace e consolazione dell'anima e del corpo. Raccomanditi a me! e i' ho bisogno d'essere raccomandata a te.

Sento pure Lodovico aranno che fare tra 'l debito di là e di qua, che poco doverrà loro rimanere di sodo.

A me anche piaceva quella da Vernia, ma i' me ne 'nformai, e mi pare abbi del zotico. Pure nella stanza qua di Lorenzo ne isaminerèno meglio; e così della nipote di Giovanfrancesco. Non sento di nessuno suo accordo co' creditori; se non che dice bene di volere fare il dovere e dà molte buone parole a ciascuno. Pure ci è chi ne dubita

spread around the things I hear, but I say you should be careful with Tommaso [Ginori] because he's a very big talker and I think Giovanni Bonsi and Marco have heard the things I write from him, because I hear them from 14[8] and 13;[9] I've also heard him discussing these things, but not much, because he's had little time to talk in these few days. But I doubt he's discussed it with his family, and as early as Tuesday he went back to San Chirico, not thinking Lorenzo would get his permit so soon, and he'll come back with Lorenzo. I'll remind him often not to speak freely to everyone the way he does, because harm could come from it. Remember this about him, and don't say it came from me.

Four short paragraphs: she has put away the gift for the Knight, whom Lorenzo says he saw in Rome; Niccolò Ardinghelli is back in Venice from the Levant; Alessandra does not want the pork butcher worrying Lorenzo, and she will reach an agreement with him herself; she has given Tommaso his letters.

I will fuss over Lorenzo as much as I can, and I wish I could do the same for both of you together. I can't do much because I'm still not well, and every day I pray to God, and I must pray that God will give me the grace to spend the little time I have left with both of you, in peace and comfort of body and soul. You should ask me to remember you kindly, just as I need to ask the same of you.

About Lodovico [Strozzi], I've heard that what with their debts here, and over there, they'll have little of substance left.

I also liked the [proposed match with the] della Vernia girl, but I was told, and it did seem to me, that she was like a peasant. But while Lorenzo is here we will look at her more closely, and Giovanfrancesco's niece too. I haven't heard anything about his agreement with his creditors, except that they say he wants to do his duty, and says many fine things to each of them. Still, there are people

che non faccia nulla. Aspettava Niccolò di Levante, che si diceva aveva sue mercatanzie. Vedrassi, ora ch'egli è tornato, quello farà. Nè altro per questa. Iddio di male ti guardi. Per la tua Allesandra Strozzi, Firenze.

Ebbi a questi dì un bariglione di susine, che mi costano tra vettura da Pisa a qui, e gabella, 30 soldi, che non gli vagliono. Aresti fatto meglio a mandarmi qualche cosa dolce, che sono piena di scesa. Pure ho caro ogni vostra; e non ti maravigliare di questa mia, che sono in fantasia aspettando Lorenzo.

22

Al nome di Dio. A dì 29 di marzo 1465.

A dì 16 fu l'utima mia. Non avendo poi tua, ho per questa manco a dire; ma solo fo perchè non mi dimentichiate, e di darvi cagione, quando avete tempo, di farmi duo versi; che non ho altra consolazione che sentire per lettere vostre, che siate sani, e facciate bene. Che Iddio sia lodato di tutto.

I' ho lettere da Roma da Lorenzo, che a dì 20 si doveva partire per costì. Arò piacere sentire si sia condotto a salvamento. Così piaccia a Dio che sia. Aspettone pelle

who doubt he'll do anything. They're waiting for Niccolò [Ardinghelli] to arrive back from the Levant and they've been saying he has his merchandise. We'll see what will happen now he's come back. Nothing more for now; may God keep you from harm. From your Allesandra Strozzi, Florence.

In the last few days I received a barrel of plums which cost 30 soldi, what with cartage from Pisa to here and the duty, which is more than they're worth. You would have done better to send me something sweet, as I've been wanting something like that. Still, I like anything you send. You shouldn't be surprised at this letter as my thoughts are wandering while I wait for Lorenzo.

---

2 2

Lorenzo had just completed his visit to Florence, and Alessandra tells Filippo of her sadness following his departure. She then repeats some gossip about Niccolò Ardinghelli's wife and the seventeen-year-old Lorenzo de' Medici. The letter then returns to her growing preoccupation with the possibility of her sons returning to Florence.

In the name of God. 29 March 1465.

My last letter was on the 16th. I don't have much to tell you in this letter as I haven't had one from you yet. I'm really only writing because I don't want you to forget all about me, and to give you a reason to write me a couple of lines when you have the time, because hearing from you that you're well, and doing well, is the only comfort I have. May God be praised for everything.

I've had a letter from Rome, from Lorenzo, saying that he had to leave for there [Naples] on the 20th, and I'll be pleased to hear that he had a safe journey; may it have

prime; e da lui entenderai delle cose passate. Dipoi che si
partì, i' non ho inteso altro di qua; se none che oggi s'a-
spetta Niccolò Ardinghelli alla porta. Ha 'vuto licenza per
dodici dì; e chi dice che l'ebbe molto largamente, e chi
dice che no. Pure Giovanni Rucellai fu il chieditore a
Piero; e forse Lorenzo suo vi s'adoperò per fare quello a
piacere alla suo' dama e donna di Niccolò, perchè ne facci
a lui; che ispesso la vede! Hanno isperanza che ancora
aranno grazia, e non passerà molto tempo. Così piaccia a
Dio che sia, no lasciando adrieto degli altri. Gioverà forse
più l'avere bella moglie, ch'e prieghi di 47! Tutto per lo
meglio sia.

L'imbasciadori si partirono iermattina per costì: conducagli Iddio salvi. Hanno dimolte buone parole, come da
Lorenzo sentirai: non so come seguiranno gli effetti; chè
oggidì è difficile a trovare uomo di fede, e che tenga sue
parole in piè. Senti' che don Federigo si doveva partire di
costà più dì sono, en modo che Lorenzo non ve l'arà trovato; e così e nostri enbasciadori: e me ne sa male, chè
qualche cosa si sarebbe di meglio inteso de' fatti tua, sen-
dosi trovati costì ensieme. Ricordoti, sopra tutto, che vadi
sodamente en questa faccenda: chè facendone impresa, e
non riuscendo, saremo la favola del popolo. Che Iddio el
meglio ti dimostri.

Per Batista da Sancasciano ebbi el fardellino cor e sei
mazzi di lino, e le due matasse di seta, che l'ebbe Tommaso. El lino mi parve bello; ma no lo posi bene mente
allora, che mi sentivo di mala voglia: chè poi partì Lorenzo no mi sono sentita bene, en modo che ho mangiato
dell'uova: non ho avuto febbre, ma i' ho molto debole il
capo, e alle volte pare che il cervello mi si volga. Ebbi della
partita di Lorenzo grande rimescolamento; e sì come viva
mi pareva essere mentre che ci stette, così mi parve essere
sanza la vita e morta quando partì: chè mi parve un soffio

pleased God to let him. I'm expecting him to get there by the end of the month, and he'll tell you everything that's happened. I haven't heard any news here since he left, apart from the fact that Niccolò Ardinghelli is expected at the gate today. He has been given a permit for twelve days, and some people say he got it very easily, though others say not. Still, Giovanni Rucellai[1] made the request to Piero, and perhaps his Lorenzo[2] exerted himself to do what he could, to please his lady and Niccolò's wife;[3] he may have done it for him [Niccolò] so that he could see her often. They hope they will be in favor again before too long; may it please God to make it so, and not to leave others behind. It might be more help to have a beautiful wife than a request from King Ferrante! Still, it's all for the best.

The ambassadors[4] left yesterday for there; may God bring them there safely. They have said many fine things, as you will hear from Lorenzo, but I don't know if anything will come of it, because these days it's hard to find a trustworthy man who is true to his word. I've heard that Don Federigo[5] had to leave there some days ago, so Lorenzo won't have found him there, and nor will our ambassadors, which seems a shame to me because they would have got a better impression of your position there, had they found you all there together. Remember, above all else, that you should go carefully in this business, because if you make an attempt and don't succeed we'll be the laughingstock of the crowd.

Batista da San Casciano brought the package, with the six bundles of flax and the two skeins of silk that Tommaso had. It seems like fine flax to me, but I haven't put my mind to it yet because I've been feeling lazy. I haven't been feeling well since Lorenzo left, so I've eaten some eggs; I haven't had a fever but my head has felt weak and sometimes it feels as if my brain is turning around. I was very shaken up by Lorenzo leaving, and if it was like living while he was here, it was like dying when he left. His visit

questa sua estanza. E del tempo che ci stette, no gli mostrai niuno mie' fatto, perchè meco non portai scrittura niuna, credendo ch'entrassi in Firenze: e dipoi quando ne fu' chiara, non volli venire per esse, per non mi partire da lui quel poco del tempo che ci stava. Ebbine consolazione: ma i' ho auto dipoi tanto dispiacere, che me ne sentirò un pezzo. Sicchè el lino non ho poi riveduto; che non ho a filare per ora. E per Batista detto, che viene costà, mando el farsetto di Lorenzo; e con esso sei sciugatoi, un poco più sottili che quegli altri. Sono quattro grandi per tenere al cappellinaio, e due piccoli per le spalle quando vi pettinate. Non ho fuori di pezza più per ora; fate a mezzo, e i' n' ho ordinati: chè si faranno ora tanti, che sarete forniti per un pezzo; e 'ngegneròmi gli abbiate per tutto maggio, se piacerà a Dio.

Escrivo a Lorenzo di parecchi fanciulle esaminate, avendo le parti che noi vorrèno, quale parentado t'aggraderrebbe più: chè Chi a tempo vole mangiare, ennanzi all'ora gli conviene pensare. Che Iddio ci apparecchi cosa buona. Nè altro per questa. Iddio di male vi guardi. Per la tua Allesandra Strozzi, Firenze.

23

seemed to go by in a flash and I didn't show him any of my business while he was here, because I didn't take any papers with me [when I went to see him], thinking that he'd be allowed to enter Florence, and then when it was clear [that he wouldn't be] I didn't want to leave him and come and get them in the short time he was here. It was a great comfort, but since then I've been so unhappy, and I will feel this way for a while. So I haven't looked at the flax yet, as I'm not doing any spinning at the moment. I sent Lorenzo's doublet by Batista (who I mentioned before) and six towels with it, which are a little softer than the others. There are four big ones to hang on the stand and two little ones for your shoulders when you comb your hair. I don't have any more at the moment but I've ordered them, and I'll have so many made now that you'll be well supplied for a while. I'll try to make sure that you have them by May, God willing.

Two paragraphs: their taxes had been paid and their bankers would send Filippo the details, while Alessandra had paid the pork butcher, who had settled for five florins; she would like Filippo to send her some oranges.

I'm writing to Lorenzo about the various girls we've considered, who have the qualities we want, and who would be a match to please you, because if you want a meal you need to order it in advance. May God prepare us something good. Nothing more for now; may God keep you from all harm. From your Allesandra Strozzi, Florence.

23

This is one of a number of letters written by Alessandra to Filippo which are dominated by the topic of finding him a wife, and it gives some examples of the detailed calculations which the choice of a wife could entail.

Al nome di Dio. A dì 20 d'aprile 1465.

A dì 13 fu l'utima mia. Ho di poi la tua de' 7 detto. Farò per questa risposta al bisogno.

Veggo che Lorenzo t'ha detto come mia volontà gli pare sia di venire a stare dove voi pure dadovero; e che per una non potresti avere maggior consolazione: che solo resta assettare el fatto della donna. A che ti dico del fatto mio, che sempre è stato l'animo mio e la mia volontà d'esser presso a voi: ma vedete la lunghezza dello spacciare le mie cose di qua; e poi che furno ispacciate, ci è stato un poco di speranza del tornare; donde n'è seguito lo 'ndugiare a tor donna: ed io, vedutomi dell'età ch' i' sono, e malsana, non credendo giugnere a questo tempo, n'ero invilita, e quasi perduto la speranza d'aver mai consolazione, se non per lettere. Pure la veduta di Lorenzo, e inteso che tu se' disposto di tor donna, e che avendo fermo l'animo a fare questo passo, mi pare ragionevole e dovere ched io estia tanto si dia effetto; che tosto si doverrà vedere. Ben ti dico, che se non fussi questo fatto della donna, niuna isperanza n'arei di stare dove voi, perchè al continovo ci sarebbe degl' impacci e degli storpi di tormi questa venuta e questa consolazione di stare dove voi. E se a voi fussi grande, pensa che a me sare' maggiore: chè, per ragione naturale, debbo aver grande amore e tenerezza più inverso di voi, che voi enverso di me. Poi ci è el bisogno! chè i' posso male fare sanza voi, e voi sanza me potete tutto fare: sì che puo' credere che a Lorenzo i' abbia detto il vero di mie' volontà. Ora i' priego Iddio che lasci seguire il meglio di tutto.

El fatto della donna, mi pare è secondo el parere nostro e di Tommaso Davizzi, che se Francesco di messer Gu-

In the name of God. 20 April 1465.

My last letter was on the 13th. Since then I've had yours of the 7th, which I'll answer as I need to.

I see that Lorenzo has told you that he thinks I still really want to come and live with you both, and [you say] nothing could give you more comfort, and that there is only the matter of the wife left to be settled. To which I say, for my part, that it's always been my dearest wish to be with you, but you saw how long it took to sell my property here, and once it was sold there was some hope of you coming back here, and the delay in getting you married came from that. And because of my age I became discouraged and lost any hope of ever having any comfort from you, except through letters. But after seeing Lorenzo and hearing that you want to get married and that you've made up your mind to do it, I think it's reasonable and my duty to stay here until it's all arranged. Then we'll have to see. I must say that [even] if it weren't for this business of finding you a wife I wouldn't have much hope of ever going to live with you, because there's always been something to stop me from having the comfort of living with you. And if it would be a big comfort to you, it would be a much bigger one to me, because in the natural course of things I love you and feel much more tenderness for you than you do for me. And the reason is because I can only do badly without you, but you can do everything without me. So you can certainly believe that I told Lorenzo the truth about what I want. Now I pray God to bring us whatever will be for the best.

One paragraph: the Florentine ambassadors will have arrived in Naples, and Filippo will have talked to them and perhaps heard something useful.

About finding you a wife, it seems to us and also to Tommaso Davizzi[1] that if Francesco di Messer Gugliel-

glielmino Tanagli volesse dare la figliuola, che sarebbe bel
parentado ad ogni tempo; e di quante ce n'è venute alle
mani, questa ha più parte. Quella da Vernia mi piaceva;
ma ell' hanno del goffo e aria di villa, secondo m'è detto.
Ora intenderò con Marco se ci fussi altro, che ci paresse
meglio; e non sendo, si farà d'intendere se volesse darla;
che non se n'è ragionato se non tra noi. Francesco è pure
estimato giovane, ed è nello Stato; ma non è della sorta
maggiore. Pure è negli uffici. E se tu dicessi: Perchè la
dare' fuori? e' ci è più cagioni da doverlo fare. La prima,
che ci è iscarso di giovani dabbene, che abbino virtù e
roba. La seconda, che l'ha poca dota: credo siano mille
fiorini; che è dota d'artefici; chè ne dà Manfredi alla sua
dumila fiorini per mettella in casa e Pitti, ed ha anni 15: e
lei n'ha 17. Sì che vedi quello si truova. La terza perchè
credo la darebbe, si è ch'egli ha gran famiglia, chè ha bisogno d'essere aiutato avviargli. E questo sarebbe la principale cagione che mi fa credere che la darebbe. Entende-
ronne qualche cosa; e non volendo, si cercherà d'altro; e
ne sarai avvisato.

Entendo che a mona Ginevra di Gino mandate libbre
80 di lino: che mi piace; che pure parrà che voi estimiate
el servigio ci fece.

Mona Lucrezia di Piero veggo t' ha scritto buona lettera per amore del lino. Fare' bene a rimunerarti in cosa
che non v' ha a spendere se no parole; e quest' è di rac-
comandarti a Piero, che ti facessi tornare in casa tua. Ringrazio sempre Iddio, chè da lui procedono tutte le cose,
ed è cagione di darci delle prosperità, e così delle avversità
pe'nostri peccati: a ogni modo si vuole ringraziare; e pre-
ghiallo che ci die grazia siàno conoscenti de' benificii ri-
ceviàno da lui.

mino Tanagli were willing to give you his daughter, it would be a good match for all seasons, and that out of those which are available, this has the most to recommend it. I liked the da Vernia match, but from what I've heard she is clumsy and looks like a peasant. Now I will talk about it with Marco, about whether there are any others who would be better, and if there aren't, about finding out whether he [Francesco] wants to give her to you; we have only discussed it among ourselves. Francesco is well thought of and he takes part in the government, though not in the more important positions. Still, he has held offices. And if you ask "but why would he give her to an exile?" there are many reasons why he might do so. First, there's a shortage of young men of good family who have both money and abilities. Second, she has only a small dowry, I think it's a thousand florins, which is an artisan's dowry; the Manfredi gave their girl two thousand florins to marry her into the Pitti family, and she is only fifteen, whereas she [the Tanagli girl] is seventeen.[2] So you see how it is. The third reason why I think he'll give her to us is that he has a big family and needs help to get them settled. This is the main reason why I think he'll agree. I'll find out more about it and if he doesn't want to, we'll find someone else. We will let you know.

I hear that you sent 80 pounds of flax to Mona Ginevra di Gino.[3] I am glad, as it will really seem as if you value the favor she did for you here.

I see that Mona Lucrezia di Piero[4] has sent you a fine letter for love of the flax you sent her. She would do well to reward you with something she doesn't have to spend anything on, apart from words, by speaking to Piero on your behalf, [to the effect] that he should return you to your family. I always thank God for everything, because he gives us our prosperity, and adversity to punish us for our sins. We should be thankful for everything, and I pray He may give us the grace to know the good things we receive from Him.

Venne mercoledì don Federigo. Sento gli hanno fatto grande onore: e giovedì mi venne a vicitare due gentiluomini, che dicono istanno presso a te; e molto ti lodorno, e dissono maraviglie di te. Ringrazia'gli della venuta loro: dipoi offersi loro la casa, e quello che per noi si poteva, pregandogli che pigliassino sicurtà nelle cose tue di qua come nelle loro propie: e così alcun'altra buona parola, come accadde: e loro il simile. E sì si partirono. I' te ne do avviso, perchè ne gli possi ringraziare quando fia tempo. Nè altro per questa m'accade dire. Iddio di male ti guardi. Per la tua Allesandra Strozzi, Firenze.

24

Al nome di Dio. A dì 26 di luglio 1465.

A dì 20 fu l'utima mia. Ho dipoi la tua de' 12 detto. Risposta.

Three short paragraphs: Alessandra is glad to hear that Filippo and Lorenzo are getting on well together; she is pleased that Piero [de' Medici] knows of the honor Filippo has shown to Messer Carlo for his sake; Niccolò Ardinghelli is taking his wife to his home tomorrow.

Don Federigo arrived on Wednesday, and I hear he has been treated with great honor. On Thursday two gentlemen[5] came to visit me who said they lived near you, and they praised you greatly and told me wonderful things about you. I thanked them for coming, and then I offered them our hospitality and offered to do anything we could for them and asked them to consider your property as their own, and said some other fine things as they occurred to me, and they did the same, and then they left. I am letting you know so that you can thank them when you have the opportunity. Nothing else occurs to me for now; may God keep you from all harm. From your Allesandra Strozzi, Florence.

Postscript: Lessandra and Giovanni have come to stay for a month; Alessandra has given Maestro Lodovico[6] cloth worth four florins and twelve soldi to mark the birth of his daughter, because of the number of times he has treated her without payment.

24

The discussion begun some months earlier about a possible wife for Filippo is continued with him here. Alessandra also discusses current Italian politics from the perspective of their likely effect on Filippo and Lorenzo's possible return to Florence.

In the name of God. 26 July 1465.

My last letter was on the 20th, and since then I have had yours of the 12th. I will answer it here.

Del none iscrivermi ispesso, non credo punto sia per non ti ricordare di me; chè è naturale che 'l figliuolo si ricordi della madre, massimo quando non è suto abbandonato da lei ne' sua bisogni: ma quando non ho vostre lettere espesso, estimo bene che le occupazioni di cose che importano vi danno tanto che fare, che il tempo vi manca a scrivere a me. E benchè mi paia ispiacevole il non avere vostre per ogni fante, quest'altra parte dell'avere voi assai che fare mi fa istare paziente. E di certo, che volentieri veggo le vostre lettere, che aspetto el mercoledì o il giovedì, che de' giugnere il fante, co piacere, credendo avere duo versi di vostra mano: e quando i' no n' ho, e l'animo mi si distende aspettare per l'altro fante; e non n'avendo, mando a sapere dal banco; se truovo abbino vostre, piglio conforto che voi sete sani e state bene. E così vengo passando tempo. E ringrazio Iddio che di voi sento buone novelle, e che avete assai faccende e d'utile e d'onore; che assai mi piace. Ed è vero quello che tu di', che tu hai, e noi teco insieme, più grazia non meritiàno: ed ho isperanza in Lui, che, conoscendo noi e benificii e la grazia che v' ha data per ensino a qui, ched e' vi prosperrà di bene in meglio. Così lo priego per sua misericordia, e al continovo fo pregare per voi; e da un pezzo in qua s'è fatte tante orazioni per la faccenda vostra, che per certo non piace a Dio ancora che noi abbiàno questo contento. Riputo tutto per lo meglio. Avevone isperanza innanzi la presura del Conte; ma di poi sento le cose sono intraversate en modo, che non è per ora da parlarne. E chi dice non essere ora tempo, credo sia vero, per quello sento: e non so pensare quando s'abbia a essere il tempo; però che si vede ogni dì traverse tra loro. E questa morte del Conte ha molto dato che dire di 47 e di 48; en modo che vogliendo e maggiori mandare imbasciadori, l'uno costà al Re e l'altro al Duca, non si vince. Darèmi poca noia queste

About your not writing to me often, I never thought it was because you'd forgotten about me, as it's natural for a son to remember his mother, particularly one who didn't desert him when he needed her help. But when I don't hear from you often, I think you're so busy with important business you don't have time to write to me. And although I'm sorry not to get a letter from [either of] you whenever the servant comes, the thought that you have so much to do keeps me patient. It's true that I'm happy to see your letters, and I'm happy looking forward to the servant coming on Wednesday or Thursday, expecting to receive a few lines from you. When I don't get them my mind reaches forward to wait for the next servant, and if I don't hear anything [again] I send a message to the bank,[1] and if they've had a letter from you I take comfort from the fact that you're well and that things are going well for you. And so I go on, passing the time. I thank God to hear such good news from you, that you're doing so much business bringing honor and profit, and I'm very pleased. What you say is very true, that you (and we too) have been given more grace than we deserve, but I put my hope in Him, that because we're aware of all the grace and favors He's given you up till now, He'll do even better for you [in the future]. I ask this of Him in His mercy, and I pray for you all the time. God has had so many prayers about your affairs lately that it's clear He doesn't want us to have this happiness just yet. I believe everything is for the best. I was quite hopeful before the Count was arrested,[2] but since then some obstacles have been put in our way and there's no point in talking about it for the moment. Those who say that now isn't the time are right, by what I hear, and I don't know when it will be, as one day follows another. And the Count's death has led to a lot of talk about the King of Naples and the Duke of Milan, so when the *Maggiori*[3] wanted to send ambassadors, one to the King and one to the Duke, it wasn't approved;[4] I wouldn't

cose, se non fussi el fatto nostro: sì che vedi a che termine ne siàno.

Siàno a dì 27; e Marco Parenti è venuto a me, ed hammi detto come più tempo fa ragionàno del darti donna, e faciemo pensiero che delle cose che ci erano, e dove noi credavamo potere andare, e quello ci pareva meglio di parentado, se l'altre cose avesse, ch'ella fussi di buono sentimento e bella, e non avesse del zotico, si era la figliuola di Francesco di messer Guglielmino Tanagli; e che perensino a oggi non ci è venuto innanzi cosa che ci paia dal fatto tuo più che questa. E in vero, non se n'è ragionato troppo, per la cagione ti sai: pure segretamente noi abbiàn cerco, e non si truova se none gente, per di fuori, che hanno mancamento o di danari o d'altro. Ora el minore difetto che sia di questo, si è e danari; e quando vi sono l'altre parti compitenti, non si de' guatare a'danari, come più volte m'ha'detto. Sì che il dì di Sa' Iacopo, essendo Francesco grande amico di Marco, e avendo una gran fede in lui, si mosse con bel modo e savie parole, avendo di già parecchi mesi sentito che noi volentieri arèno veduto la figliuola, a domandare Marco di questo, e che stimava che se ne domandassi per te, e che quando noi avessimo il capo a ciò, che ci veniva volentieri; perchè tu se' uomo da bene: che avendo fatto sempre be' parentadi, e avendo poco che dargli, più tosto la vuole mandare di fuori a persone da bene, che darla qui a di quegli che si truovano, chi ha pochi danari: e no si vorrebbe abbassare.

worry much about these things if it wasn't for our business. So you see the position we're in.

Two short paragraphs: she had told him in another letter about the oranges he sent to Piero [de' Medici]; she is glad that the King's business is now settled.

It is now the 27th and Marco Parenti has come to see me. He has been talking to me about how we discussed finding you a wife a long time ago, and how we discussed the possibilities and where we thought we'd be able to go, and how it seemed to us that the best match, all other things being equal—if she had the right ideas and was beautiful, and wasn't rough or uncouth—was Francesco di Guglielmino Tanagli's daughter. We haven't heard of anything, up to the present, which would suit you better than this. And, to tell you the truth, we haven't discussed it too much, and you know the reason.[5] However we have looked into it secretly, and we've found that there aren't any girls [whose families would marry them] to an exile, who don't have some shortcoming or other, whether [lack of] money or something else. Now the least serious drawback is the money, and when the other things we want are there we shouldn't look askance at the money, as you've said to me a number of times. So on St. Jacob's Day, as Francesco is a great friend of Marco's and trusts him greatly, having already heard several months ago that we were willing to have a look at the girl, he asked Marco about it in a fine manner and choosing his words well. He said that if he [Marco] asked for her on your behalf, when we had made up our minds, she would come to us willingly, because you're a man of substance and [his family] having always made good matches, as he had little to give her he would sooner send her away to someone of substance rather than give her to whoever he could find here, someone who would have little money, and that he wouldn't want to lower [his family's status]. He wanted

E volle che Marco andassi co lui a casa sua, e chiamò giù la fanciulla en gamurra: la vide; e profersegli che ogni volta ched io la volevo vedere, e così la Caterina, che ce la mosterrebbe. Dice Marco ch'ell' ha bella persona, e parvegli che fussi ricipiente fanciulla: e noi abbiàno informazione ch'ell' è di buono sentimento e atta, che ha a governo brigata assai, chè sono dodici figliuoli, sei maschi e sei femmine; e, secondo sento, ella governa tutto, chè la madre sta sempre grossa, e non è da molto. Ècci porto da chi usa in casa, che la governa la casa lei; chè così l'ha avvezza el padre, ch'è tenuto d'assai, ed è stato de' puliti giovani da Firenze. Sì che pensando che si ha 'ndare per la lunga, non mi pare che sia tempo d'aspettare a fare questo passo: e pertanto avvisa di quello s'ha a fare; e sarebbe buono, a mio parere, che tu ne domandassi Pandolfo: chè sendo el più presso avemo a questa fanciulla, ne de' assapere el tutto; e così della condizione del padre. Non gli direi che noi n'avessimo nulla ragionamento; ma, avendo el pensiero, se te ne consigliassi: e se te ne dicesse bene, come è stato detto a noi, sare' da credere; e fermarsi qui, e deliberare d'uscire di questo pensiero: chè Preso el partito, passato l'affanno. Credo da Marco sarai di questo fatto avvisato più particularmente che non ho fatto io, perchè la praticò, e intende meglio di me. Metti in ordine le gioie, e belle, chè la moglie è trovata. Essendo bella, e di Filippo Strozzi, è di bisogno di belle gioie; chè come tu hai l'onore nell'altre cose, en questo non vuole mancare.

Lorenzo non mi scrive; chè no n' ho da lui da' 27 di giugno en qua; che mi fa pensare che non sia di buona voglia: avvisa che n'è, e s'egli ha avuto reda, chè mi disse Tommaso che l'aspettava. Credo starete tanto sanza donna,

Marco to go with him to his house, and he called the girl down, and he [Marco] saw her, and he [Francesco] said that if Caterina or I wanted to see her at any time he would show her to us. Marco says she looks beautiful and that she seemed suitable to him. We've been told that she has the right ideas and is capable and that she runs the household to a large extent because there are twelve children, six boys and six girls, and according to what I hear she runs it all because her mother is always pregnant and doesn't do much. Those who know the household say she manages the house and that her father has trained her to do it, and he is very well thought of and one of the best-mannered young men in Florence. So as it seems to me that we will have to wait a long time, I don't think we should put off taking this step, so let us know what we should do. And it would be good, to my way of thinking, if you asked Pandolfo [Pandolfini] about it, as he is the closest contact we have with this girl, [and ask him] to tell us all about it, and about her father's circumstances. I wouldn't tell him that we haven't discussed anything, but [say] that we have the idea, and if he would give you advice about it. And if what he says to you is favorable, like what we've heard, I would believe it, and decide to stop all this thinking, because once the decision has been made all your suffering will be over. I'm sure you will hear all about this business from Marco in much more detail than you have from me, because he discussed it and understands it better than me. Get the jewels ready and let them be beautiful, because we have found you a wife. As she is beautiful and the wife of Filippo Strozzi, she will need beautiful jewels. Just as you have honor in other things, she doesn't want to be lacking in this.

Lorenzo isn't writing to me; I haven't heard from him since the 27th of June, which makes me think he isn't in a good frame of mind. Let me know how he is and if he has had an heir,[6] because Tommaso told me he was expecting

che ne troverrèno qualche serqua. Iddio vi presti pur vita, come disidero. Nè altro per questa m'accade dirvi, se no che attendiate a star sani; che Iddio di male vi guardi. Per la vostra Allesandra Strozzi, in Firenze.

25

Al nome di Dio. A dì 17 d'agosto 1465.

A dì 9 fu l'utima mia. Ho dipoi la tua de' 7. Risposta al bisogno.

Dall'amico tuo ha' buone lettere, e dimostra avere fede in te: che mi pare buon segno. E se farà un dì dimostrazione del bene che dice volerti; non se ne starà poi en dubbio. Priego Iddio che sia presto l'effetto, se 'l me' debb'essere per noi. Ancora non si sa se manderà il figliuolo costà; che si dice che ancora Madonna tornerà indrieto: chè siàno come un farnetico in questo mondo: che a Dio piaccia darci la salute dell'anima e quella del corpo. E se il Conte Iacopo morì, Iddio gli perdoni. Così andassino gli altri che ci fanno male, se dovessi essere el meglio.

Di quello Della Luna, sento che sono tremila di dota e millecinquecento di donora. S'egli è vero, ha sceso un

one. You'll both be unmarried for so long that you'll have a dozen of them. May God still give you a long life, as I wish. Nothing else occurs to me to tell you for now, except that you should try to stay well. May God keep you from all harm. From your Allesandra Strozzi, in Florence.

25

In this short letter to Filippo Alessandra describes the daughter of Francesco Tanagli—her name is not mentioned at any stage—who was being considered as a wife for him.

In the name of God. 17 August 1465.

My last letter was on the 9th, and since then I've had yours of the 7th, which I'll answer as I need to.

One paragraph: she is sorry she gave Filippo and Lorenzo some news which turned out to be false.

You've had some fine letters from your friend [Piero de' Medici], who shows he has faith in you, and that looks like a good sign to me. And if one day he shows publicly the good will he says he feels for you, we won't have to doubt it any longer. I pray God that the result may come soon, and it will be all the better for us if it does. No one knows yet whether he will send his son there [to Naples], as they say Madonna will still go back.[1] We all live like madmen in this world; may it please God to keep our bodies and minds healthy. And if Count Jacopo died, may God pardon his sins. And all the others who do us harm may follow him, if it's for the best.

About that member of the della Luna family, I've heard that there's three thousand florins in dowry and one thousand five hundred in trousseau. If it's true then he's taken

grande iscaglione della dota, da quello dicevano di principio. Non è se non da biasimarlo, aver fatto parentado co' preti. E si dice anche, ch'e fatti loro non ci è grascia; che forse si ripareranno con questi. E' murano una bella casa, a vedere di fuori; drento non so.

Avvisoti, che andando domenica mattina a l'avemmaria in Santa Liperata alla prima messa, come vi son ita parecchi mattine di festa per vedere quella fanciulla degli Adimari, che la suole venire alla detta messa; ed io vi trovai quella de' Tanagli. E non sappiendo chi ella si fussi, mi gli posi allato, e posi mente a questa fanciulla; che mi parve ch'ell'avesse una bella persona e ben fatta: è grande come la Caterina, o maggiore; buone carni, none di queste bianche: ma ell' è di buon essere; ha il viso lungo, e non ha molto dilicate fattezze, ma no l'ha rustiche: e mi parve nell'andare suo e nella vista sua, ch'ella non è addormentata: tanto è, che mi pare che, piacendoci l'altre parti, ch'ella non è da sconciare mercato; che sarà orrevole. I' gli andai drieto fuori della chiesa, tanto ch' i' vidi ch'ella era quella de' Tanagli. Sì che sono di lei pure un poco alluminata. Quella degli Adimari, mai l'ho trovata; che mi pare un gran fatto, chè son ita tanto alle poste, e non esce fuori, com'ella suole: e andando coll' animo diriet' a questa, e' mi venne quest' altra, che non vi suole venire. Credo che Iddio me l'apparecchiò innanzi perch'io la vedessi; che no ci avevo il pensiero a vederla ora. Per altra, da Marco e da me ne se' avvisato: e di' che l' è materia che bisogna adoperare il cervello; e così mi pare ancora a me. Tu hai avviso delle parti ch'ell' ha, e degli incarichi che vi sono: pènsaviti su, e piglia el partito tu credi sia il meglio: che Iddio te lo dimostri.

Per Francesco di Benedetto Strozzi ti mando per mare un sacchetto co cento mazzi di finocchio: è segnato di

a big step up the dowry ladder from what was mentioned at the start. He's nothing if not to blame in having married himself into a family of priests. And they also say that their business isn't profitable, perhaps they will fix it up this way. And they are building a beautiful house, at least it looks that way from the outside.

One paragraph: the new Florentine ambassadors.

I must tell you how, during the Ave Maria at the first Mass at Santa Liperata,[2] having gone there several times on feast mornings to see the Adimari girl[3] as she usually goes to that Mass, I found the Tanagli girl there. Not knowing who she was, I sat on one side of her and had a good look at her. She seemed to me to have a beautiful figure and to be well put together; she's as tall as Caterina or taller, with good skin, though it's not white, and she looks healthy. She has a long face and her features aren't very delicate, but they're not like a peasant's. It seemed to me, from looking at her face and how she walks, that she isn't lazy, and altogether I think that if the other consid- ⌒ erations suit us she wouldn't be a bad deal and will do us credit. I followed her out of church and saw that she was one of the Tanagli, so now I know a bit more about her. I've never seen the Adimari girl, something which seems difficult because I've gone to all the places and she hasn't been there as she usually is. And going there with my mind on her, the other one came, who doesn't usually do so. I think God arranged it so I could see her, as I hadn't any thought of doing so. You've been told [about this] in other letters, by Marco and by me, and you say it's something where you need to use your brain, and I think so too. You've been told what she looks like, and what the disadvantages are. Think about it and take whatever decision you think is for the best; may God show it to you.

I am sending you a little sack by sea, by Francesco di Benedetto Strozzi, containing one hundred heads of fen-

vostro segno, che venne già col lino. El finocchio non è
quest'anno molto dolce: e però te ne mando poco. Non
era bene secco; che per mandartelo presto e bene, per non
indugiar per le piove, lo mando ora. Quando l'hai avuto,
fallo trarre del sacco, e tiello quindici dì al rezzo, chè ha
del verde, e diventerà più bigio. Avvisa come lo truovi.
Che Iddio di male vi guardi. Per la tua Allesandra, in
Firenze.

26

Al nome di Dio. A' dì 13 di settembre 1465.

A dì 7 fu l'utima mia, e dirizza' la a Lorenzo: chè non
avendo tue, non avevo che dirti. Ho avuto dipoi a dì nove
una tua de' venzei dì del passato. Risposta al bisogno.

I' no mi maraviglio che tu vada a rilento al fatto della
donna; chè, come tu di', è cosa di grande importanza, e la
maggiore che si possa fare: chè l'avere buona compagnia
fa istar l'uomo consolato l'anima e 'l corpo: e così pel contradio; chè quando sono moccieche o cervelline, o come

nel; it has your insignia on it because you sent me flax in it. The fennel isn't very sweet this year so I've only sent you a little. It wasn't well dried, but so I could send it to you quickly, rather than waiting for the rain, I'm sending it now. When it arrives take it out of the sack and keep it in the shade for fifteen days because it's green, and it will become grayer. Let me know how you find it. May God keep you from harm. From your Alessandra in Florence.

26

It appears that Filippo was finding it difficult to come to a decision about marrying Francesco Tanagli's daughter. In this letter Alessandra at first appears sympathetic to his concerns, but then expresses her exasperation when it appears that the delay has led to the collapse of their negotiations.

In the name of God. 13 September 1465.

My last letter was on the 7th and it was addressed to Lorenzo; because I hadn't heard from you I didn't have anything to tell you. Since then, on the 9th, I've had one of yours of the twenty-sixth of last month. I will answer as I need to.

Two paragraphs: she has heard nothing about Lorenzo's affairs; Marco has not yet spoken to Francesco Tanagli because they have both been in the country.

I'm not surprised that you're proceeding cautiously in this business of acquiring a wife; it is, as you say, very important, the most important thing you can do, because having a good companion is a comfort to a man, both in body and soul, and the opposite is also the case, if you have a wife who is silly or a sniveller, or like the one

quella ch'ebbe Filippo, si sta mentre che si vive in assai
tribolazione. A quella che ebbe Filippo, gli fu detto insino
quando e' ci era, che la vide, e piacquegli tanto la cervel-
linaggine sua, che di niun'altra volle dire di sì; e volevala,
quando era qui, torre: ma la madre non volle acconsentire
di mandarla fuori. Poi avemo per le mani parecchi fanciulle da bene; ma non ne volle nessuna. Escadde che la
madre morì, e messer Manno la teneva: fece ta' portamenti, che parve loro mill'anni di levarsela dinanzi; e sì
per non aver dota: e dierolla a Filippo. Sì che non era da
maravigliarsi di lei; ma fu da maravigliare di lui, mocci-
cone, che tanto se la lasciò salire in capo, e tanto se n'at-
taboccò, ch'ella fece vergogna a sè e a lui. Gli uomini,
quando hanno simile col cervello leggiere, le fanno istare
a siepe: e ch'un uomo, quando è uomo, fa la donna
donna; e non se n'ha attaboccar tanto; che, quando nel
prencipio elle fanno de' piccoli errori, riprenderle a ciò
che non abbino a venire ne' maggiori. E la buona compagnia ischifa ria ventura. Assai sono quella che, per non
avere persone sopra capo, fanno de' mancamenti; che ogni
piccola cosa di guardia le scamperebbe, e no le lascerebbe
isdrucciolare. Sì che, pensando a tutte le parti; che mi di'
che chi più sa, lo dimostra ne' casi d'importanza; che se'
tu uno di quegli che le sai, e che lo dimostri (che mi piace)
en tutte le cose; i' credo, esaminato tutto, e per quanto ho
'nteso, che questa non è cervellina: chè vi sono passata
tante volte, e mandatovi, e non si vede tutto dì su pelle
finestre; che mi pare buon segno. E n'ho auto tanto di lei,
che no ne potrei aver più. Aspetto che te n' arà detto Pandolfo, per vedere se appone a nulla: chè la moglie no vi sa
apporre, se no che la madre non è una saccente cosa; e
però il padre l'ha avvezza a fare la masserizia e governare

Filippo [1] had, your life will be a burden to you. About the one Filippo had, it was said that when he was here he saw her and liked her extreme silliness so much that he wouldn't agree to marry anyone else, and he wanted to marry her, but her mother wouldn't agree to send her away [to Barcelona]. We found various other suitable girls for him, but he didn't want any of them. Then her mother happened to die, and Messer Manno [2] was her guardian. She carried on in such a way that it seemed like a thousand years before they could get rid of her, and she didn't have a dowry so they gave her to Filippo. There was no need to wonder at her, the wonder was at him, the silly old fool, that he let her do what she liked, and was so besotted with her that she brought shame on both herself and him. Men, when they have such a feather-brained wife, manage to hold them in check, and a man, when he is a real man, makes his wife a wife, and he can't do that if he is too infatuated with her. When in the beginning she makes little mistakes, he corrects them so they don't become bigger ones. And sensible people don't take any chances. There are plenty of women who, because there's no one to boss them about, make mistakes, so they should be picked up on every little thing and not allowed to let things slide. So, considering it from every angle, you tell me that the wise person must show his wisdom in important matters; you are one of those people who knows these things, and you show it in everything, which pleases me. Having looked at everything and judging by what we've heard, I believe she isn't a scatterbrain, because I've passed there many times, and sent a servant there, and you don't see her there all day at the window, which seems to me a good sign. And I've heard so much about her, I couldn't have heard more. I'm waiting for you to talk to Pandolfo about it, to see if he can add anything, because his wife can't, except that her mother isn't up to much and so her father has brought her up to do the house-

la casa. I' ti conosco libero, e none ismemorato; che se tu l'hai, e la sia di sentimento come m'è detto, credo che insieme arete consolazione. I' non so quello s' hanno a fare le persone per l'avvenire; ma al presente è da stimare bene. Ora i' ho fatto quello s'appartiene a me: Iddio lasci seguire il meglio.

Ho scritto la lettera, e Marco è venuto a me; e dice essersi accozzato con Francesco Tanagli: e che Francesco n' ha parlato molto freddamente, en modo che comprendo n' ha levato il pensiero; e che dice, che ne vuole ragionare con messere Antonio Ridolfi, ch' è suo cognato, che è in ufficio, ed ha a tornare per Ognisanti. E disse che gli era gran cosa a mandare una sua figliuola tanto di lunge, e in una casa che si può dire sia uno abergo. E parlò in modo, che si vede ha mutato proposito. E questo istimo che ne sia suto cagione l'andar tanto per la lunga a dargliene risposta; sì per la lunghezza tua, e poi quella di Marco; che quindici dì fa gliene poteva dargliene un poco di speranza. O questa lunghezza l'ha fatto isdegnare, o egli ha alle mani cosa che gli aggrada più ch'e fatti tua. A me pare ci sia sì gran carestia di fanciulle, che abbino le parti che ha questa; che noi faremo sanz'essa, chè arà trovato meglio, ma non già noi non abbiàno a trovar meglio. I' n'ho auto sì gran dispiacere di questo fatto, ch' i' non so

keeping and run the household. I know you well, and I haven't forgotten [what you're like]; if you marry her and she's the sort of girl I've been told she is, I think you'll be happy together. We don't know what's going to happen to people in the future, but for the present we can judge well. Now I've done my part; may God let you do whatever's for the best.

Seven paragraphs: Filippo wanted her to order household linen; more about fennel; Bettino[3] *had returned from seeing Giovanfrancesco, who spoke fairly but would act badly, and who was living in high style; there was a delay about a financial settlement; she hadn't written to Niccolò about the marriage negotiations; Filippo would need another slave in his household once he was married; someone who was more knowledgeable than she was would let Filippo know what was happening in Florence.*

I had finished writing this letter when Marco came to see me. He says he bumped into Francesco Tanagli, and that Francesco spoke about it [the projected marriage alliance] in a very unenthusiastic way, so I gather he's had second thoughts, and he says he wants to discuss it with Messer Antonio Ridolfi, his brother-in-law, who is [away] holding an office and has to be back by All Saints' Day [1 November]. And he said it was a big decision to send a daughter so far away, to live in a house which was almost like a hotel.[4] And he spoke in such a way that you could see he had changed his mind. I think this has happened because it has gone on for so long without us giving him an answer, because of the time you took to decide, and Marco as well. Fifteen days ago he [Marco] could have given him some reason to feel hopeful about it, but now he's taken offense and has some better prospect in view. It seems to me there's a great shortage of girls who have the qualities this one has. We will have to do without her because he will have found someone better, but we haven't found anyone better. I've been very upset by this busi-

quando me l'avessi tale; chè mi pareva questa fussi così el nostro bisogno, come qualche altra si potesse trovare; che ma' più ci abbiàno abbattere, se bene s'avessi di quelle di Cosimo. Era questa più il bisogno. Troppo mi duole che per lentaggine ci sia uscita di mano; e non so, com' io m' ho detto a Marco, dove mi rivolga ora; chè no ci è venute altro che nebbete alle mani, e per me non so s'abbia a fare. Sì che non arò a trovare e pannilini, nè tu le gioie: che quando credevo essere a mezza via, ed io l' ho ancora a trovare. Sia col nome di Dio tutto! Marco vi doverrà avvisare di qualche cosa; chè a me è cascato il fiato, che tanta fatica n' ho durata, e perduta tutto.

27

Al nome di Dio. A dì 19 d'ottobre 1465.

A dì 12 fu l'utima mia. Ho poi la tua de' 3 di detto; e questa mattina una di Lorenzo de' 12. Risposta al bisogno.

ness, I don't know when I've been more upset, because it seemed to me that she suited us better than anyone else we might find. We'll never come across such a girl again, unless we get one of Cosimo's.[5] This one was just what we needed. I really regret the delays which made us lose her, and as I said to Marco, I really don't know where we can turn now, because there are only stupid girls available, and so far as I'm concerned I really don't know what we should do. Anyway, I won't have to find linen and you won't have to find jewelry, as I thought we would when it all seemed to be under way; but I still have to find a wife. May it all happen in God's name. Marco will have to let you know about something because this has knocked all the wind out of me, I've worked so hard and lost everything.

27

In this comparatively short letter, written to both Filippo and Lorenzo, Alessandra concentrates on the rather depressing theme of the uselessness of human wishes in the face of God's plans. This somber mood had been brought about partly by the collapse of the marriage negotiations and partly by the death of their friend and distant relative, Pandolfo Pandolfini, while in Naples as Florentine ambassador.

In the name of God. 19 October 1465.

My last letter was on the 12th and since then I've had yours of the 3rd, and this morning one from Lorenzo, written on the 12th. I will answer as I need to.

One paragraph: she has given the letter Filippo sent to Romolo to Marco to give to him.

Per questa di Lorenzo intendo come Pandolfo era allo stremo della vita: che n' ho auto dispiacere assai; che poi che morì el mio figliuolo, non ebbi tal dispiacere di parente che mi morissi, quanto ho 'uto di lui: chè troppo mi duole per amore della donna giovane, e tanti figliuoli che lascia; chè è morta quella casa! E assai mi duole per vostro amore; chè s'era riconosciuto il parentado, e aggiuntovi una amicizia e una grande benivolenza; che sendo vivuto, t'arebbe dato grande aiuto al fatto tuo: chè aveva buona grazia co' principali, ed era qua el bisogno vostro. Ora Iddio non ha guardato nè al bisogno della sua famiglia, che mi pareva maggiore che il nostro. Pazienza bisogna avere: chè credo, e son certa, che Iddio l' ha chiamato a sè per salute dell'anima sua. E se gli ha 'uto pazienza della sua malattia, e dell'essere fuori di casa sua e fuori del governo della donna, e non si vedere la sua famiglia intorno (che son certa n' ha auto passione), credo arà meritato assai: però che era amorevole molto della sua famiglia, e gran dolore arà auto a lasciarla. Altro non si può fare: Iddio abbia auto misericordia dell'anima. Avete fatto gran perdita. Iddio vi guardi da più danni.

I' ho sentito del Consolo fatto costà: qua vogliono il consolo usato de' Lottieri; e di costà non si patisce. E sento hanno fatto Lorenzo; che istimo no l'arà accettato: chè non fa per voi; chè di qua non si patisce nulla de' vostri fatti, chè sete a noia a molta gente: chè poi sete nel grado che sete, non si può ricordarvi, se no quando fate qualche cortesia, o servendo altri. E pertanto qua ci è chi n'è malcontento, e dàvvi contro; sì che per verun modo no l'accettare; che non avete bisogno acquistare per questa piccola cosa la nimicizia d'alcuni di qua. Marco n'ha auto dispiacere, che sia fatto Lorenzo. Per Dio, non pigliate queste punte contro a questi di qua, chè non fa per voi, e avete onore assai nell'altre cose: sicchè, non avendo ri-

I heard from Lorenzo's letter how Pandolfo was almost dead, which has upset me very much. I haven't been so upset about the death of a relative since my son died, as I've been about this. I'm very upset for his young wife's sake, and because he's leaving so many children; [1] it's as if the whole Pandolfini family were dying. And I'm also sorry for your sake, because you had revived your relationship with him, and made a good friend, one who wished you well. Had he been alive he could have been a big help to you because he was in the good graces of the leading citizens and that was what you needed. But God hasn't even taken his family's needs into consideration, and their needs are greater than ours. We must resign ourselves to what has happened, because I believe, and I'm sure, that God has called him back for the sake of his soul. And if he was resigned to his sickness, and to being away from his wife's care, and to not seeing his family around him, which I'm sure would have given him pain, then I believe he will have deserved a great deal, because he loved his family very much and will have been very sad to leave them. There's nothing to be done. May God have mercy on his soul. You've had a great loss; may God keep you from more harm.

I've heard about the election for consul [2] there; here they wanted the previous consul from the Lottieri family [to be reelected], but he wasn't wanted there. And I've heard that they chose Lorenzo, and I don't think he will have accepted it; it won't do for you [to accept it] because they won't stand for anything like that where you're concerned. A lot of people would dislike it because you're legally what you are, and they don't want to be reminded about you, except when you do someone or other a favor. And there might be someone here who is hostile to you, or has a grudge, so you certainly shouldn't accept it. You've no need to make enemies here for the sake of such a small thing. So if you haven't already refused it, do so

nunziato, all'auta di questa fatelo; che avete bisogno di grazia e non di nimicizia!

Di gravezza non si ragiona: dell'altre cose si sentono dì per dì, ma non sento di quelle che mi dieno isperanza delle cose disidero; che non piace ancora a Dio: e le cose vanno a pian passo; e co lunghezza di tempo si potrà vedere delle cose: ma chi ha fretta, l'aspettare gli è pena. Confortimi a star sana, e ch'io mi dia buon tempo: i' mi posso male rallegrare, che sto tuttavia in pena; e dello star sana m' ingegno, per più rispetti. Ma a voi si vole ricordare che stiate sani; chè io sanza voi sono morta, e voi sanza me vivete e potete istare in filice istato. Se sete privati de' vostri disegni, riputate tutto per lo meglio; chè ogni volta non ci dà Iddio quello che disideriàno, perchè non è il meglio; e alle volte ci adempie il nostro disidèro, e poi ci torna in danno. E vedilo in Pandolfo; che parecchi mesi fa ebbe di tornare; e cercorono di raffermarlo: che sendo tornato, era sano: e se pure fussi infermato e morto, moriva con altro contento che non debb'esser morto. Sì che, quando noi non abbiàno ciò che vogliamo, abbiàno pazienza. I' ho auto un grande dispiacere che Filippo non ha preso donna, e massimo sendoci profferte delle cose che mi parevano pel fatto suo. Ora, veduto la cosa intorbidata, e il tempo che vuole aspettare, i' mi conforto con dire: Forse che non è il meglio! E honne posto l'animo in pace. Quella degli Adimari, Marco gliele pareva avere in mano, rispetto el mezzo che ci era. E l' è maritata a uno Bernardo Buonaguisi, e cugino di Matteo: sicchè le cose no riescono come uomo crede. Tutto rimettiàno in Dio. Marco ha 'uto tre dispiaceri en de' fatti vostri in duo dì: l'uno, la morte di Pandolfo, che gli pare che vi fussi molto affezionato, e disiderava la tornata sua, perchè sapeva quello aveva a dire di voi: l'altro dispiacere è, che Lorenzo

when you get this. It's goodwill you need, not enemies.[3]

Taxes aren't being discussed at present. I hear about other things day by day, but I haven't heard anything to give me hope of getting what I want. So far God hasn't wanted to do it and things are moving at a slow pace. All things come to those who wait, but waiting hurts if you're in a hurry. You tell me to stay well and keep cheerful, but it's difficult to be cheerful when I'm still in pain all the time, but I do try to stay well for various reasons. I want to remind you two to stay well, because without you I'm dead, but without me you will go on living and be happy. If your plans don't work out you must believe it's all for the best, because if God doesn't give us what we want it's because it wouldn't be good for us. And sometimes He gives us what we want and it does us harm. You can see this in Pandolfo's case: he had to come back a few months ago, and they sought to have his term of office renewed. When he came back he was well and if he is sick or dead now, he died with the dubious satisfaction that he needn't have done so. So when we don't get what we want we should be resigned to it. I've been very upset about Filippo not getting married, particularly because there were matches on offer here which would have suited him. But now, seeing how everything has been messed up and how long he wants to wait, I comfort myself by saying that perhaps it's all for the best, and I've calmed down about it. About the girl from the Adimari family, Marco seemed to have that in hand, considering what means were available. But now she has been married to one Bernardo Buonagiusi, who is a cousin of Matteo's, so things never turn out as you'd expect.[4] We must put everything back in God's hands. Marco's had three disappointments in two days, where your affairs are concerned: first, Pandolfo's death, as he [Marco] thought he was very fond of you, and he wanted him to come back to Florence because he knew what he would have said on your behalf; another disap-

sia consolo; e maravigliasi che tu, Filippo, lo lasci pigliare questo: e il terzo dispiacere è, che questa fanciulla degli Adimari sia maritata; che sendo la minore, e non sendo maritata la maggiore, gliene pare esser rimaso ingannato; che aspettava si maritassi la maggiore, e poi arebbe ragionato della minore. Ora non ci bisogna pensare: forse che non è il meglio ched io abbia a mie' dì questa consolazione d'avere una bella fanciulla. Iddio faccia la sua volontà di tutto. Nè altro per questa. Iddio vi guardi di male. Per la vostra Allesandra Strozzi, Firenze.

28

Al nome di Dio. A dì 2 di novembre 1465.

Dicestimi per la tua de' 28 di settembre, che t'era capitato costì una ischiava, ch' era qui di Lionardo Vernacci, e che l'aresti tolta, se non per rispetto della vecchia che tu hai en casa. A che ti dico, che non è pel fatto tuo, a mie' parere; che l'ha tenuta la donna di Lionardo quattro o vero cinque anni; e perchè non apparava, ed era di mal

pointment is Lorenzo being consul, and he is surprised that you, Filippo, should have let him take it, and the third disappointment is that the Adimari girl has been married. As she is the younger and the older one isn't married he was fooled, as he had been waiting until they married the older one and then he was going to start discussions for the younger one. Now we don't need to think about it. Perhaps it's all for the best that I'm not going to have this comfort before I die of having a beautiful girl [for my daughter-in-law]. Everything is as God wills. Nothing more for now; may God keep you from harm. From your Allesandra Strozzi, Florence.

28

The somber mood continues here, in a letter which ranges over a discussion of unsatisfactory domestic slaves, political gossip, the poor agricultural season, and the plague. Alessandra ends on an equally dark note by telling Filippo of the despair felt by Pandolfo Pandolfini's widow.

In the name of God. 2 November 1465.

One paragraph: her last letter was on the 26th of October, she is writing now to tell Filippo that Niccolò Soderini is the new Gonfalonier of Justice, and to discuss marriage prospects.

You told me in your letter of the 28th of September that there was a slave there who used to belong to Lionardo Vernacci, and that you would have bought her if it hadn't been for the old one you have in your house. To that I say that she wouldn't be what you need, as I see it; Lionardo's wife had her for four, or really five, years, and because her appearance was dubious and she had bad

sangue, en modo che dubitavano non facessi qualche male a sè o ad altri, cavoronsela di casa: ed era disonesta. Venderolla 'Antonio della Luna; e poco vi stette, che no la vollono; e rimandorolla: sicchè l'hanno mandata di costà. La donna di Lionardo la teneva per cucire, e non ha 'vuto el cervello a ciò: che s' ella fussi buona serva, l'are' tenuta per sè. Di' che n' hai una in casa, che fu di Filippo degli Albizzi. Cotesta era tenuta dassai e saccente messo: ma e' la venderono perchè el vino gli cominciava a far noia, e facevala istare molto allegra: e poi non era onesta: e avendo le moglie loro fanciulle, no la vollono en casa: lodavalla di lealtà, e di saper fare. Ora fa' che ti pare: i' t' ho detto quello ch' i' so. No me ne sono ricordata di dirtelo per altra mia; ma scrivendoti ora di 33, me ne ricordo, venendomi alla mente il bisogno. 32 e 56 vanno pure piggiorando, en modo che si stima che 'l male gli nocerà: chè di nuovo el parente di Lionardo Ginori, che altre volte disse a 56 quello ch' egli era, e dipoi raffreddò, ora di nuovo, perchè hanno fatto il parentado ti scrissi per l'utima, gli dà caldo che possa me' cantare. E non domandare come espranga bene contro a 56. Dicesi ch' egli è invilito: aspettasi che 18, che gli è nimico, quello che farà. Che Iddio dia loro a pigliare il meglio.

E' s'ha a pagare per ensino a dì 6 di questo el 47 catasto, che s'è sostenuto il dì per ensino ad ora; che è parecchi mesi lo pagò chi ha Monte: e così per tutto dicembre se n'ha a pagare el 46: che va a perdere. E credo che da questi in là, si pagherà di quegli otto che son posti per tre anni. A Dio piaccia por fine a tanto pagare! Dicesi che Niccolò ne leverà qualcuno di questi catasti; sì che per ora piglierò

blood—so that you wondered whether she'd do harm to herself or someone else—they got her out of the house. She was immoral as well. They sold her to Antonio della Luna, but she only stayed there for a little while because they didn't want her and they sent her back; so she was sent there [to Naples]. Lionardo's wife used her for the sewing, but she didn't have the brains for it. If she'd been a good servant she would have kept her for herself. You say you have one [slave] in the house, who used to belong to Filippo degli Albizzi. They thought she knew a lot, but they sold her because the wine was starting to do her harm and she was always tipsy, and she was immoral as well, and the wives had their daughters to think of, so they didn't want her in the house. They praised her as trustworthy and knowledgeable. Do what you think is best; I've told you all I know. I didn't remember to tell you [about this] in my other letter, but writing now about 33 [1] reminded me, as the need for it came to mind. 32 [2] and 56 [3] are getting even worse, so that it's thought that it will do them harm; Lionardo Ginori's relation, who on other occasions has told 56 what he was, and then cooled down, well, now, because he has made this marriage alliance that I told you about in my last letter, he has told him heatedly that he should crow less. And you shouldn't ask about the blows he dealt 56. They say he is disheartened, and they are waiting to see what 18, [4] who is his enemy, will do. May God let them choose the best path.

Payment of the 47th *catasto* [5] is due on the 6th of this month, as they have extended the due date until now. Those who have *Monte* shares paid it several months ago, and so they have to pay the 46th for December, which will be lost. [6] And I believe that from these [taxes] onward we will pay eight of these, which have been imposed for three years. May it please God to put a stop to us having to pay so much. They say that Niccolò [7] will raise one of these taxes, so for the moment I'll take the money for them out

dal banco e danari per questo catasto, che sono fiorini 9 e
10 danari a oro: e più piglierò fiorini 5 per fare dire ufficio
e limosine per l'anima del vostro padre e del mio figliuolo,
e ancora per mio padre e madre, e degli altri nostri passati
(chè da un pezzo in qua non fo, come solevo), in questo
dì de' Morti. Avvisandoti, ch' i' ho ricolto staia 27 e
mezzo di grano e barili nove di vino a Pazzolatico, tra
bianco e vermiglio, e nove a Quaracchi: en tutto, ho barili
18. E se non fussi la carestia del pane, el vino varrebbe un
fiorino largo el barile; ma vale 3 lire e soldi. Abbiàno un
magro anno pe' pover' uomini: e con questo ce ne muore
di pesta. È morto parecchi a questi dì. Un figliuolo di
Meo Pecori, d'anni ventotto, in duo dì; e uno a Saracino
Pucci, di quattordici. En casa Rinieri da Ricasoli, dopo la
madre, la schiava e una figliuola loro no ligittima. Ancora
ce n' è en due case qui appresso; che pochi n' è rimasi. Sì
che ella comincia, e siàno nel verno. Iddio ci aiuti.

Ben ti so dire che la moglie di Pandolfo è mezza dis-
perata, e non si può per verun modo accordarsi: e se nulla
gli mancava, tornò Priore e gli altri, e dissono come e'
morì mal volentieri: che ha fatto doppie pazzie. È da
'ncrescere di lei. Iddio, che può, la conforti; ch'era in
tanta allegrezza quando ebbe il figliuolo maschio, e tosto
gli tornò in amaritudine. Niuna isperanza si può porre in
questo mondo, che non venga meno. In Dio solo debb'essere; e ce lo dimostra per molte vie. Sicchè pensiàno al
fine, che Iddio ce lo dia a far buono. Nè altro per questa.
Iddio di male vi guardi.

Di' a Lorenzo, ch' i' ho una sua de' 17 passato; e perchè
istetti all'ufficio tardi, non ho tempo di fare risposta. Farolla, se piacerà a Dio, pel primo. Altro. Per la tua Allesandra Strozzi, Firenze.

of the bank, which will be 9 and 10 gold florins. I'll also take out 5 florins, to have masses said and give alms on behalf of the souls of your father and my son, and the other departed members of our family—because for a time I didn't do it, as I used to—on this All Souls' Day.[8] I must tell you that I harvested 27 and a half bushels of grain and nine barrels of wine [9] at Pazzolatico, some white and some red, and nine at Quaracchi, so altogether I have 18 barrels. If it weren't for the shortage of bread, wine would be worth one large florin a barrel, but as it is it's only worth something over 3 lire. It's been a hard year for poor men, and there's plague as well; several people have died of it in the last few days. A son of Meo Pecori, twenty-eight years old, [died of it] in two days, and one of Saracino Pucci's, who was fourteen. In Rinieri da Ricasoli's house his mother died of it, and then a slave and an illegitimate daughter. Now it's in two houses close to here and it's leaving few survivors. So it is beginning, and it is winter. God help us.

I must tell you that Pandolfo's wife is nearly in despair, something which I can't possibly agree with, and so as not to spare her anything, Priore [10] and the others have returned [from Naples] and told her that he died very unwillingly and was doubly desperate,[11] which has increased her despair. May God, who has the power to do so, comfort her. She was so happy when she gave birth to a boy, but it has so soon turned to bitterness. All our hopes in this world come to little, and we can only hope in God, who shows us this in many ways. We must think about our end, so that God may let us make it a good one. No more for now; may God keep you from harm.

Tell Lorenzo that I have his letter of the 17th of last month and that because I was out late at Mass I don't have time to answer it now. God willing I will do so at the first opportunity. From your Allesandra Strozzi, Florence.

29

Al nome di Dio. A dì 15 di novembre 1465.

A dì 2 e 9 vi scrissi l'utime mie. Ho di poi quattro vostre, de'28 e 30 e 31. Farovvi, per questa, risposta.

I' ho inteso per le vostre l'animo vostro esser diritto a tramendue a fare il passo che vi s'è tocco più volte, e quello ch'io ho disiderato più tempo fa; che estando fermi in tal proposito, e avendo effetto a' mie' dì, credo che di tal cosa sarebbe consolazione a voi, e a me grande conforto; chè avendo duo figliuoli, e sendovi affaticati tanto tempo, e no vedendo altri di voi, mi davate alle volte che pensare: Per chi s'affaticano costoro? Se estanno a questo modo, endureranno l'animo, e fermerannosi così; e me terranno in queste pratiche tanto, che io mancherò! Ed ho auto molta battaglia nella mente, e da duo mesi in qua mi recavo, che pe' mia peccati che Iddio non volessi ch' i' avessi questa consolazione. Sommi rimessa nelle man sue, e pregatolo, e fatto pregare al continovo (e così si fa), che disponga la mente mia e le vostre a pigliare quello partito che debba essere el meglio per l'anima e pel corpo. Ora avendo le vostre lettere, e intendendo la diliberazione

29

Alessandra's brother-in-law Niccolò Soderini had become Gon-falonier of Justice at the end of October 1465. As he was one of the leaders of the movement opposed to Piero de' Medici, it was widely believed that political changes would finally occur. Floren-tines usually rejoiced to have a close relative in this position of supreme honor, but Alessandra did not have a friendly relation-ship with Niccolò and could not ask him directly to help her sons. This letter is addressed to both Filippo and Lorenzo.

In the name of God. 15 November 1465.

. I wrote to you last on the 2nd and the 9th, and since then I've had four letters from you, of the 28th, 30th and 31st. I will answer you both in this letter.

I've gathered from your letters that you've made up your minds to take this step you've discussed so many times, and which I've wanted for so long. If you keep to your resolution and do so while I'm still alive, I think it will be a comfort to you and a great consolation to me. Having two sons who have worked so hard for so long, and not seeing any children of yours, sometimes makes me wonder "who are they doing all this work for? If they go on as they are they'll harden their hearts and stay as they are, and they'll keep me in all these negotiations for so long that I'll die!" And I've had many battles in my mind and for the last two months I've brought myself to the point of thinking that God, for my sins, doesn't want me to have this consolation. I've put myself in His hands and prayed to Him, and prayed continually (as you do) for Him to make up my mind and yours to take that decision, which must be best for our bodies and souls. Now, having your letters and hearing the decision you've made be-

fatta tra voi, credo certo che gli è volontà di Dio che abbiate preso tale partito: e per ensino a qui i' n' ho preso
piacere di queste vostre lettere; con isperanza che tu, Filippo, non ci farai più difficultà, e non ci pagherai più
d'inchiostro. E, come per altra iscrissi a Lorenzo, siamo
tanto informati di vostra volontà, e siamo persone che
amiamo l'onore e l'utile vostro, come voi medesimi; e più
diligenza ci mettiàno che non faresti voi, essendo alla presenza: sì che state di buona voglia, e lasciate fare a noi; che
sopra tutto vogliàno le parti più volte ragionate, e sopra
tutto belle. Ancora mi va per l'animo quella di Francesco
per te, Filippo; e per Lorenzo, quella degli Adimari, ch'è
di meno tempo. Potendo averle, sono delle più belle che
ci sieno, e amendue buone parti in loro: ma essendosi
amendue ragionato per Filippo, non so se si mutassino a
volerla dare a te, Lorenzo. Tutto si tasterà; e quando non
si potessi avere, si cercherà d'altro; e di cosa che noi cre-
derrèno faccia per te, e di quella de' Borghini, tutte ci
recherèno innanzi. La sirocchia di quella degli Adimari,
non si dice per noi nulla perchè vi sia mancamento; è di
tempo d'anni sedici; ma di primo avemo la minore per più
bella, e quivi ponemo l'animo: chè, potendo, ve le vorremo dare belle. Parmi che ancora tu sia, di questa diliberazione fatta, del tor donna, tu sia molto impaurito, e
veggo che dimostri avere poco animo; chè di', che poi
che 'l diliberasti, t'è entrato nell'animo cento pensieri. I'
priego Iddio che v'aiuti di tanta paura, quanto avete; chè
se tutti gli altri uomini avessino auto la paura del tor
donna come voi, sare' di già ispento el mondo. E però è
da darvi espaccio, a ciò che veggiate che il fistolo non è
nero come si dipigne, e trarvi di questa paura. Tu di',

tween yourselves, I believe it's God's will that you should take that decision, and I've been pleased by these letters of yours. And I'm hoping that you, Filippo, won't make any more difficulties and that you won't waste any more ink on it. And, as I said in another letter to Lorenzo, we know so much about what you both want, and we are people who care about both your pride and your pocket as much as you do, and we're more diligent than you would be, actually being here, so you should hope for the best and leave the details to us. More than anything else we want the qualities we've so often discussed, and beauty more than anything. I would still like Francesco Tanagli's daughter for you, Filippo, and the Adimari girl, who is younger, for you, Lorenzo. They're among the most beautiful girls there are, if we could get them, and both of them have good qualities, but as we have had discussions about both of them as a wife for Filippo, I don't know whether [her family] would want to change the arrangement and give her to you, Lorenzo. We'll sound all this out and if we can't have her we'll look for someone else. And those we think might be for you, like the Borghini [girl], we'll parade them all in front of you. With the Adimari girl's sister, nothing has been said about her and there may be something lacking there; she's sixteen, but from the beginning we gathered that the younger one is more beautiful and we set our heart on her, because if we can we would like to give you beautiful wives. It seems to me [Lorenzo] that you're still terrified of getting married, despite the decision you've come to, and you show how little inclined you are. You say that as soon as you decided a hundred different thoughts entered your mind, and I pray that God will help you with such fear, because if all men were so afraid of getting married the world would be empty by now. You must go ahead with your purchase, so that you can see that the devil's not as black as he's painted, and free yourself from this fear. You ask

se mi paressi che tu indugiassi ancora uno o duo anni a torla. Dicoti, a mio parere, di no: e se Marco arà il mandato da voi di poter fare, e non ci nasca altro di nuovo, te n'avvedrai. E delle ispese, tu farai quello che il tempo richiederà, e così Filippo: e del sodamento delle dote, e tutto, si seguirà quello ci parrà il meglio.

Non vi maravigliate se Marco non ritocca Francesco: l'una, perchè da voi non ha libera commessione; l'altra, perchè messere Antonio Ridolfi non è tornato da Pisa. De' tornare ora in questi dì. E l'altra cagione si è, che tutti gli uomini sono in pensiero di quello che s' ha a fare in Palagio nel dirizzare lo Stato, e 'n che modo s' ha a vivere: e tutto dì si pratica, e stanno in aspetto quegli che furono tratti delle borse nel 58, d'essere rimessi nelle borse: e 13 se n'affatica molto; e così fanno degli altri assai, che si metta il partito. E questo è il maggiore pensiero ch'egli abbia. Dicesi che riuscirà; e dipoi si dice che, fatto questo, si ragionerà di ristituire gl'innocenti confinati; che ci è pure di questi popolani che dicono, che s'ha a fare. E domenica, cioè a dì 10, partendosi Giovanni di qui, e andando alle Selve, s'accozzò per la via con Luigi Pitti; e vennono a ragionamenti de' fatti vostri, e che disse averne ragionato col Gonfaloniere della ristituzione vostra, e che il Gonfaloniere rispose, gli era buono a fare in genero per tutti gl'innocenti. Parvemi una buona novella, se così disse. E così sento che Francesco di Nerone ne toccò in genero la prima volta che Niccolò fe' Richiesti. Sì che, essendo così, sare' forse buono che tu, Filippo, ti ricordassi per lettera agli amici tua; e scrivendo mandare le lettere a Marco, se gli pare da darle o no: chè iscade alle volte delle cose, che non vi se ne può dare così avviso presto. Sì che le cagioni dette fanno tenere a drieto e ragionamenti

me if I think you should wait a year or two longer to get married, and I tell you, in my opinion, no. And if Marco has your authority to do so, and if no new prospect turns up, we will let you know. About the cost, you'll do whatever's needed at the time and so will Filippo, and about the dowry settlement and everything, it will all be arranged as seems the best.

Don't be surprised if Marco hasn't taken up this matter with Francesco [Tanagli] again yet. For one thing, he doesn't have full authority to speak for you, and for another Messer Antonio Ridolfi hasn't come back from Pisa yet; he's expected any day now. Another reason is that everyone's mind is on what is happening in the Palazzo,[1] to put the government back on track and decide how we are going to live. They're discussing it all day and those who had their names taken out of the bags in 1458 are expecting to have them put back in.[2] Marco is working hard on this and so are the others who are putting it to the vote. They say it will be passed, and then they say that if this is done, they'll discuss allowing the innocent exiles[3] to return, although it's only the *popolani*[4] they're talking about doing this for. On Sunday, that is the 10th, Giovanni [Bonsi] left here, and he met Luigi Pitti on the way to Le Selve, and they talked about your affairs, and he [Luigi] said he had discussed your return with the Gonfalonier, and the Gonfalonier said it seemed to him a good thing to do for all those who were innocent. That seems to me to be good news, if he did say it. And I also heard that Francesco di Nerone[5] raised the matter in general terms the first time Niccolò called a group of leading citizens together to consult with him. So, this being the case, it might be a good idea if you, Filippo, sent a letter to your friends to remind them of your position and then sent the letters to Marco to send or not, according to what seems best to him, because sometimes things happen which we can't let you know about quickly. So the things that I've mentioned are holding up discussions about the marriage.

179

della donna. 13 ti doverrebbe avvisare d'ogni cosa che segue, che è quattordici dì nollo vidi; chè il mio male m' ha tenuto en casa parecchi dì. Pure iermattina mi sforzai d'andare alle Murate, e parlai co Madonna, perchè è molto di Niccolò, e portagli grande divozione; il perchè i' la pregai che gli dovesse iscrivere una lettera piena d'amore e di carità, e ch'ella gli ricordassi la buona fama gli acquistava dal popolo per l'opere buone faceva; e che si teneva che farebbe dell'altre; e ricordassigli e poveri innocenti, e massimo voi, che sete sua nipoti. Ella molto allegramente disse di farlo, e che farebbe aggiugnere molto più orazioni per questo. E più mi disse, che v'era stato a lei a fare fare dell'orazione dell'altre, che di questo avevano isperanza. Sì che i' fo quello ch'io posso: così fate voi, e a Dio vi raccomandate, che ci farà grazia: così n' ho isperanza, non pe' nostri meriti, ma per sua misericordia: e ci faccia questa grazia, se 'l meglio debb'essere.

Dello stagno, ho saputo da Lodovico, dice è ben tre mesi lo vendè a uno linaiuolo; e il detto linaiuolo l' ha tutto ispacciato: ma e' dice che ispesso gliene viene alle mani, de' cittadini che ne vendono; e capitandogliene del bello, che me lo farà vedere: sì che aspetterò. Se a Dio piacessi che voi tornassi, i' ho dieci scodelle e dieci scodellini e duo piattegli da 'nsalata, e uno maggiore; che sono begli, che furono di quegli mi diè Anton Strozzi: che il resto mi fu tolto, e' candellieri, e santelene, quando ero

Marco must have let you know about everything that's happened, but I haven't seen him for a fortnight because I've been sick, which has kept me at home for several days. But yesterday I made the effort to go to the Murate [6] and speak to the Mother Superior because she is a friend of Niccolò's and is extremely fond of him. I asked her if she would write him a letter full of love and charity and remind him of the good reputation he has gained among the people for the good works he has performed, and [saying] that she believed he would do more, and reminding him about the poor innocents and you most of all, who are his nephews. She was very happy to do so, and said she would also offer many more prayers for this. And she also told me that other people had come to ask her to pray for this, because they had been given some hope. So I do what I can and so do you, and you recommend yourselves to God, so that He will give us grace. I hope He will, not because we deserve it but through His mercy. May He give us this grace, if it is for the best.

Four paragraphs: while she was at the Murate she met a young boy, the brother of Pietro Pagolo's wife, and she comments that he [Pietro Pagolo] [7] had done well out of the marriage; Filippo will have heard of Alessandra di Lorenzo's death; [8] he will have received the letter from the Signoria about the consulate, a matter which has been resolved; so only one of Marco's three disappointments remains, the death of Pandolfo.

About the tinware, I've found out about it from Lodovico [Strozzi]. He says it's a good three months since he sold it to a linen merchant, who has since sold it again. But he says he often gets hold of some, from citizens who are selling it, and if he comes by some which is beautiful he will show it to me; so I'll wait for that. If it pleases God to let you come back, then I have ten soup bowls and ten little bowls and two small salad plates and one larger one [which we can use]. They're beautiful, and part of what Antonio Strozzi gave me. The rest were taken from me

en casa Francesco; e, se te ne ricorda, sai che dubitammo di Marco Rota; e Francesco perdè le berrette. E quando si fece la giostra, Matteo (Iddio gli abbia perdonato) andando in casa Marco, riconobbe e candellieri, e vide le santelene. Sì che certo egli ebbe lo stagno. Sento che gli è morto. Avendo da ritrarvi di questo, lo fate; che lo trarrete di peccato. Sicchè, come dico, ho quello stagno, ch'è bello; ed ho dell' altro, che è assai orrevole; e parecchi piattelletti e de' piattegli grandi; e sono begli, essendo qui. Sì che istarò a vedere un poco come le cose passano. Maisì, che abbattendomi a dodici piattelletti begli, gli torrò; chè non ho che sei.

Attendiàno pure a raccomandarci a Dio; e disponetevi di fare qualche bene a onore suo e della sua benedetta madre Vergine Maria e dell'Angiolo Raffaello, che come guardò Tubbiuzzo da pericolo e da inganni, e poi lo rimenò al padre e alla madre, che così rimeni voi a vostra madre, che con tanto disiderio v'aspetta. I' ho speranza che, raccomandandovi di buono animo e con fede, che noi arèno questa grazia. E di così lo priego per sua misericordia. Nè altro per questa. Che Iddio di male vi guardi. Per la vostra Allesandra Strozzi, in Firenze.

Sono a dì 16, e altro non ci è per me da dirvi.

30

Al nome di Dio. A dì 4 di gennaio 1465.

A dì 30 passato fu l'utima mia, e avisa'vi quanto per ensino a quel dì avevo sentito da 13 del fatto di 60: e altro non ho di poi, di 59; sì che per questa non ho da dirne

when I was in Francesco's[9] house, and if you remember you'll know we suspected Marco Rota, and Francesco lost the caps. And while the joust was going on, Matteo, may he rest in peace, went into Marco's house and recognized the candlesticks and saw the medallions.[10] So I am certain he took the tinware. I've heard he's dead; if you can get these things back you should, and you will free him of the sin. Anyway, as I was saying, I have that tinware, which is beautiful, and some more which is very respectable, and some little plates and big plates which are beautiful because they already belong to us.

We must pay attention to recommending ourselves to God, and you should arrange to do some good works to honor Him and His Blessed Mother the Virgin Mary, and the Angel Raphael, so that just as he looked after Tobias and kept him from danger and deceit and then brought him back to his father and mother,[11] so he may return you both to your mother, who is so eager to see you again. I hope that if you commend yourselves to Him in good heart and faith we will have this grace, and so I pray to Him in His mercy. May God keep you from harm. From your Allesandra Strozzi, in Florence.

It is the 16th, and I have nothing else to tell you.

30

Alessandra's main theme here is the great good fortune Filippo had been given by God, despite his exile, and the need for him to show his gratitude.

In the name of God. 4 January 1466.

My last letter was on the 30th and in it I told you as much as I'd heard up till then from Marco about the business of the Tanagli girl, and since then I've heard nothing about

nulla. Ho poi la tua de' 17, tenuta a dì 19; che alla parte di 33, come ha' 'nteso per altra, s'ha aspettare tempo: e per questo non ci è risposta. Ma i' son d'animo, che s'io vedessi da potere andare altrove per le parti che noi vorremo, che 60 si lascerebbe istare; e 59 vuole ispacciare la prima, e poi ragionerà della seconda: che l'ho veduta, e piacemi; e non pare però tanto semprice, come m'era detto; che è buona carne, e assai savore. Quando altro sentirò, ne sarai avvisato.

Al figliuolo di Brunetto desti mangiare; e rivestitolo, e riscaldatolo, e datogli danari, lo rimandasti en qua: facesti delle sette parti le tre dell'opera della misericordia, e facesti molto bene a non guardare a l'opere del padre fatte inverso di voi allo sgravo; chè chi ha seco la carità non può capitare che bene, e Iddio v'aiuterà e prospereravvi di bene in meglio. Così ve ne conceda Iddio la grazia, che voi possiate fare el simile a degli altri che v'hanno fatto male; che daresti loro aiuto, e voi salveresti l'anima; chè renderesti bene per male. E non è dubbio che i' ne piglio conforto assai, quando sento che del bene e delle prosperità che v'ha concesse Iddio, che voi ne siate conoscenti inverso di chi ve lo dà; e sete molto obrigati a Dio; e specchiandovi negli altri vostri pari, come istanno: che oltre l'essere privati della patria, sono disfatti dell'avere; e voi sete in termine, che pochi n'è fuori che sieno di riputa-

the Adimari girl, so I've got nothing to tell you about that here. Since then I've had your letter of the 17th which you kept until the 19th. So far as the business of finding wives is concerned, we have to wait and see what happens, as I told you in another letter, so I've no answers to give you here. But I'm of the opinion that if we look elsewhere for what we want, we should leave the Tanagli girl alone and buy the Adimari girl first and look for a second. I've seen her and I'm pleased with her and she doesn't seem so ordinary to me, unlike what someone told me; she's good meat with lots of flavor. When I hear anything else I'll let you know.

Two paragraphs: Filippo has heard about the new Signoria and the new Gonfalonier,[1] *who is a good man; she has spoken to Gostanza di Pandolfo [Pandolfini], who is considering whether she should send one of her sons to the court of King Ferrante of Naples.*

You gave Brunetto's son[2] food to eat and clothes to wear, and you gave him shelter and money and sent him back here; out of the seven acts of mercy you have performed three. You have done very well and you didn't hold what his father had done to you against him. God will help you prosper even more, because he who is charitable can only meet with good in return. And God may give you grace so that you may do the same thing for others who have done you harm, so you can help them and save your own soul and pay back good for bad. And there's no doubt about it, that when I hear about the blessings and wealth God has given you I take great comfort from it. You should acknowledge who has given them to you, and that you owe everything to God; when you compare your position with that of other exiles, who as well as being deprived of their homeland have been ruined financially, whereas you're in such a position that there are few outside the city who have a better reputation or

zione e di roba più di voi. E ancora en questa terra n' è sì pochi, che di roba estieno meglio di voi; ch'è una maraviglia, che si dice per chi ha a maritare delle fanciulle, e con gran dote, che non ci è venti giovani, di persone da bene, che tocchi per uno, in suo' parte, più che mille cinquecento fiorini. Sì che vedi come voi estate! Ringraziate Iddio, che avete altra riputazione, e dell'avere, più che questi che sono in casa o vero nella patria loro. Iddio ci ha dato questo iscontento della patria; ma e' v' ha dato tante dell'altre cose, che avete da stare contenti; e tanto più, quando fussi accompagnati di buona compagnia: che Iddio ve l'apparecchi, quella che sia il meglio; che si farà pure pensata, e none in fretta.

Di' a Lorenzo, ch' i' none scrivo a lui per questo fante, chè non ho da dirgli se none che Marco sta desto al fatto tuo e suo; e bene che noi abiàno gran freddi, non s'è freddo a' fatti vostri; che s'aspetta che noi siàno chiamati: e essendo, forse si farà qualche concrusione; che a Dio piaccia che s'esca di tante pratiche. Nè altro per questa m'accade dire. Iddio vi guardi di male lungo tempo, com'io disidero. Per la vostra Allesandra, Firenze.

---

3 I

a bigger fortune than yours. And even here there are very few better off than you are, which is a miracle. And they say that among those looking for a wife, and one with a big dowry, there aren't twenty young men of good birth who could lay their hands on more than 1500 florins.[3] So you see how well you stand. You must thank God that you have a reputation and financial circumstances different from those of these men who are in their own homes and their own country. God has given us this burden of exile, but he has given you so much else; you should be happy and so much more so when you have good friends to keep you company. May God prepare for you whatever is for the best, but He will do it deliberately, not in a hurry.

Three paragraphs: payment of taxes; the purchase of cattle, stakes for vines, and manure for the farm at Pazzolatico; Marco tells her that none of Brunetto's sons has been successful in the scrutiny.

Tell Lorenzo I haven't written to him by this messenger because I've nothing to tell him, except that Marco is still wide awake on his business and yours, and that although it's been very cold it isn't cold for your business. We're waiting until we're sent for, and when we are perhaps we'll reach some conclusion, if it pleases God to let us escape from these endless negotiations. Nothing else occurs to me for now; may God keep you from harm for a long time, as I wish. From your Allesandra, Florence.

---

3 1

During the last months of her sons' exile Alessandra was preoccupied with certain themes, which are in evidence here: the need for them to marry, but the difficulty of doing so satisfactorily while they were in exile; the chances of the ban of exile being lifted; and political events in Florence which might help bring this about. This letter was written to Filippo.

Al nome di Dio. A dì 11 di gennaio 1465.

A dì 4 fu l'utima mia. Ho di poi la tua de' 28 passato; che veggo che mi scrivi più perch' io abbia quel contento d'avere vostre lettere, che per bisogno che ci sia: e a me ne fate grande appiacere, poi che non vi posso vedere colla presenza. Ringrazio Iddio di tutto, che è forse el meglio. Risposta alla tua.

Dissiti per altra mia quanto era seguito di 60; e altro non ci è poi di nuovo: e di 59 se' avvisato che non se ne ragiona, per aspettare lo spaccio della maggiore. Altro non pare a 13 di fare ensino non siamo chiari di queste due, che cammino piglieranno: che, secondo el tempo che l'hanno, non doverrebbono troppo indugiare a uscirne. Egli è vero che il mio disidèro sarebbe di vedervi tramendue accompagnati, come altre volte v' ho detto; che, morendo, mi parrebbe che voi fussi ridotti a quel passo che si disidera per le madri, di vedere e figliuoli ammogliati; e che quello che voi con fatica e affanno avete per lungo tempo acquistato, e vostri figliuoli l'avessino a godere: e a quella fine io mi sono ingegnata di mantenere quel poco ch' i' ho auto, lasciando indrieto delle cose ch' io are' potuto fare per l'anima mia e de' nostri passati: ma per la speranza ch' i' ho, che voi togliate donna (e l'effetto è per avere figliuoli) sono contenta d'aver fatto così. Sicchè il mio disidèro sarebbe quello vi dico: e da poi che intesi la volontà di Lorenzo, come era disposto per mio contento di torla, ma che lui volentieri starebbe ancora due anni a legarsi a la donna; i' mi v' ho pensato su più volte, e mi pare che non ci sendo una cosa molto vantaggiata, e avendo tempo di potere aspettare questi due anni, che sia buono a starsi così; se già non venissi qualche gran ventura: ma altrimenti non mi pare da darsene ora pensiero, e massimo essendo il temporale che corre al presente; che

In the name of God. 11 January 1466.

My last letter was on the 4th and since then I've had
your letter of the 28th of last month. I see you're writing
to me more often, not because you need to but so I can
have the happiness of receiving your letters. You give me
great pleasure by doing so while I can't see you in person.
I thank God for everything, which may be for the best. I
will answer your letter.

I told you in another letter what had happened about
the Tanagli girl, and so far there's no more news about
that, and you know we're not having any discussions
about the Adimari girl until they sell off her older sister.
Marco doesn't think there's anything else to do until we're
clear about those two and what path they will take; depending on the time they have, they wouldn't want to delay too long in getting through with it. It's true that I want
to see you both married, as I've said before, so that when
I die I can feel that you've got to that stage that mothers
want for their sons, to see them married, so that your children will benefit from all you've gained over a long time
by your hard work and trouble. And for that reason I've
tried to keep what little I have, and I haven't done things
I should have, either for my own soul or for those of our
departed, and because I've hoped that you'll both marry
and have children I've been happy to have done it. So this
is my wish. Since I heard what Lorenzo had decided, that
he wanted to get married for my sake, but that he would
still be happy to put it off for two years before tying himself to a wife, I've thought about it many times, and it
seems to me that it's not of any great advantage to us, [but]
if we have the time to wait these two years it might be a
good idea to do so, if some great piece of luck hasn't come
our way. Otherwise it doesn't seem a particularly good
idea to think about it now, and above all given the present

de'giovani che sono nella terra, volentieri si stanno sanza
tor donna: e la terra è in cattivo termine; e mai si fece le
maggiori espese en dosso alle donne, che si fa ora. Non è
sì gran dota, che quando la fanciulla va fuori, che tutta l'ha
in dosso, tra seta e gioie: sicchè non sarebbe el bisogno
suo per noi di qua. Benchè i' no glien' abbia iscritto nulla,
non se n' è cerco per lui di nulla; che s'aspettava se per te
prima riusciva niuna delle due pratiche: essendo riuscita
quella di 60, si sare' tastato quest' altra per lui; che v'è
della biada, se la dessino, a ogni tempo sare' stato com-
mendato. Ora andando le cose come le vanno, mi pare di
stare a vedere un poco di tempo per lui. E veggo che, secondo mi scrive per ogni sua, se ne contenta di stare ancora due anni: che alla buonora sia tutto; che forse a quel
tempo saranno gli animi in pace: e in questo mezzo potre'
seguire delle cose, che non si proferrebbe la donna sanza
danari, come si fa ora; che pare a chi l' ha a dare, di super-
chio dare dota a 50. 13 t' ha scritto che 'l padre di 60 lo
ritoccò, e nel modo ch' io ti scrissi. Di' che del vedere e
praticare te ne stai a noi: io dal canto mio ho fatto la mia
diligenzia, e non saprei farne più ch' i' m'abbia fatto: e
per vostra consolazione più che mia; chè il tempo mio è
brieve, e il vostro debb' esser lungo, secondo la ragione.
Così piaccia a Dio che sia. E Marco ancora v'attende con
diligenza. Iddio ne lasci seguire il meglio. E a Lorenzo di',
che riposi l'animo in pace, della donna.

Uscì Niccolò, e pure fece alcune cose buone; ma non
di quelle arei voluto. A lui e gli altri usciti è suto fatto
poco onore, e mentre che erano in seggio e poi che uscirono. Lo squittinante nostro n'ebbe assai disagio, e noi
ancora: ma sento che ciò che s' è fatto andrà a terra, e si
crede si farà di nuovo. Ha questa Signoria fatto parecchi

state of things. Young men here are happy to stay single; the country is in a bad way and men have never spent so much money on dressing their wives as they do now. If a girl doesn't have a really big dowry she wears it all when she goes out, what with silk and jewels, and that isn't what we need here. Although I haven't written anything to him about it, we're not looking for anyone for him: we're waiting to see if we have any success for you with either of the two we've had discussions about. If we managed to get the Tanagli girl for you we could sound out the possibility of the other one for him. And I can see he's happy to wait for two years more, as he tells me in every letter, so everything will be done in the fullness of time. Perhaps our minds will be at peace by then, and this way we'll be able to pursue other possibilities, [people] who wouldn't offer a wife without money, as they're doing now,[1] because it seems superfluous to whoever has to give it, giving a dowry to an exile. Marco has written to tell you that the Tanagli girl's father has had second thoughts about it, of the kind I wrote to you about. You say that so far as looking at [any prospective wife] and negotiations are concerned, you will leave it to us. For my part, I have done as much as I can, and I don't know how to do more than I have, and I've done it for your sake more than my own, because I haven't got much time left but you have a lot, it stands to reason. May it please God to let it be so. Marco is still giving it his best efforts; whatever is for the best, may God let it happen. Tell Lorenzo he needn't worry about getting married just yet.

Niccolò has left office, and he really did do some good things, but they weren't the things I wanted. He and the others who are leaving office now have been little honored, either while they were in it or now they've left it. The scrutiny is in a mess,[2] and so are we, but I hear they're going to throw out what's been done already, and start all over again. This Signoria has spent several days in con-

dì pratica; e nulla si può intendere: chè hanno fatto pena di rubello a chi rivela nulla, a chi si truova di questa pratica: sì che va molto segreto le cose. E' m' è detto che 58 è il tutto; 54 nonn' è così; e per tanto 56 si tornerà ne' primi termini, secondo mio giudicio, andando le cose come si vede al presente. Iddio, che può, ponga rimedio a questa città, ch'ella sta male. Niccolò entrò fiero, e poi s'invilì; e, come disse il fratello a 14, «Egli è entrato lione e uscirà agnello»; e così gli è intervenuto: che come vide che le fave no gli riuscivano, e'cominciò a umiliarsi: e poi ch' egli uscì d'uficio, va accompagnato quando con cinque e quando con sei armati presso a sè, per sospetto o de' Conti di Maremma o d'altri. Era el suo meglio che non fussi estato; che no si sarebbe iscoperto tante nimicizie.

Altro non c' è, ch' i' sappia, da dirti; se no che ara' sentito d'alcuno parentado fatto di nuovo, della figliuola di messer Piero de'Pazzi a Braccio Martegli, e quella d'Antonio a Priore Pandolfini; e ciascuna n'ha dumila di dota. Quella di messere Piero ha un occhio che none vede bene. Di quella di Giovanfrancesco non sento dirne nulla per qui; ma sento da Pierantonio, ch'ella si darà a Mantova al figliuolo di messer Benedetto Strozzi. Non so donde se l' ha sentito. E così mi disse Giovanni di ser Francesco, quando tornò. Debbano recare di costà questa novella; e non sendo vero, fa' pensiero, se ti paressi, da farne toccare da Niccolò Strozzi un motto a Giovanfrancesco per 45. Ben ch'io non credo che degnassi sì basso, pure alle volte

sulting with leading citizens, and no one has heard anything, because anyone who reveals anything will be declared a rebel and so everything has been kept very secret.
Someone told me that Piero de' Medici wields all the
power and not Luca Pitti, while Antonio Pucci will return
in fine state, as I see it, if things go on as they are at present. God, who can, may cure this city, which is sick.[3] Niccolò went in boldly but then he lost heart, and as his
brother [Tommaso Soderini] said to Giovanni Bonsi, "he
went in like a lion and will leave like a lamb," and so it
happened. As soon as he saw the beans were not in his
favor[4] he began to humble himself, and since he left office
he goes around with sometimes five and sometimes six
armed men nearby, for fear of the Counts of Maremma,[5]
or others. He should have done the best he could, and
then he wouldn't have revealed so many enemies.

*Two paragraphs: Filippo had been told about the 14 florins
withdrawn from the bank; he should tell Giovacchino[6] that the
flax for the nuns had arrived on the 4th of January.*

There's nothing else to tell you that I might know about,
except that you will have heard about the marriage alliances
which have just been made, Messer Piero de' Pazzi's daughter with Braccio Martegli and Antonio's [daughter] with
Priore Pandolfini. Both of them have a dowry of two
thousand florins; Messer Piero's daughter can't see properly out of one of her eyes. I haven't heard anything about
Giovanfrancesco's girl [Marietta Strozzi] from here, but
I've heard from Pierantonio that she will be marrying the
son of Messer Benedetto Strozzi in Mantua.[7] I don't know
where he heard it. And Giovanni di Ser Francesco told
me the same thing when he came back. They must have
brought the news back from there, but if it's not true and
it seems like a good idea to you, you should think about
sending a message to Giovanfrancesco by Niccolò Strozzi
on Lorenzo's behalf. Although I don't think he would

si va in luogo che altri no l' are' stimato, pelle cose che occorrono, o per morte o per altri casi. Si che pensavi su. Nè altro per questa. Iddio di male vi guardi. Per la tua Allesandra Strozzi, Firenze.

32

Al nome di Dio. A dì 25 di gennaio 1465.

A dì 17 fu l'utima mia e iarsera ebbi dua tue de' 6 e de' 13; che appresso farò risposta di quella parte saprò.

Di' ch'io debbo avere inteso da Giovanni el pensiero avete fatto di lui per aiutarlo sollevare: che vi pare, essendo dell'età ch'egli è, questo sia più onorevole per lui e per voi, e che se ne debba più contentare, che avere a stare di fuori: e duo cose vorresti da me ennanzi che si strignessi la cosa. La prima, che me ne pare, e se istimo che ve

stoop so low, still sometimes things turn out unexpect-
edly, because of something which happens or because
someone dies, or for some other reason. So you can think
about it. Nothing more for now; may God keep you from
harm. From your Allesandra Strozzi, Florence.

32

*A large part of this long letter, written to Filippo, deals with the
plight of Giovanni and Lessandra. They were in debt and living
in very straitened circumstances, due to Giovanni's lack of success
at business and, according to Alessandra, his inability to handle
money.*

In the name of God. 25 January 1466.

My last letter was on the 17th and yesterday evening I
received two of your letters, one of the 6th and one of the
13th; I will answer what I can here.

*Six paragraphs: there was still no progress with the marriage
negotiations; the matter of the new scrutiny had not yet been
resolved; Piero de' Medici had been afraid of Niccolò Soderini's
reforms, and Filippo should not put too much faith in him because he was untrustworthy; more gossip about Niccolò Soderini,
who now went about accompanied by seven armed men; she con-
gratulated Filippo on helping two guests; she has heard that the
galleys from the Levant have arrived in Naples.*

You say I must have heard from Giovanni about Lorenzo's and your idea for helping him pick himself up, and
that being the age he is, this seems more honorable for
him and for you, and that he would be happier not having
to live away from Florence,[1] and that you'd like to hear
two things from me before it's settled. The first is what I

n'abbia a rendere buon conto. La seconda, che vi scrive aver debito fiorini 200 larghi, e che accenna che vorrebbe voi ne lo servissi; e voi lo faresti volentieri, per un anno, per aiutarlo; ma per riavergli en capo dell'anno co' 40 v' ha a dare. E perchè sapete ch'io v'amo, ed è ragione ch'io vi consigli e esamini e fatti sua se è da servillo, che al tempo voi non avessi avere iscandolo insieme, come interviene al più delle volte; e servendolo, donde gli arebbe a trarre per rendergli al tempo; e se ha più debito che questi fiorini 200: en prima ti dico, che il pensiero fatto della bottega, mai me n'ha detto nulla; ma io sentendolo da Giovanni di ser Francesco quando tornò di costà, gliele dissi; e mi disse, che il detto Giovanni di ser Francesco glie l'aveva detto. E altro non ho dipoi sentito; se no che ieri, avendo la lettera di Lorenzo de' 10 dì, e dice «No' vorremo pure fare, potendo, del bene a Giovanni»; e dissiglile. E' rispose: «E' vogliono fare una bottega d'arte di lana con Carlo e Giovanni di ser Francesco». E in altro non entrammo: sì che questo è quanto ho sentito da lui. E alla parte del trovarvisi Giovanni Bonsi a governare, credo che per via di governo la farebbe bene; chè mi pare sollecito e intendente: ma l'avere a trassinare danari, non posso giudicare se si rendesse buon conto; chè ha pure de' bisogni. È vero che per ensino a qui, e per quello ho veduto, fa pure il dovere: e così quando ha presi mia danari, o quando glien' ho prestati, benchè sieno pochi, pure ne rende sempre buon conto: e così sento per chi ha a fare co lui. Ora i' non so, avendo avere danari nelle mani, come si facessi. Ha la famiglia grande, che sono otto bocche: e

think about it, and whether I think he would keep a careful record of what he did with your money. The second is that he has written to tell you he has a debt of 200 large florins,[2] and he's hinted that he'd like you to help him with it, and [you say] you'd do this willingly for a year, to help him, but [you'd want] to have it back at the end of the year, with the 40 [florins] he [already] owes you. And you know I love you, and that's why I'm giving you advice and looking into his affairs, if you want to help him, so you won't all get into a mess over it, which is something that often happens. If you do help him [with the debt], where is he going to get it from to repay it then? And what if he has other debts besides this 200 florins? In the first place I must tell you that where the idea about the [wool] business[3] is concerned, he has never said anything to me about it, but when I heard about it from Giovanni di Ser Francesco when he came back here, I mentioned it to him [Giovanni Bonsi] and he told me that Giovanni had told him about it. I haven't heard anything else about it since then, except yesterday when I received Lorenzo's letter of the 10th, which says, "We would still like to do something if we can to help Giovanni." I told him this and he answered, "They want to set up a wool business with Carlo and Giovanni di Ser Francesco." We didn't go into it any further. So this is all I've heard about it from him. So far as having Giovanni Bonsi run it is concerned, I think he would run it well because he's energetic and understands business, but if he had to handle money I can't be sure he'd be responsible with it because he still needs it himself. It's true that so far from what I've seen he's done the right thing, and when he's had money of mine, though they were only small amounts, still he has always kept careful account of them, and I've heard the same thing from those who do business with him. Now I don't know how he'd go, having to handle large sums of money. He has a big family, there are eight mouths to feed, and

tre ricolte in qua non ha avuto, tra per la tempesta e temporale tristo, e l'avere a dare grano e vino a quel Della Luna pel baratto fe' de' drappi, non n' ha auto el bisogno della sua famiglia: i' dico del vivere, sanza che sono male in ordine del vestire; che gli è l'Allesandra, che quando ha bisogno di ricucire la gamurra, si mette la cioppa in sulla camicia tanto che l' è racconcia. Sicchè, sendo el bisogno suo grande, i' non so giudicare quello si facessi. Pure avendo qualche avviamento di guadagno, e' stare' meglio che sanza; e non è ismemorato, e teme vergogna. Alla seconda parte de' fiorini 200 larghi, che dice aver debito, i' credo sieno quello o più. Egli è persona che non dice troppo e fatti sua; e veggo che alle volte egli empegnerà di que' pochi panni ch'egli ha, e guardasi da me, che se ne vergogna, ch' io lo sappia. I' non so che altro debito e' s'abbia, che con Marco fiorini 80, che gli prestò l'anno passato per fare una dota alla fanciulla: e per questo non ha bisogno d'accattargli da voi per rendere a lui. Ha debito un panno tolse l'anno passato al tempo dell'anno, e vendello a contanti per piatire; e tutto s'ha perduto. I' credo che n'abbia tolti più de' panni che questo; chè ha 'uto poca rendita e grande ispesa. E ancora levò a credenza panno rosato; che si fece il mantello per lo Squittino; che l' ha anche a pagare. Sì che istimo che n'abbia debito qualcuno più: chè nel numero de' 200 non credo sieno e tua 40, nè gli 80 di Marco. I' non so suo debito: ma volendo vendere le Selve, e Marco domandò s'egli aveva altro debito che si sapessi, e' disse di no: e ne lo isconfortò, e 'l mercato tornò indrieto. I' vorrei che voi l'aiutassi: d'altro canto penso, che servendolo voi di questi danari, non so al termine donde se gli avessi a trarre per rendervegli; chè

for the last three harvests he hasn't had what he needed to feed them; because of the bargain he made with that della Luna for the cloth, he's had to give him grain and wine.[4] I'm talking about what they need to live, not about the fact that they're in a bad way for clothing; the fact is that Lessandra, when her underskirt is worn out, puts a flowing gown over her skirt so that it still looks respectable. Because his need is so great I can't say what he might do. But if he had some way of earning money he'd be better off than he would be without it, and he isn't scatterbrained and he doesn't want to disgrace himself. Where the second question is concerned, about the 200 florins he says he owes, I believe it is that much or more. He's someone who doesn't say much about his own business, but I know he sometimes pawns the few clothes he has and hides the fact from me because he is ashamed to have me know about it. I don't know what other debts he may have, apart from one with Marco for 80 florins, which he borrowed last year to make a dowry investment for his girl, and he doesn't need to borrow that from you to repay him. He owes money for some cloth he took last year, which he agreed to pay for after a year and which he sold for cash to pay for some legal proceedings, and he lost it all. I think he may have taken more cloth than this, because he's had little income and a lot of expenses. And he still bought some cloth on credit, to have a cloak made for [when he was a member of] the Scrutiny Council, and he has to pay for that as well. So I would estimate that he owes rather more than this, because I don't think your 40 or Marco's 80 are included in the 200. I don't know what his debts are but he wanted to sell Le Selve,[5] and Marco asked him if he had any other debts that he knew of and he said no, and he [Marco] talked him out of it and he withdrew from the deal. I would like you to help him, but on the other hand if you do help him with this money, I don't know whether he will be able to repay you when it's

no lo veggo in istato che, se altra ventura no gli viene, che di qui a un anno egli abbia da por mano in su tanta quantità di danari; e non facendo, o non potendo rispondere, e' ne nasce iscandolo. E' sare' meglio istarsi. I' mi do a 'ntendere ch'e termini di questi 200 fiorini gli corrono addosso (e però ve ne richiede), come dico, di panni. I' ho 'nteso bene lo scriver tuo. E per volergli al termine, credo non sia da 'mpacciarsene. Da altro canto, è tanto buono e servente, che i' non vorrei ch'egli avesse avere danno o vergogna. E del salaro, che avessi a stare a bottega, non è da scontar debiti nè da farvi su assegnamento. I' t' ho detto quanto i' ne so de' fatti sua; e tu no mi scrivi ch' io dimostri di saperlo che ti richiegga: chè sendo contento, glien' arei detto apertamente: «Giovanni, tu richiedi Filippo di tanti danari. Tu sai ch' egli è il migliore servigio, e il più scandoloso, che si faccia, quando e' non si risponde al tempo. Per verun modo i' non vorrei che tra vo' avessi a nascere iscandolo niuno; che i' ne starei male contenta: sì che dimmi donde faresti pensiero a trargli per rendergli loro». E vedrei tosto quello n'avesse a seguire, chè so appresso quello ch' egli ha. Ma non me ne avendo tu avvisato, no gliene dirò ensino non ho altro da te; e m'ingegnerò, s' i' potrò, in questo mezzo, d'intendere se ha altro debito, e ve ne darò avviso. Chè è da 'ncrescere di lui, ch'è tanto buono, ch'è troppo; ed ha auto di queste ricolte picchiata quest'anno, per la qua' credette essere disfatto. Pure non ha tanto danno quanto credette; Iddio lodato! Nè altro per ora. Iddio di male vi guardi. Per la tua Allesandra, Firenze.

Pazienza a leggere, chè nel mio dire sono lunga.

due, because I don't see him being in a position in a year's time to lay his hand on that amount of money. And that being the case, if he was not able to pay it would disgrace him. So it might be better not to get involved. I'm trying to find out when the 200 florins are due, which is the reason why he's asking you for it, as I said, because of the cloth [he bought on credit]. I understand what you've written very well, but I think he would be embarrassed if I asked him when it's due. On the other hand it's right and proper for me not to want to see him injured or humiliated. And about the salary you would pay him to work in the [wool] shop, it wouldn't be to repay his debts or to repay you in installments. I've told you all I know about his affairs, and you haven't written to me that I can make it clear to him that I know what he is asking from you, because if you were happy for me to do that I would have said to him openly "Giovanni, you are asking Filippo for so much money. You know it would be a great help to you, but that it would also be a very disgraceful thing if it wasn't repaid in time. I wouldn't want anything disgraceful to happen between you, and it would make me very unhappy. So tell me where you intend to find the money to repay them." And then I would soon see what would come of it, because I know, near enough, what he has. But as you haven't said that to me I won't speak to him about it until I hear from you, and I'll try if I can, in this way, to find out if he has other debts and I'll let you know. You have to feel sorry for him, he's so good, only too much so. He has been hit by these harvests this year; he thought he was ruined but perhaps he has not been hurt as much as he thought, God be praised. Nothing more for now; may God keep you from harm. From your Allesandra, Florence.

Be patient reading this because I've gone on for a long time.

33

Al nome di Dio. A dì 4 di marzo 1468.

A dì 18 del passato fu l'utima mia: ho dipoi dua tue de' XI e XXIII detto. Risposta.

Per altra ti dissi dell'essere di Lorenzo, della persona; e veggo ti dispiace che pigliando lui el lattovaro, no gli faccia frutto. Pure avendolo di poi continovato, non è peggio che si fussi quando te ne scrissi: chè della magrezza s' è al

Postscript: Piero Antonio had been there this morning, and had told her that Filippo should stick with Piero [de' Medici] and Messer Agnolo [Acciaiuoli].

33

More than three years separate this letter from the previous one. In August and September 1466 the struggle for power between Piero de' Medici and his main opponents had finally come to a head. After several days of tension during which Florence was full of armed men employed by one side or the other, a new Signoria was drawn which was favorable to the Medici. Repressive, pro-Medicean measures were implemented, and almost all of Piero's opponents exiled. Piero felt the need to cultivate the friendship of the King of Naples, however, and hence agreed to lift the sentence of exile on Filippo and Lorenzo Strozzi. It also balanced the internal politics of the city: having just created a new group of exiles, it was diplomatic to allow some earlier ones to return. Filippo returned to Florence in November 1466. By March 1469 he had married Fiammetta Adimari,[1] their first child, Alfonso, had been born, and another baby was expected. Lorenzo, still unmarried, was living in Florence, but Filippo (to whom the letter is addressed) was making an extended visit to Naples to look after their business interests there.

In the name of God. 4 March 1469.

My last letter was on the 18th of last month and since then I've had two of yours, written on the 11th and the 23rd. I will reply here.

I told you in another letter how Lorenzo was, in himself, and I see you're upset that he should have taken the medicine and not had any benefit from it. He's gone on with it since then and isn't any worse than he was when I

modo usato; ma è migliorato assai di colore. È vero che, poi che fu quaresima, non è come mi pareva prima: ed è ragionevole; chè questi cibi sono contradi a chi sente d'oppilato; e al continovo non si può estare a vita iscelta o a latte di mandorle; che rincresce, e massime a chi è vago de' cibi della quaresima. Pure m'ingegno per la Fiammetta e per lui e per la balia di fare vivande più sane ch' i' posso. Che Iddio ci conduca a pasqua, con salute dell'anima e del corpo.

Alfonso si sta pure con un poco di quello omore: è stato come guarito parecchi dì; e da dua dì en qua è un poco rifigliato: non è però cosa da farne istima; ma pure non posso dire sia guarito affatto. Egli sta per altro benissimo della persona, è rischiarato delle carni, e comincia andare duo passi sopra di sè. Non s'assicura ancora; ma presto doverrà andare liberamente.

La Maria di Ramondo è duo dì ch' ell' è venuta in Firenze: è malata: androlla a vicitare, e sì gli ricorderò e tua danari; e dandomigli, gli darò a Lorenzo, come mi di' ch' i' faccia.

Entendo per più tue quello di' della balia per quest'altro che ha fare la Fiammetta. Lei gli pare, secondo che la dice a me, di trovare una balia di fuori col latte fresco: e anche a me pare; chè non si può sapere quanto Alfonso sarà a poppa; che secondo istarà della persona, secondo farete: e vogliendolo ispoppare a settembre, e recarvi l'altro in casa, ogni volta si troverrà balia: sì che per ora cerchiamo d'una balia qui presso a Firenze; che Iddio ce l'apparecchi buona.

Dell' errore del non essere ito a Monte più che fiorini

wrote to you about it. He's as thin as he always is, but has a better color. It's true that since it was Lent it isn't how it seemed to me at first, and it's not surprising because these foods are bad for anyone who feels constipated; and you don't want to limit yourself continually to a restricted life or to [drinking] milk of almonds, which is harmful, most of all to those who [don't] like the Lenten foods. Still, I try my hardest for Fiammetta and for him and the wet nurse,[2] to make the most nourishing dishes I can. May God bring us to Easter with healthy bodies and souls.

One paragraph: Alessandra was waiting to hear from Filippo what she should do about his business.

Alfonso[3] still has a slight cold; he seemed completely better for a few days, but two days ago it started again. I can't say he's completely better, although it isn't anything to worry about. Otherwise he's well in himself and his skin is clearer, and he's starting to take two steps by himself. He isn't steady yet but soon he should be able to walk freely.

Maria di Raimondo[4] arrived in Florence two days ago. She is sick so I will go and visit her, and remind her about your money. If she does give it to me I will give it to Lorenzo, as you told me to.

I've heard from several of your letters what you say ⟵ about the wet nurse for this other baby Fiammetta is having. It seems to her, from what she tells me, [that we should] find a wet nurse who has fresh milk outside [the city] and I think so too, because we can't know how long Alfonso will stay on the breast; what you do will depend on how he is in himself. And if you want to wean him in September and bring the other one back to the house,[5] you will find a wet nurse at any time. So for now we will look for a wet nurse here, close to Florence. May God make a good one ready for us.

About the mistake of only 225 florins going to the

225, credo sia ritrovato, e Lorenzo te ne debba avere avvisato dov' è suto il mancamento.

La Fiammetta sta bene: el corpo cresce, ed è un poco aggravata della persona; che è ragionevole. Sta bene per altro. Stassi volentieri en casa, ed io co lei al continovo; che dalla messa in fuori, non vo altrove, se non m' è nicistà d' andare.

Di' che non ti pare di mandare ora Giovanluigi, e assegnine buone ragioni; ed è quello che tu di'; e conosco el fanciullo arebbe assai disagi: ma a me pareva quanto più tosto si levassi dalla madre, tanto più tosto si leverebbe el pensiero l'uno dall' altro. Lorenzo mi pare resterà contento non lo mandi ora.

Non ti maravigli che Alfonso sia sì reo, ensegnandogli io leggere. A che ti dico, se tu lo vedessi, ti parrebbe ancora più ch' i' non dico: chè ti prometto non bisogna dirgli la cosa più d'una volta, che l' ha 'ntesa. E' mi venne dettogli una sera nell'orecchie: El babbo è a Napoli. Non bisognò dirglielo più; che come n'è domandato, e' dice: Bambo a Napi. E così d'ogni cosa fa: che è segno ha buona memoria. So che tu ti riderai di questo mio scrivere, e dirai ch' i' sia una bestia: ma i' so che da altro canto n' arai piacere e consolazione; e tanto più voglia arai di vederlo. Che Iddio ci die grazia sia tosto, e con allegrezza e consolazione. Nè altro per questa. Iddio di male ti guardi. Per la tua Allesandra Strozzi, Firenze.

La Fiammetta si porta bene. 13 e 14, ognuno attende a fare e fatti sua; che sta bene. Non accade altra risposta alla tua. Aspettiàno per Batista le frutte, che di' che mandi per lui.

Monte,[6] I believe we can recover it, and Lorenzo must have told you where the failing occurred.

Fiammetta is well; her body is getting bigger and she is a little weighed down, which is not surprising. Otherwise she is well and she stays at home willingly and I stay with her all the time. I go nowhere if I don't have to, except to Mass.

You say you don't think it's a good idea to send for Giovanluigi[7] now and you give good reasons. What you say is right and I know it would be hard for the boy, but it seems to me that the sooner he leaves his mother, the sooner they will stop thinking about each other. But I think Lorenzo will be happy for you not to send him now.

Three paragraphs: Marco and Lorenzo will have told him that they are going to sell 3500 florins' worth of Monte *shares in Alessandra's name; the new tax has been revealed; Guasparre, son-in-law of Jacopo degli Orsi, has been in Florence.*

You shouldn't be surprised that Alfonso is so advanced for his age, and that I am teaching him to read. I must tell you that if you saw him he'd strike you as even more advanced than I've said. I promise you, you don't need to tell him anything more than once for him to understand it. One evening I said to him "Daddy is in Naples." I didn't need to say anything more to him about it because when he was asked he said "Dada in Nape." He is like that with everything and it shows he has a good memory. I know you will laugh at what I've written and say I'm a fool, but I know it gives me pleasure and comfort and will make you want to see him even more. May God let it be soon and let it bring us happiness and consolation. No more for now; may God keep you from harm. From your Allesandra, Florence.

Fiammetta is behaving well. Both Marco and Giovanni do everything for her and she is well. Nothing else occurs to me in answer to your letter. We're waiting to get the fruit from Batista which you say you're sending by him.

34

Al nome di Dio. A dì 8 di maggio 1469.

A' 29 di marzo fu l'utima mia: ho di poi dua tue del primo e 12 del passato. Risposta.

En prima tu mi di' del fatto della donna, che Lorenzo ti scrive avere riferito Marco di quest'utima pratica, e che gli amici ed io ne lo confortiàno: e quello ne di' ho 'nteso, e così per altre tue. A che ti dico, che quando me ne ragionò nel prencipio, che non mi dispiacque punto; e parevami che, ben che ci fussi delle parti che fussino d'alcun carico, che ce ne fussi anche delle buone: e però ti scrissi. Dipoi, veduto la risposta che tu mi facesti, i' ne stetti sopra di me, e no ne lo confortai; e stetti un pezzo, ched io no ne ragionai a lui nè lui a me. Dipoi, avendo da loro che

34

Lorenzo had succeeded in delaying his marriage for some time, but had finally decided to act on his long-held desire to marry Marietta Strozzi, whose few surviving male kinsmen, most notably her uncle Giovanfrancesco, were still exiled from Florence. Alessandra seems to have had mixed feelings about the prospect, and in this letter to Filippo she refers to it in a very guarded manner. Marietta's father and grandfather had been her husband's close friends and her mother had been Alessandra's own friend, but Filippo was too young to remember any of this and was opposed to the match on pragmatic grounds. Marietta's uncle Giovanfrancesco was a disgraced bankrupt and political enemy of the Medici, and Marietta herself was by now older than most Florentine girls of this class were when they married.

In the name of God. 8 May 1469.

My last letter was on the 29th of March and since then I've had two of yours, of the first and 12th of last month. I will answer here.

First you tell me about this business of a wife [for Lorenzo], that Lorenzo has written to you and said he had told Marco about this last discussion and that I and our friends had advised him about it and that I had heard what you had to say about it; and the same is true of your other letters. To which I say to you, that when he discussed it with me in the beginning I didn't dislike it at all, and it seemed to me that although there were aspects to it which might be a burden, there were also good things about it, and so I wrote to you. After that, seeing the answer I got from you, I thought about it a great deal, but I haven't given him any [more] advice about it, and I left it for a while and I didn't discuss it with him and he didn't discuss it with me. Since then [I've been given advice] from those

ci venivano volentieri, e Marco e Lorenzo me lo dissono, quello che pareva a me; risposi, che loro se ne intendevano meglio di me. E, secondo si vede, non ci è grascia nell'altre che ci sono, vogliendo tor donna che no diminuissi d'onore. E pertanto dissi pigliassino quel partito paresse loro il meglio; e che vedevano quello tu ne scrivevi. E come t'ho detto pel passato, così ti dico, ch'io non me ne travaglio, nè no ne lo domando di questa nè d'altra; nè lui ne dice a me: sì che, quello si seguirà non te ne so avvisare di nulla, nè che sia seguito da dua mesi en qua. Priego bene Iddio che gli dia a pigliare el meglio.

Di' che non mi raccomandi la Fiammetta, perchè sai non bisogna: e così è il vero; chè fo inverso di lei più che non farei a una delle mie figliuole. E così si fa guardia d'Alfonso, quant'è possibile: è un pericoloso fanciullo; va sopra di sè, e sta magruccio, ma pure è forte della persona. La Fiammetta fece la fanciulla, e partorì bene; ed è per ensino a questo dì sana; e sta meglio che non fè in Alfonso. Iddio lodato.

Lorenzo ebbe poco che fare a scriverti del dispiacere che i' ebbi del por nome Allesandro al fanciullo, s'egli era maschio; e bene che dicessi el vero, non te lo doveva iscrivere; perchè, come e' mi disse, «E' no' staremo freschi, se a' nostri figliuoli noi non potessimo por nome a nostro modo!» E dice il vero. Ed i' ho auto tanti degli altri dispiaceri, ed hogli passati, e così passo questo; e sare' passato avendo fatto Allesandro, come passò Alfonso: benchè allora v'era ragione rispetto di chi lo battezzò. Insino allora m'avvidi, che 'l nome di tuo padre non ti piaceva. Ora Iddio provvide che fece la Lucrezia: ed è una bella fanciulla, e somiglia la Fiammetta; bianca come lei, e così di fattezze è tutta lei: ed è più grossa che non fu Alfonso. Iddio gli presti lunga vita.

who have wanted to come and see us, and Marco and Lorenzo have asked me about it, about how it seemed to me, and I said that they understood it better than me. And, from what we can see, the other girls here aren't up to much, not for anyone who wants to marry without losing status. And for that reason I said they should take whatever decision seemed best to them and that they had seen what you'd written about it. And as I said to you in the past, so I say now, I'm not tormenting myself about this and I'm not asking him anything about this girl or any other one, and he doesn't want to talk about it to me. So I can't tell you anything about it or what will happen or might happen two months from now.

You say you don't ask me to look after Fiammetta because you know you don't need to and that's true, because I do more for her than I would for one of my own daughters. And we try to keep our eyes on Alfonso as much as we can, because that boy's a great danger to himself. He's growing too fast and stays very thin, but he's still a strong child. Fiammetta had a girl [1] and gave birth easily and she's been well, up to the present. She's been better than she was with Alfonso, God be praised.

Lorenzo had no business writing to tell you how displeased I was about calling the baby Allesandro, if it had been a boy, and although what he wrote may have been the truth, he should not have written it to you. Still, as he said to me, "we will get ourselves in a mess if we can't name our sons in our usual way!" What he says is true. [2] I've had many other griefs and I've endured them, and so I endure this one; I would have put up with having him called Allesandro just as I put up with Alfonso, although in that case there was a reason, because of his godfather; but I realized then that you didn't like your father's name. Now God has decreed that Lucrezia should be born and she's a beautiful girl and like Fiammetta, fair like her and like her in the face as well, and she's bigger than Alfonso was. May God give her a long life.

Mon' Antonia venne, come fusti avvisato. Andammola a vicitare, e volemmola levare di 'n sull'abergo: e perchè era in compagnia della donna di messer Giovanni Bentivogli, non si volle partire da lei. Giunse il dì a ore 20, e l'altra mattina cavalcò. Fecigli offerte di danari o d'altro, che avesse di bisogno. E così senti' avea fatto Lorenzo. Aspettiàlla di ritorno a dì 12; e se ci soprastarà niun dì, farèno a ogni modo si stia qui en casa, e farogli quello onore ci fia possibile di fare: e la Fiammetta fia di tre settimane di parto, che sarà fuori del letto: sicchè farèno nostro isforzo. Non m'è briga nè noia niuna, quando potessi fare e aiutarmi della persona più ch' io non posso; ma i' no sono però cotale come mi scrivesti in questo verno, ch' io avevo messo un tallo; e di poi è passato, che mi senti' male insino pella settimana santa; e così fatto pasqua: dipoi mi purgai, ma non molto bene. Son pur vecchia, e credo migliorare, ed i' peggioro: tanto farò così, io finirò e mie' debiti. Sicchè non t'avendo iscritto ispesso, come solevo, fu la cagione in prima il non mi sentir bene, e poi ho pure da fare. E la Fiammetta partorì, e delle genti ci capitano assai; e a me tocca tutto. E s'io non avessi altro iscioperìo che Alfonso, non me ne bisognere' più: ma questo è con piacere. Sempre m' è drieto, come il pulcino alla chioccia. Sicchè i' non posso così escrivere ispesso: ristoreratti la Fiammetta.

Dissi a Lorenzo che t'avvisassi come mona Lucrezia di Piero invitò duo volte la Fiammetta alle nozze, prima ch' ella facessi la fanciulla. Risposi, che l'avesse per escusata, ch'ella aveva a fare il fanciullo; e che perventura lei sarebbe in parto. Dipoi, come sentì ch'ella l'ebbe fatto, ella ci rimandò, che 'n ogni modo la voleva, e che non si gli dicessi di no. Ella non ha voglia d'andarvi, e a me non pare ch'ella debba andare. La prima, perchè tu non ci se'; l'altra, che s'ella v'andasi, bisognerebbe espendere parecchi

Mona Antonia came, as you were informed.[3] We went to visit her and we wanted her to leave the inn, but because she was there as one of the retinue of the wife of Messer Giovanni Bentivogli[4] she didn't want to leave her. She arrived at 3 p.m. and left the next morning. I offered her money or anything else she needed and so, I gather, did Lorenzo. We expect her to come back on the 12th and if she won't stay here at all, we'll try in every way possible to have her here in the house, and I'll show her every honor I can. It will be three weeks by then since Fiammetta gave birth, and she'll be out of bed so we'll make every effort. It's no trouble or annoyance to me when she's able to help me, [and she does] more than I can do myself. But I'm not as I was during the winter, when I was feeling young again; that's gone and I've been feeling ill since Holy Week, and then we had Easter. After that I purged myself, but not very well. I'm old, and I think I'm getting better and I get worse. But I'll do what I can and I'll pay off my debts. The reason why I haven't written to you often, like I used to, is that I haven't been feeling well and I still have things to do. And Fiammetta had the baby and we had lots of people here, and I had to do everything. And if I had nothing to do except for Alfonso I still wouldn't need anything else. But that's a pleasure, he follows me around like a chicken follows the mother hen. So I can't write to you often, but Fiammetta will make it up to you.

I told Lorenzo he should tell you how Mona Lucrezia di Piero [de' Medici] had invited Fiammetta to the wedding[5] twice before she had the baby. I replied that she'd have to excuse her as she was expecting a baby and she might still be in bed. Since then, as she'd heard that Fiammetta had had the baby, she sent us another message to say she really wanted her to come, and we shouldn't say no. She doesn't want to go, first because you're not here and also because if she does go we'll have to spend several

centinaia di fiorini. Avvisandoti che si fa assai robe e cotte di broccato; che così si richiederebbe fare ancora a lei: e poi delle gioie è mal fornita. Sì che tu ha' 'nteso: avvisa che ti pare. Envitorono pe' 4 dì di giugno; ma dicono che prolungheranno insino a San Giovanni: sicchè ci è tempo assai, chi s'ha a vestire.

E la mi dice la Fiammetta ch'io ti scriva, ch'ella vorrebbe farsi una giornea di saia nera melanese per questo San Giovanni, e che tu ordinassi a Lorenzo che gliele levassi. E invero, ella n'ha bisogno, chè non è tempo allora di portare le cioppe: e poi potrà portar la cotta. Sì che ordina che la se la possa fare, e averla al tempo; che, a mie' parere, n'ha nicistà. Nè altro per questa. Iddio di male ti guardi. Per la tua Allesandra Strozzi, in Firenze.

---

3 5

Al nome di Dio. A dì 14 d'aprile 1470.

A questi dì passati ho 'vuto più tue lettere, per le quali mi di' della tua partita di costà, e secondo mi di' per l'utima tua de' 30 del passato, che fia a mezzo questo, e che ne verrai a Roma: che Iddio v'accompagni. E più ho 'vuto lo 'nventario d'una balla di panni, e lino, e greco, che

hundred florins. I must tell you that they are having a lot of brocade gowns and robes made, and we'd have to have them made for her as well, and she doesn't have much jewelry. So now you know; let me know what you think. They've invited her for the 4th of June but they say it will go on till St. John's Day,[6] which is a long time to provide enough clothes for.

Fiammetta tells me I should tell you that she'd like to make herself a cloak of black Milanese twill, and that you should tell Lorenzo to buy it. She really needs it because it's not the season for wearing gowns with a hood, and [with such a cloak] she'll be able to wear a lighter gown. You should arrange it so she can make it and have it soon, because it seems to me she needs it. Nothing more for now; may God keep you from harm. From your Allesandra Strozzi in Florence.

35

This is Alessandra's last surviving letter, written to Filippo nearly a year after the last, and about ten months before her death. Lorenzo had given up his ambition to marry Marietta Strozzi, either in obedience to Filippo's wishes or because he had not reached an agreement with her family, and was betrothed to Antonia Baroncelli in June 1470.

In the name of God. 14 April 1470.

In the past few days I've had several letters from you, in which you told me how you were leaving there, and according to what you told me in your last letter, of the 30th of last month, that may be in the middle of this month, and [you say] you will go to Rome; may God go with you. And I've also had the inventory for a bale of

mandi per la via di Pisa. Questi non sono ancora compa-
riti: non mi pare di mandargli a Lari, chè sare' di noia
assai; e non sendovi cose nuove, non v' è troppa gabella di
panni: el greco si pagherà in ogni modo; e 'l lino è poca
gabella. Quello che mandasti per Biagio, cioè un paio di
forzeretti e 'l lino, abbiàno secondo lo 'nventario riscon-
tro, e tutto istà bene. Faciemone quanto tu ci ordinasti.

Di' che arai a mente di pigliare forma e modo della
schiava; che mi piacerà.

Se Lorenzo è provvisto delle cose arà di bisogno, ha
fatto bene.

Della biada, cioè della spelda, n'ho comperata da diciotto estaia soldi 9 lo staio, e mille dugento covoni di
paglia d'orzo: ècci cara, che vale più di soldi 10 el cento;
chè è rincarato il grano soldi 20 lo staio: chè è la ventura
nostra, che sempre ci abbattiàno a comperare quando le
cose rincarano. Così farèno del vino per la state; che per
noi ne bisognerà comperare parecchi barili. E rispetto il
gran freddo ch'è stato, ed è ancora, le viti non mettono; e
dicono che assai ne secca: sì che è rincarato. Sono degli
altri nostri provvedimenti. Iddio vi dia pur grazia torniate
sani. E se non hai mandato di quella polvere da nettare
ariento, non ne fo caso, perchè son certa n'arete qua pel
bisogno. Io v'ho fatto fare in quella casa dirieto una man-
giatoia e rastrelliera en su 'l pulito, che vi starà alla larga
tre cavagli. Sì che venite a vostra posta; e avvisateci a
punto quando ci credete essere, a ciò che mettiàno in
punto per voi quello che fia di bisogno.

Alfonso e noi altri siamo sani.

Arete sentito delle novità seguite di qua. E 'n prima,
duo volte rotto le Stinche, cioè le prigioni: e la prima

cloth and flax, and *greco* wine,[1] that you are sending via Pisa. They haven't turned up yet and I don't think it's a good idea to send them to Lari[2] because it would be too much trouble. Because it's not new there's not too much duty to pay on the cloth; we will pay for the *greco* in any case, and there's little duty on the flax. We have received what you sent with Biagio, as described on the inventory, and it's in good order. We did what you asked us to do with it.

You say you're thinking about taking the slave's position and style [of living] away [from her];[3] I'd be pleased by that.

If Lorenzo is provided with the things he is going to need, he will have done well.

About the fodder, that is the spelt,[4] I've bought 18 bushels at 9 soldi the bushel, and one thousand two hundred sheaves of barley straw. It's dear here, worth more than 10 soldi the hundred, because the price of grain has gone up to 20 soldi the bushel. That's our luck, we're always having to buy things once they get dear. We'll have to do the same with the wine for the summer, as we'll have to buy several barrels for our own use. Because it's been so cold and still is, the grapevines aren't setting fruit and they say it's very dry for them, so they've got dearer. (These are among our other supplies.) God give us grace that things may still turn out well. If you haven't sent that powder for cleaning silver I won't be needing it, because I'm sure you'll have as much here as I need. I've had a trough and a hayrack made in that house at the back,[5] [which is finished] as far as the cleaning up; it will be wide enough for three horses. So you're coming [home] to your place; let us know exactly when you expect to be here so we can get things ready for you.

Alfonso is well, and so are the rest of us.

You will have heard about the revolt which took place here.[6] To begin with they broke out of the Stinche twice,

volta ruppono le finestre, e uscirono nella corte: furono ripresi, e fu perdonato loro. La seconda volta arsono gli usci delle prigioni, e ruppono il muro dove ruppono quando Matteo di Giorgio n' uscì; ma non riuscì loro, chè furono sentiti, e vi corsono de' provigionati che stanno in Piazza, e colle balestra ne saettorono uno che voleva uscire per quelle buche. Poi furono presi, e fu tagliato la testa a tre, e gli altri vi furono rimessi. E dipoi, a dì sei di questo, la mattina a ore 14, ci fu che quello de' Nardi era entrato in Prato con ben dugento fanti, e che Prato era perduto. Oh non domandare el viluppo che fu in questa terra! che per du' ore era tutta ravviluppata la gente che correvano le vie, e massimo quella da casa Lorenzo di Piero; e quanto pane cotto si trovò, tutto si portò tra casa Lorenzo e 'n Palagio, en modo che non si trovava nè pane nè farina. A me pareva istar male, che non ho grano, e poca farina in casa. Dipoi, per grazia di Dio, e' ci fu novelle che questo de' Nardi era preso con tutta la sua gente; che dicono erano da sessanta; e 'l dì medesimo ne fu menato preso: e dipoi l'altro dì, a dì 7, ne venne 15 tutti legati a una fune: e lunedì, a dì 9, fu tagliato il capo a quello de' Nardi; e 'l dì medesimo ne venne presi tre, pure da Prato. E là dicono che 'l Podestà ne 'npiccò quattordici. E questa mattina se n'è impiccati quattro di questi medesimi: e lunedì che viene, dicono che n'andrà sette. E non so poi che si faranno del resto. È suto un grande ispavento a tutto il popolo: pare una iscurità, tanta gente morta e straziati. E oltre a questa tribolazione, ci è suto e tremuoti: che quella mattina che gli entrò in Prato quello poverello, venne un tremuoto molto ben grande. Tra l'una paura e l'altra, e' mi pare essere mezza fuori di me: credo che noi siàno

the prison that is;[7] the first time they broke the windows and got out into the courtyard. They were retaken and pardoned. The second time they burned down the doors of the prison and broke down the wall where it was broken down when Matteo di Giorgio got out,[8] but they didn't succeed because they were heard and some of the guards who live in the Piazza[9] ran there and shot one of them with their crossbows while he was trying to get out through the holes. Then they were taken, and three of them were beheaded and the others were put back inside. And later, on the sixth of this month, at 8 o'clock in the morning, we heard that one of the Nardi[10] had entered Prato[11] with a good two hundred soldiers and that Prato was lost. Oh, don't ask about the confusion that reigned in this land: for two hours there was complete confusion, with people running about the streets, and particularly around Lorenzo di Piero's house,[12] and they carried all the bread they could find between Lorenzo's house and the Palazzo,[13] so there was neither bread nor flour to be found;[14] I thought things were looking bad, because I had no grain. Later, by the grace of God, news came that this Nardi had been taken with all his men; they say there were about sixty of them. And he was imprisoned the same day, and later, the next day, on the 7th, 15 of them came [to Florence], all tied to a rope, and on Monday the 9th Nardi was beheaded. And the same day three more men were captured, but from Prato, and they say the Podesta[15] has hanged fourteen of them there. This morning four of them have been hanged, and they say seven more will go this coming Friday. I don't know what they'll do with the rest. All the people have been terrified, and it seems a very dreadful thing, with so many people dead and tortured. And apart from this great trouble, there's been an earthquake: the very morning that poor man entered Prato, there was a very big earthquake. Between one fear and the other I seem to have been half

presso a finimondo. Sì che è buono acconciarsi dell'a-
nima, e stare apparecchiato. Che Dio ci guardi da più tri-
bolazioni. Sento ancora, che a Pistoia è suto non so che;
en modo che si dice, ch'e Panciatichi di là si sono tutti
partiti per paura: che a Dio piaccia por fine. Nè altro per
questa. Iddio di male vi guardi. Per la tua Allesandra
Strozzi, in Firenze.

beside myself; I thought we were close to the end of the world. So it's good to put your soul in order and be ready. May God keep us from further troubles. I also hear there's been I don't know what [happening] in Pistoia,[16] and they say the Panciatichi [17] have all left in fear. May it please God to bring it to an end. No more for now; may God keep you from harm. From your Allesandra Strozzi in Florence.

Notes

Letter 1

1. He had held office in one of the two magistracies which constituted the "Colleges" of the Signoria, or Priorate, which assisted and advised the priors: the "Twelve Goodmen" and the "Sixteen Gonfaloniers of Companies," popularly known as the Twelve and the Sixteen.

2. The Dowry Fund was established in 1425, allowing parents of some means to deposit a sum on their infant daughters' behalf, to mature after a set term. This was paid to her husband after the marriage had been consummated or after the term of the investment was completed, if that was a later date.

3. If a girl died before her marriage, or after it but before a Dowry Fund investment matured, only the deposit was returned to her relatives.

4. The elite group who held high office and enjoyed real political power.

5. Filippo had raised the question of whether Matteo, who was eleven, should leave Florence to begin learning merchant practice in one of the branches (in Naples, Bruges, and Barcelona) of the bank of Niccolò, Filippo, and Jacopo di Lionardo Strozzi. They were first cousins of Alessandra's husband, Matteo.

6. The head tax.

7. That is, he was learning to write business letters, and also to write a clearer script.

8. The Florentine state or government.

9. Branches or divisions of the Florentine government, in charge of its various fiscal functions.

10. Filippo Maria Visconti, Duke of Milan (died 13 August 1447), had spent much of the previous three decades at war with Florence.

11. Alfonso I of Naples (Alfonso V of Aragon), ruled 1443 – 58.

12. In the Val d'Arno, about forty-five kilometers to the southeast of Florence.

13. Niccolò di Lionardo Strozzi, for whom Filippo worked in Naples at this time.

14. Her remark at the end of this paragraph suggests that this misdemeanor involved carelessness with money.

15. Giovanni della Luna and Antonio di Benedetto Strozzi. Antonio had been only a distant relation of Matteo Strozzi, but was one of Alessandra's closest friends and advisers at this time.

16. Alessandra forgot to sign this letter.

Letter 2

1. The "plague" which is frequently referred to in four-teenth- and fifteenth-century Italian sources has generally (but not universally) been considered to be bubonic plague and two variants, pneumonic and septicemic plague. The mortality rate among victims was high (between 60 and 90 per cent for bubonic plague), and death usually occurred within a week of symptoms appearing.

2. The *contado* or rural districts immediately surrounding and ruled by Florence.

3. That of her son-in-law, Marco Parenti.

4. Her second surviving son, Lorenzo; see below, Letter 8.

5. Instead of going into business for himself, as he did later.

6. This may be a reference to the fact that she no longer had access to politically influential friends or relations to help her in this area.

7. Filippo frequently sent flax to female relatives and friends in Florence, who spun it into linen thread as a pastime.

8. That is, he had to pay eleven florins each time the tax was levied, which happened as frequently as the government judged necessary.

9. Considered a sign of ill health and undesirable.

10. Under Florentine law, if an urban property was to be sold, those with an adjoining property were supposed to be given an opportunity to purchase it. This property was finally purchased by Filippo in 1477 as part of the site of the Strozzi palace.

11. Jacopo Strozzi, brother of Niccolò Strozzi, for whom Lorenzo worked in Bruges.

Letter 3

1. Soldo di Bernardo Strozzi, a distant cousin of her husband. Matteo was supposed to travel to Naples with him.

2. These seem to have been for cutting pens.

3. A man of great political influence who had been a friend of her husband.

4. A laborer from their farm at Quaracchi, a district to the west of the city.

5. Alessandra's half-sister.

6. It is not clear why she had dealings with these Communal officials.

7. If Filippo left Naples to escape the plague.

Letter 4

1. A village to the southeast of Florence.

2. Formerly a business partner of Alessandra's husband, he now worked for Niccolò Strozzi and his brothers.

3. The Strozzi lineage.

4. Husband of Alessandra di Messer Filippo Strozzi, who was an aunt of the Filippo Strozzi whose death has just been mentioned.

5. A first cousin of Alessandra's husband.

6. To discuss the administration of their brother's estate.

7. This money belonged to Alessandra because she had paid Marco 500 florins of her own money at the time of the marriage.

8. Pilgrims to Rome could obtain a plenary or full indulgence which remitted all temporal punishment for their sins up to that time.

Letter 5

1. The new year did not begin until March 25, so all letters written before March 25 actually bear the date of the previous year, in this case 1449.

2. The whole Strozzi family or lineage.

3. As he was dead, this house now belonged to his sons.

4. The son of Niccolò's first cousin, Maria di Piero Strozzi.

5. Niccolò's sister.

6. Checca di Piero Strozzi, Niccolò's first cousin.

Letter 6

1. In his own household, where Filippo also lived.

2. Francesco di Benedetto Strozzi, brother of Antonio Strozzi.

3. The Strozzi lineage.

4. Antonio was the first Strozzi to hold office as a member of the Signoria since the Medici regime took power in 1434.

Letter 7

1. Meat, a food considered desirable for invalids, was not eaten during Lent.

2. Only the betrothal had in fact taken place.

3. The ducat was a Neapolitan coin, while the lira was a Florentine silver coin of account; there were about five lire to the florin (a gold coin) at this time, and 20 soldi to the lire.

4. Dried smoked fish roe, generally mullet.

5. A domestic slave; Alessandra was considering selling her. Slaves, mainly Tartars, were quite common as domestic servants at this time in Tuscany.

6. From Jacopo Strozzi's household.

Letter 8

1. Lorenzo must have intended to start a book of family records of his own.

2. Devotees had wax images of themselves or their relatives placed in this church, one of the most celebrated shrines of the Virgin in Italy.

Letter 9

1. This business had been begun by Filippo in August 1456. It is likely that he also continued to do some business in Naples for Niccolò Strozzi, who now lived in Rome.

2. One *braccio* was .3364 of a square meter.

3. Apparently the proceeds of a sale of property.

4. Benedetto di Francesco Strozzi.

Letter 10

1. During the second half of 1458 the Medici regime sought to strengthen its position (among other measures) by renewing the sentences of exile imposed on their enemies in 1434. In the case of some families, including the Strozzi, the sentence was also extended to the male descendants of the original exiles. Initially those affected were obliged to stay one hundred miles from the city, but this was then reduced to fifty miles.

2. The Eight of Watch (or Guard), a committee of state security.

3. Battista di Francesco Strozzi, a brother of the Benedetto Strozzi whose death is described in Letter 9.

4. Her illegitimacy.

5. Probably Francesco di Benedetto Strozzi, a business associate of Jacopo.

6. Although it is not mentioned here, Isabella would also have received a dowry from her father.

Letter 11

1. Francesco di Piero Strozzi.

2. Matteo di Giorgio Brandolini.

3. Malaria; later Alessandra believed that Matteo had died of the plague, although the description given does not seem to support this conclusion.

4. Because they had no time to confess and receive the last rites.

5. As legal exiles.

6. A rod was a linear measurement of varying length.

7. A boy who worked for Filippo.

8. Matteo had left a sum in his will to be used for good works, and Alessandra felt that this young woman would be a suitable recipient of the intended charity.

9. Messer Giannozzo Manetti, a humanist scholar and formerly a wealthy Florentine merchant, who was living in Naples.

10. Probably drawn from classical or Christian literature.

11. Also called Bernardetto, he was a personal friend of Alessandra and was connected to the Strozzi by marriage.

Letter 12

1. The Olivetans were an order of friars.

2. See above, Letter 8.

3. It seems likely that this garment (a sleeveless vestment worn by the priest officiating at the mass) was to be given to the church of the Florentine community in Naples.

4. Florentine men, in their wills, usually gave their daughters or sisters the right to return to their parental home if they needed to do so. In fact Matteo's will does not specifically refer to this.

5. Under Florentine law it was possible to refuse the inheritance of an estate. If she had accepted it, Alessandra would also have become liable for Matteo's debts.

6. Lorenzo had lived in Barcelona (in Catalonia) when he first left Florence.

7. Checca di Piero Strozzi.

Letter 13

1. Probably Pagolo di Benedetto Strozzi.

2. A church close to Florence which possessed a reputedly miracle-working image of the Virgin Mary.

3. To take Lorenzo's place in the business.

4. Alfonso I of Naples had wrested the throne of Naples from the French incumbent, Rene of Anjou, in 1443. When Alfonso died in 1458, his bastard son Ferrante (Ferdinand) succeeded him, unsuccessfully contested by Rene in a further war.

5. November 3, the day after the previous passage had been written.

6. To Italy, but not of course to Florence, from which he was legally exiled.

Letter 15

1. He died on 26 March 1461.

2. Lionardo di Jacopo Strozzi, the heir of his uncle Niccolò Strozzi.

Letter 16

1. Probably a mistake for Marco, Filippo's most frequent correspondent.

2. Marina.

3. It is not clear who this is.

4. A distant cousin and celebrated beauty. Born in about 1448, she was the daughter of Lorenzo di Messer Palla Strozzi and Alessandra dei Bardi and the niece of Giovanfrancesco Strozzi, who became her guardian after her parents' death.

5. From this time onward there are fairly constant references in Alessandra's letters to the need for her sons to marry. It later became clear that Lorenzo wanted to marry Marietta; see in particular Letter 34 below.

6. This is probably a reference to the fact that Filippo liked to have a great deal of cash in his coffers.

7. Niccolò Ardinghelli was related to Alessandra's sons through his mother, Caterina di Niccolò Strozzi. He was also a very close friend of Lorenzo de' Medici.

8. Spectacles had been in use in northern Italy since at least the early fourteenth century.

Letter 17

1. This could have been Filippo's own godmother, or the mother of a child to whom he had stood as godfather.

2. Francesco Strozzi; see Letter 16.

3. Probably Andrea di Carlo Strozzi, who was sixteen in 1464.

4. Tommaso di Francesco Ginori, a son of Maddalena di Filippo di Lionardo Strozzi and hence a nephew of Niccolò Strozzi; he was an employee of Filippo and Lorenzo at this time.

5. The manager of the Medici bank and the brother-in-law of Piero de' Medici.

6. Marry Marietta Strozzi, the granddaughter of an anti-Medicean exile.

Letter 18

1. Miraballi appears to have been a courier or messenger employed by the Strozzi, who travelled between Florence and Rome or Naples.

2. Piero de' Medici.

3. A hospital which admitted plague victims during epidemics.

4. A young male employee or servant.

5. The Eight of Guard, who had wide powers during a plague epidemic to limit the spread of the disease.

Letter 19

1. Cosimo de' Medici died on 1 August 1464, at the age of seventy-five.

2. Dietisalvi Neroni, previously a prominent supporter of Cosimo, became one of the leaders of the opposition to Piero de' Medici. He was exiled in September 1466.

3. The opponents of Piero de' Medici.

4. Messer Agnolo Acciaiuoli, also previously a leading Medicean and now one of the leaders of the opposition to Piero de' Medici.

5. Giovanni d'Antonio di Salvestro Serristori; this family had only recently gained high political office under the Medici.

6. The priors themselves had no power to choose the Gonfalonier of Justice. Here Alessandra probably refers to the *accoppiatori* or electoral scrutineers, who were the key officeholders of the Medici regime. When the electoral bags were "open," as they were at this time, they had the power to sort through the names of eligible citizens until they found a candidate they considered suitable.

7. A cousin of her husband.

8. Antonio Pucci. The Pucci were a family of *gente nuova* and loyal followers of the Medici.

9. The Stinche was primarily a debtors' prison, but also housed some criminals.

10. Alessandra was staying with Lessandra and Giovanni at their villa.

Letter 20

1. In their role as bankers to the Neapolitan court, Filippo and Lorenzo had acquired the friendship and gratitude of King Ferrante, who had, unsuccessfully, requested the Signoria to revoke their exile.

2. The company of Lodovico di Francesco Strozzi and his brothers had just "failed," unable to meet its immediate financial obligations.

3. That is, they would eventually pay their debts in full.

4. Giovanfrancesco di Messer Palla Strozzi, whose company had also failed.

5. This is meant with bitter irony, as she believed that his behavior had disgraced the Strozzi lineage.

6. As possible husbands for Marietta.

7. The Florentine state-funded debt; certain taxes took the form of the compulsory purchase of shares in this, and a low rate of interest was paid on them. These could be bought and sold by Florentine citizens, but for much less than their face value.

8. An oratory, or small chapel, in the parish of Brozzi in the Florentine countryside, patronage of which was held jointly by some members of the Strozzi lineage; a new priest needed to be chosen for it.

9. Under Florentine law a widow was not liable to pay the debts of her husband's estate from her restituted dowry.

10. The courts of the Roman Curia (the papal administration) could issue a decree of excommunication against an individual who refused to pay a creditor.

11. A minor legal professional, mainly employed to draw up documents.

Letter 21

1. Probably Agnolo Acciaiuoli.

2. Probably Messer Luca Pitti, who had been one of the most important and powerful followers of Cosimo de' Medici, but who became one of the leaders of the anti-Medicean reform party at this time.

3. Probably Piero de' Medici; if this identification is correct, Alessandra must have written brother (*fratello*) by mistake for son (*figliuolo*), as Piero had no brothers alive at this time.

4. A son of Dietisalvi Neroni.

5. The measure had first to be put to the vote in the Council of One Hundred and receive 44 votes, a two-thirds majority of the likely quorum of 66 (two-thirds of the council's total membership). It then had to be passed by the two ancient councils, of the People and the Commune.

6. King Ferrante had written to Piero de' Medici on Lorenzo's behalf in this matter.

7. Probably Messer Agnolo Acciaiuoli.

8. Giovanni Bonsi.

9. Marco Parenti.

Letter 22

1. A wealthy merchant and important patron of the arts, and formerly a close ally of the exiled Strozzi; his wife, Jacopa di Messer Palla Strozzi, was a first cousin of Niccolò Ardinghelli's mother. In 1461 Giovanni had allied himself to Piero de' Medici by betrothing his son Bernardo to Piero's daughter Nannina.

2. Lorenzo di Piero de' Medici (1449 – 92), now popularly called Lorenzo the Magnificent.

3. Lucrezia Gondi.

4. The Florentine ambassadors to Naples, Messer Luigi Guicciardini and Pandolfo Pandolfini. Pandolfo was a friend of Marco Parenti and also distantly related to these Strozzi by marriage.

5. Younger son of the King of Naples, he was on his way to Milan (via Florence) to collect his brother Alfonso's bride, Ippolita, daughter of Francesco Sforza, the Duke of Milan.

Letter 23

1. A cousin of her husband, and also a relation of Tommaso Ginori.

2. Patrician girls were married at sixteen or even younger, if possible.

3. Probably the wife of Gino di Neri Capponi.

4. Lucrezia Tornabuoni, wife of Piero de' Medici.

5. Rinaldo and Carlo Mormino, members of Don Federigo's retinue.

6. Her doctor.

Letter 24

1. The bank with which Filippo "corresponded" or did business in Florence.

2. The *condottiere* Jacopo Piccinino had been arrested and murdered in Naples, apparently on the orders of King Ferrante. Alessandra believed that this episode had damaged Ferrante's credit in Florence.

3. The three greater magistracies, the Signoria, the Twelve, and the Sixteen.

4. By the councils, which could ratify or veto certain decisions made by the magistracies.

5. Because they had hoped the sentence of exile would be lifted, following Don Federigo's visit to Florence.

6. Lorenzo had two illegitimate children, but it is not clear which of them was born on this occasion. His son Giovanluigi may not have survived infancy; his daughter Violante was married to Stefano di Cino, a shoemaker, in 1486.

Letter 25

1. It was uncertain whether Francesco Sforza would allow the Neapolitan marriage of his daughter to go ahead, because of the murder of Jacopo Piccinino. If he did, Piero de' Medici would send his son Lorenzo to Naples to attend the wedding.

2. Santa Maria Reparata, the Florentine Cathedral.

3. Fiammetta Adimari.

Letter 26

1. Filippo di Lionardo Strozzi, who married his second wife, Filippa Bischeri, in 1449, two years before his death.

2. Probably Messer Manno Temperani.

3. Bettino Ricasoli, a brother-in-law of Niccolò Strozzi.

4. This seems to be a reference to the fact that Filippo and Lorenzo had numerous employees who lived in their house with them.

5. There were no daughters of Cosimo de' Medici of marriageable age or status in 1465, so this is a definition of the unattainable.

Letter 27

1. Pandolfo and his wife Gostanza had eleven children.

2. The Florentine community of merchants in Naples (and in other cities) periodically elected one of their number to act as their representative.

3. It is not clear whether Lorenzo gave up this office, or whether he was required to do so by the Florentine Signoria.

4. This report was incorrect.

Letter 28

1. Matrimonial negotiations.

2. Piero de' Medici.

3. Antonio Pucci.

4. Niccolò Soderini.

5. During the period in which a certain tax measure was current (which could be a number of years), each occasion on which it was levied was numbered.

6. A direct tax, not yielding shares in the *Monte*.

7. Niccolò Soderini, who had just become Gonfalonier of Justice.

8. All Souls' Day, November 2, when prayers were said and offerings made for the souls of dead relatives presumed to be still in Purgatory.

9. A barrel of wine was of standard capacity, holding about 45 liters.

10. Pandolfo Pandolfini's brother.

11. It was believed that the only appropriate attitude for the devout Christian, when faced with death, was resignation and faith in God and the Church; to despair was considered a sin.

Letter 29

1. The Palazzo della Signoria, the seat of the Florentine government.

2. In 1458 up to 1500 eligible citizens had had their name-tickets removed from the electoral bags, in a purge of possible opponents of the Medici regime. These could be restored by holding a new scrutiny or process of political qualification, which was now to take place.

3. Those who had been exiled for political reasons only.

4. Since the late thirteenth century there had been a division of the wealthy and powerful families of Florence into *grandi,* or nobles, and *popolani,* or those of non-noble origin, such as the Strozzi; by the fifteenth century this division was largely anachronistic.

5. Francesco Neroni, brother of Dietisalvi Neroni.

6. The Madonne Murate were a group of nuns who lived in sealed cells.

7. Possibly Pietro Paolo Tommasi, a Florentine merchant who had a company in Naples during this period.

8. Alessandra de' Bardi.

9. This could be one of a number of Strozzi with this first name.

10. Tin medallions called *santeleni,* which had images of saints on them.

11. On the instructions of Raphael, his guardian angel, Tobias caught a fish which had attacked him on the River Tigris, and then cured his father's blindness by applying the fish's gall to his eyes; from the Book of Tobit, part of the Old Testament Apocrypha.

Letter 30

1. Francesco Bagnesi.

2. I have not been able to identify this person.

3. By contrast, Filippo and Lorenzo began a new company in this year, with a joint capital of 16,000 ducats.

Letter 31

1. A reference to Francesco Tanagli, who seems to have offered his daughter to Filippo almost without a dowry, at least by the standards of their class.

2. There was a fundamental division between those who wished to create a larger class of politically eligible citizens and those who did not. The Scrutiny Council (with more than 500 members initially) was also generally felt to be too large.

3. This "sickness" was probably the domination of the city's political life by an increasingly narrow circle of the Medici family and their close allies, to the exclusion of other patrician families such as the Strozzi.

4. Votes were cast with beans, black for yes and white for no.

5. Niccolò Soderini owned considerable property in the Tuscan Maremma, and this feud with the Counts of Maremma was originally over stock and grazing land.

6. Giovacchino Guasconi, a first cousin of Niccolò Strozzi and an employee of Filippo and Lorenzo.

7. A branch of the Strozzi lineage had been established in Mantua since the previous century. This information proved to be incorrect.

Letter 32

1. Either Alessandra or Giovanni himself had suggested he might move to Naples to work for Filippo and Lorenzo.

2. The large gold florin was made the obligatory currency for large financial transactions from 1464 onward.

3. An enterprise which coordinated all the manufacturing processes involved in producing woolen cloth, as well as selling the finished product.

4. Giovanni had bartered (in advance) some of the produce of his farm for cloth and had done badly out of the deal, as it had been a poor harvest and the price of grain was high.

5. Giovanni's villa.

Letter 33

1. Fiammetta Adimari must have been about sixteen at the time of her marriage. Filippo recorded the receipt of her dowry (of 1500 florins) on 14 February 1467. She bore him seven children and died on 23 August 1476.

2. For a woman of this social class to breast-feed her own child was very unusual, although not unknown.

3. Alfonso was born on 11 December 1467 and was named after his godfather, Alfonso of Aragon.

4. Maria di Piero Strozzi, wife of Raimondo Manelli.

5. Babies and toddlers of this class were breast-fed by their wet nurses until well into their second year of life, and many were sent away to live with their wet nurses in the country and did not return until they had been weaned.

6. Either the Florentine state-funded debt or the Dowry Fund.

7. Lorenzo's illegitimate son.

Letter 34

1. Lucrezia was born on 20 April 1469 and was probably given her name as a compliment to Lucrezia Tornabuoni. She died in 1481, at the age of twelve.

2. It was usual for a man whose father had died to name his first son after him, or otherwise after some other deceased male relative, or his wife's father, if dead. It was highly unusual for a boy to be named after his grandmother or any other female relation.

3. I have not been able to identify this person or the nature of her connection with the Strozzi.

4. The de facto ruler of Bologna from 1463 to 1506.

5. Of Lorenzo de' Medici and Clarice Orsini.

6. That is, 24 June, the feast day of St. John the Baptist, patron saint of Florence.

Letter 35

1. Made in Tuscany from what were called *greco,* or Greek, grapes.

2. A small town to the southeast of Florence, near Livorno.

3. Probably Marina.

4. Two-row barley, which was apparently used as horse feed.

5. A separate small house near their main residence, converted for use as a stable.

6. Piero de' Medici had died on 2 December 1469, and the events described here showed continuing discontent with Medici rule in some quarters.

7. Alessandra connects this escape attempt with the more obviously political episodes which followed it.

8. Matteo di Giorgio Brandolini.

9. Probably Piazza Santa Croce.

10. Bernardo Nardi was one of the anti-Medicean exiles of 1466 and had also been condemned as a rebel.

11. A town about 16 kilometers to the northwest of Florence, which had been part of the Florentine territorial state since the mid-fourteenth century.

12. The Medici palace in the Via Cavour.

13. The Palazzo della Signoria.

14. At times of open opposition to their rule, it seems to have been a Medici tactic to secure the support of the poor by monopolizing all supplies of bread and flour in the city.

15. The Florentine official who governed Prato.

16. A town about thirty-four kilometers to the northwest of Florence, which had come under permanent Florentine rule from 1341 onward.

17. The leading family of Pistoia.

Selected Bibliography

ALBERTI, LEON BATTISTA. *The Family in Renaissance Florence.* Columbia, S.C.: University of South Carolina Press, 1969.

BORSOOK, EVE. "Ritratto di Filippo Strozzi il Vecchio." In *Palazzo Strozzi Meta Millenio 1489–1989, Atti di Convegno di Studi*, edited by Daniela Lamberini, 1–14. Rome: Istituto della Enciclopedia Italiana, 1991.

BRUCKER, GENE. *Florence, 1138–1737.* London: Sidgwick and Jackson, 1983.

———. *Giovanni and Lusanna: Love and Marriage in Renaissance Florence.* Berkeley: University of California Press, 1986.

———. *Renaissance Florence.* New York: Wiley, 1969.

———. *The Society of Renaissance Florence: A Documentary Study.* New York: Harper Torchbooks, 1971.

CARMICHAEL, ANN G. "The Health Status of Florentines in the Fifteenth Century." In *Life and Death in Fifteenth-Century Florence*, edited by Marcel Tetel, Ronald G. Witt, and Rona Goffen, 28–45. Durham and London: Duke University Press, 1989.

———. *Plague and the Poor in Renaissance Florence.* Cambridge: Cambridge University Press, 1986.

CASSANDRO, MICHELE. "Affari e uomini de affari fiorentini a Napoli sotto Ferrante I d'Aragona (1472–1495)." In *Studi di storia economica toscana nel Medioevo e nel Rinascimento in memoria di Federigo Melis*, 103–23. Biblioteca del Bolletino Storico Pisano, Collana Storica 33. Pisa, 1987.

CLARKE, PAULA C. *The Soderini and the Medici: Power and Patronage in Fifteenth-Century Florence.* Oxford: Clarendon, 1991.

CRABB, ANN MORTON. "A Patrician Family in Renaissance Florence: The Family Relations of Alessandra Macinghi Strozzi and her Sons." Washington University, St. Louis: University Microfilms International, 1980.

DA BISTICCI, VESPASIANO. *Renaissance Princes, Poets and Prelates: The Vespasiano Memoirs.* Edited and translated by W. G. and E. Walters. New York: Harper and Row, 1963.

———. *Le Vite.* Vol. 2, edited by Aulo Greco. Florence: Istituto Nazionale di Studi sul Rinasimento, 1976.

GOLDTHWAITE, RICHARD A. "The Building of the Strozzi Palace: The Construction Industry in Renaissance Florence." *Studies in Medieval and Renaissance History* 10 (1973): 99 – 194.

———. *Private Wealth in Renaissance Florence: A Study of Four Families.* Princeton: Princeton University Press, 1968.

GORDON, BENJAMIN LEE. *Medieval and Renaissance Medicine.* New York: Philosophical Library, 1959.

GREGORY, HEATHER. "Chi erano gli Strozzi nel Quattrocento?" In *Palazzo Strozzi Meta Millenio 1489 – 1989, Atti di Convegno di Studi*, edited by Daniela Lamberini, 15 – 29. Rome: Istituto della Enciclopedia Italiana, 1991.

———. "Daughters, Dowries and the Family in Fifteenth Century Florence." *Rinascimento* 2d ser., 27 (1987): 215 – 37.

———. "A Florentine Family in Crisis: The Strozzi in the Fifteenth Century." Ph.D. diss., London University, 1981.

———. "The Return of the Exile: Filippo Strozzi and Medicean Politics." *Renaissance Quarterly* 38 (1985): 1 – 21.

GUTKIND, CURT S. *Cosimo de' Medici, Pater Patriae, 1389 – 1464.* Oxford: Clarendon Press, 1938.

HERLIHY, DAVID. *Cities and Society in Medieval Italy.* London: Variorum Reprints, 1980.

———. "The Florentine Merchant Family of the Middle Ages." In *Studi di storia economica toscana nel Medioevo e nel Rinascimento in memoria di Federigo Melis*, 179 – 201. Biblioteca del Bolletino Storico Pisano, Collana Storica 33. Pisa, 1987.

———. "The Making of the Medieval Family: Symmetry, Structure and Sentiment." *Journal of Family History* 8 (1983): 116 – 30.

HERLIHY, DAVID, AND CHRISTIANE KLAPISCH-ZUBER. *Tuscans and their Families: A Study of the Florentine Catasto of 1427.* New Haven, Conn.: Yale University Press, 1985.

KENT, DALE V. "The Florentine *Reggimento* in the Fifteenth Century." *Renaissance Quarterly* 28 (1975): 575 – 638.

———. *The Rise of the Medici: Faction in Florence, 1426 – 1434.* Oxford: Oxford University Press, 1978.

KENT, FRANCIS WILLIAM. *Household and Lineage in Renaissance Florence: The Family Life of the Capponi, Ginori and Rucellai.* Princeton: Princeton University Press, 1977.

―――. " 'Più Superba de quella de Lorenzo': Courtly and Family Interest in the Building of Filippo Strozzi's Palace." *Renaissance Quarterly* 30 (1977): 311–23.

KIRSHNER, JULIUS. "Pursuing Honor While Avoiding Sin: The *Monte delle Doti* of Florence." *Studi Senesi* 41 (1978).

KIRSHNER, JULIUS, AND ANTHONY MOLHO. "The Dowry Fund and the Marriage Market in Early Quattrocento Florence." *Journal of Modern History* 50 (1978): 403–38.

KLAPISCH-ZUBER, CHRISTIANE. *Women, Family and Ritual in Renaissance Italy.* Translated by Lydia Cochrane. Chicago: University of Chicago Press, 1985.

KUEHN, THOMAS. *Emancipation in Late Medieval Florence.* New Brunswick: Rutgers University Press, 1983.

―――. "Law, Death and Heirs in the Renaissance: Repudiation of Inheritance in Florence." *Renaissance Quarterly* 44 (1991): 213–56.

MARTINES, LAURO. *The Social World of the Florentine Humanists, 1390–1460.* Princeton: Princeton University Press, 1963.

―――. "A Way of Looking at Women in Renaissance Florence." *Journal of Medieval and Renaissance Studies* 4 (1974): 15–28.

MOLHO, ANTHONY. "Deception and Marriage Strategy in Renaissance Florence: The Case of Women's Ages." *Renaissance Quarterly* 41 (1988): 193–217.

―――. *Marriage Alliance in Late Medieval Florence.* Cambridge, Mass.: Harvard University Press, 1994.

ORIGO, IRIS. "The Domestic Enemy: Eastern Slaves in Tuscany in the Fourteenth and Fifteenth Centuries." *Speculum* 30 (1955): 321–66.

―――. *The Merchant of Prato: Daily Life in a Medieval Italian City.* Harmondsworth: Penguin, 1963.

PARK, KATHARINE. *Doctors and Medicine in Early Renaissance Florence.* Princeton: Princeton University Press, 1985.

PHILLIPS, MARK. *The Memoir of Marco Parenti: A Life in Medici Florence.* Princeton: Princeton University Press, 1987.

ROSENTHAL, ELAINE G. "The Position of Women in Renaissance Florence: Neither Autonomy nor Subjection." In *Florence and Italy: Renaissance Studies in Honour of Nicolai Rubinstein*, edited by Peter Denley and Caroline Elam, 369–81. Lon-

don: Westfield College, University of London Committee for Medieval Studies, 1988.

Ross, James Bruce, "The Middle-Class Child in Urban Italy." In *The History of Childhood: The Evolution of Parent-Child Relationships as a Factor in History*, edited by Lloyd de Mause. London: Souvenir Press, 1976.

Rubinstein, Nicolai. *The Government of Florence under the Medici, 1434–1494*. Oxford: Clarendon Press, 1966.

Strocchia, Sharon. "La famiglia patrizia fiorentina nel secolo XV: la problematica della donna." In *Palazzo Strozzi Meta Millenio 1489–1989, Atti di Convegno di Studi*, edited by Daniela Lamberini, 126–37. Rome: Istituto della Enciclopedia Italiana, 1991.

————. "Remembering the Family: Women, Kin and Commemorative Masses in Renaissance Florence." *Renaissance Quarterly* 42 (1989): 635–54.

Strozzi, Alessandra Macinghi. *Alessandra Macinghi Strozzi, Tempo di affetti e di mercanti: Lettere ai figli esuli*. Edited by Angela Bianchini. Milan: Garzanti, 1987.

————. *Una lettera della Alessandra Macinghi negli Strozzi in aggiunta alle LXXII pubblicate da Cesare Guasti nel 1877*. Edited by Isidoro del Lungo. Florence: Carnesecchi, 1890. Appended to the 1972 Licosa reprint of Guasti's edition of the letters.

————. *Lettere di una gentildonna fiorentina del secolo XV ai figliuoli esuli*. Edited by Cesare Guasti. Florence: Sansoni, 1877. Reprint, Florence: Licosa Reprints, 1972.

Trexler, Richard. "In Search of Father: The Experience of Abandonment in the Recollections of Giovanni di Pagolo Morelli." *History of Childhood Quarterly: Journal of Psychohistory* 3 (1975): 223–52.

Twigg, Graham. *The Black Death: A Biological Reappraisal*. London: Batsford, 1984.

Ulysse, Georges. "De la séparation et de l'exil: Les lettres d'Alessandra Macinghi Strozzi." *L'Exil et l'exclusion dans la culture italienne*, 89–112. Aix en Provence: Publications de l'Université de Provence, 1991.

Index

Biblioteca Italiana
The First Bilingual Editions

GIAMBATTISTA DELLA PORTA
Gli Duoi Fratelli Rivali
The Two Rival Brothers
Edited and translated
by Louise George Clubb
1980
*

TOMMASO CAMPANELLA
La Città del Sole:
Dialogo Poetico
The City of the Sun:
A Poetical Dialogue
Translated by Daniel J. Donno
1981
*

TORQUATO TASSO
Tasso's Dialogues:
A Selection
with the Discourse on
the Art of the Dialogue
Translated by Carnes Lord
and Dain A. Trafton
1982
*

GIACOMO LEOPARDI
Operette Morali
Essays and Dialogues
Translated by Giovanni Cecchetti
1983
*

CARLO COLLODI
Le Avventure di Pinocchio
The Adventures of Pinocchio
Translated with an Introduction
and Notes by Nicolas J. Perella
1986
*

MATTEO MARIA BOIARDO
Orlando Innamorato
Translated with an Introduction and Notes
by Charles Stanley Ross
1989
*

RUZANTE (ANGELO BEOLCO)
L'Anconitana
The Woman from Ancona
Translated with an Introduction
and Notes by Nancy Dersofi
1994
*

LUDOVICO ARIOSTO
Cinque Canti
Five Cantos
Translated by Alexander Sheers and David Quint
with an Introduction by David Quint
1996
*

ALESSANDRA STROZZI
Selected Letters of Alessandra Strozzi:
Bilingual Edition
Translated with an Introduction and Notes
by Heather Gregory
1997

Composition: G & S Typesetters, Inc.
Text: 10/12 Bembo
Display: Bembo
Printing and binding: Thomson-Shore, Inc.